Serving
Children and
Adolescents with
Developmental
Disabilities in the
Special Education
Classroom

Serving Children and Adolescents with Developmental Disabilities in the Special Education Classroom

Proven Methods

by

Sebastian Striefel, Ph.D.
Exceptional Child Center
Psychology Department
Utah State University
Logan, Utah

and

Mary J. Cadez, M.Ed.
Exceptional Child Center
Special Education Department
Utah State University
Logan, Utah

·P·A·U·L·H·
BROOKES
PUBLISHING Co. Baltimore · London

Paul H. Brookes Publishing Co.
Post Office Box 10624
Baltimore, Maryland 21204

Copyright 1983 by Paul H. Brookes Publishing Co., Inc.
All rights reserved.

Typeset by Brushwood Graphics, Baltimore, Maryland.
Manufactured in the United States of America.

Library of Congress Cataloging in Publication Data

Striefel, Sebastian, 1941–
    Serving children and adolescents with developmental disabilities in
the special education classroom.

    Includes bibliographical references and index.
    1. Handicapped children—Education.   I. Cadez, Mary J.,
1947–   II. Title.
LC4015.S77   1983   371.9   83-3632
ISBN 0-933716-32-X

Contents

8

9

10

Preface

This book was written to fill the need for a single, comprehensive source of proven methods for working with children with developmental disabilities. The methods described in the following chapters are in use today. They have been developed over an 8-year period in the clinical classrooms at the Exceptional Child Center at Utah State University and were field tested in other locations throughout the state of Utah. Many of the methods are also currently being employed in other states throughout the country.

This text explains the process for setting up classrooms for children and adolescents with developmental disabilities, and it identifies general operating procedures and philosophies for such classrooms. Specific practices for working with these children are also detailed. The book includes valuable information on suggested policies and procedures, samples of forms and record sheets, and recommended lists of materials.

This text is geared to administrators, special education teachers, psychologists, speech and language therapists, occupational and physical therapists, parents, and all professionals and paraprofessionals who are faced with the task of educating children and adolescents with developmental disabilities. An administrator may be interested in the text for its broad array of proven methods; the professional and paraprofessional because of the detail for day-to-day intervention; the parent in order to better understand the education process and how to help his or her child's "team" function better; and the college student because of the text's value as a source of useful, up-to-date information.

An earlier version of this book, directed specifically toward working with school-age severely and profoundly mentally retarded children, was partially developed with funds from contract no. 300-77-0258 from the Bureau of Education for the Handicapped, United States Office of Education, Department of Health, Education, and Welfare. The earlier version has been totally revised to expand the applicability of these proven methods to individuals with all types of developmental disabilities and to children and adolescents from birth to 21 years of age. The book is now in a more general format, and relevant published literature is cited throughout; thus, this volume has more utility in other settings.

Appreciation is expressed to several individuals who contributed to the writing of one of the many earlier versions of this book, including Michael J. Fimian, Donna Lake, Mark Weaver, Richard Whitney, Charles Ray Owens, Joseph Hoffman, Connie Morgan, and Chris Hencinski. Appreciation is also extended to all of the professional staff in the Exceptional Child Center and field-test sites who, through their efforts in serving handicapped children and youth in an exemplary manner, have helped to develop and field test the content of this book; without them, this book could never have become a reality. A thank you is also extended to Juanita Stokes who typed the many revisions of the final product. In addition, we would like to thank the professionals who reviewed and provided feedback useful in the development of the final product, including Grayson Osborne, Frank Ascione, Daniel Morgan, Richard Baer, Joseph Stowitschek, Gus Hamerlynck, Phyllis Cole, Susan Cassady, David Shearer, and Carol R. Beasley.

Serving
Children and
Adolescents with
Developmental
Disabilities in the
Special Education
Classroom

1

Introduction to Proven Methods in Serving Individuals with Developmental Disabilities in the Classroom

After reading this chapter, you should have an understanding of:

1. The impact of Public Law 94-142
2. The importance of special education programs being implemented in both the classroom and the community
3. The components of a comprehensive special education classroom program
4. The importance of having a description of these components available to staff in written form
5. The service philosophy of one model program
6. The model program goals
7. The model program description
8. The common areas and methods for individual assessment and programming in special education
9. Instruction and management in the classroom, including the importance of generalization
10. The importance of parent involvement

THIS CHAPTER PROVIDES the necessary basis for developing a comprehensive special education program. While providing a context for the chapters that follow, it has also been written to stimulate readers to compare this information with their own ideas of special education as they prepare to serve children and adolescents with developmental disabilities.

PUBLIC LAW 94-142

Since 1975, appropriate, individualized, and specialized services for individuals with developmental disabilities in special education settings have been mandatory rather than optional because President Ford signed into law that year the Education for All Handicapped Children Act of 1975 (PL 94-142), 1976. Prior to that time, special education students were often relegated to basements and other inferior, undesirable, or inappropriate environments, and often were provided with minimal services of a "babysitting" nature and lacked individualized and specialized attention. Because they had no legal basis for asserting their rights, individuals with developmental disabilities had traditionally been treated as second or third class citizens at best. Today, many individuals with developmental disabilities are receiving individualized services in the least restrictive environment as mandated by law now that they have achieved a legal basis for their rights. The least restrictive environment means that, to the extent that it is appropriate, handicapped children are educated in the same classes as nonhandicapped children, and that handicapped children are removed from regular classes only when they cannot be educated there satisfactorily. Handicapped students are approaching a level of equality with normal students in the sense that they are receiving not only a free, but an appropriate education. This is not to say that there is total compliance with the law, or that parents of children with handicaps can now sit back and relax, or that continued lawsuits will not be necessary to maintain or expand current services. However, a turning point seems to have been reached in that many school administrators, teachers, legislators, and parents accept and support the premise that individuals with developmental disabilities have specialized needs that can be met only with specialized services. Many believe that even the severely and profoundly handicapped can be effectively served in the public schools (Sontag, Burke, & York, 1973; Sontag, Certo, & Button, 1979).

Because PL 94-142 mandated services based on client need rather than availability of service (Laycock, 1982), many program administrators and staff found themselves trying to obtain and secure services in order to comply with the law. Due to the emphasis on obtaining funding and services, many programs did not establish a firm instructional model, and even programs that were in compliance with the law often operated in a disjointed manner when they lacked the necessary established written model. This lack of system clarity is cited as one of the largest contributing factors to stress and burnout for service delivery staff (Shaw, Bensky, & Dixon, 1981). As such, a great need exists for developing effective models for providing the requisite specialized educational and related services in the form of well developed procedures, forms, and materials. The major aim of this book is to describe some proven methods for serving individuals with handicaps in classroom settings while programming for generalization of acquired skills into community settings.

IMPLEMENTATION IN THE CLASSROOM AND COMMUNITY

Wehman and Hill (1980) have stressed the importance of an instructional model for programs serving individuals with handicaps, a model that is implemented both within the classroom and within the local community. They specified eight reasons why such a model should be implemented. In a slightly modified form, these included: 1) a higher probability of skill generalization to other people and locations, 2) a greater exposure to the natural communities of reinforcers that exist in the "real world", 3) an increase in the interaction of handicapped and nonhandicapped people, 4) additional availability of and exposure to appropriate role models, 5) an increased level of teacher expectation and interest, 6) increased parental hope for improvement in the future, 7) a demonstration of competence by handicapped students in different skill areas, and 8) an appropriate selection of functional curricula. It would appear that the potential benefits of education occurring in both the classroom and in the community far outweigh the negative reception often experienced by individuals with developmental disabilities when they venture into the community, including social ridicule, embarrassment, and the ability to participate only partially in community activities.

COMPONENTS OF A COMPREHENSIVE
SPECIAL EDUCATION PROGRAM

Much effort goes into the organization and implementation of the many "classroom parts" or classroom components that, when taken as a whole, are experienced as a smoothly run, effective, and efficient classroom. Many of these component parts have been analyzed and will be discussed at some point in this book. The basic components of the classrooms include: a) service staff, b) classroom organization and coordination, c) program entry, d) the individualized education program, e) behavior management, f) data collection, g) curriculum, h) paraprofessional training, and i) parenting.

A comprehensive education program for individuals with developmental disabilities should address at minimum the following major categories:

1. The staff needed for a comprehensive program
2. The use of consultants in the classroom
3. Classroom organization and operation

4. Identification and assessment of children needing special education services
5. Development, monitoring, and evaluation of individualized education programs (IEPs)
6. The modification of behavior
7. Data collection and analysis
8. Curriculum development and use
9. Utilization and training of paraprofessionals
10. The role of parents in educating their child

In addition, it should also address the following specific characteristics (Wehman, Bates, & Renzaglia, 1980):

1. Generalization of skills across people and locations
2. Maintenance of skills across time
3. Functionality and age appropriateness of skills trained
4. Development of specific goals and objectives
5. Interaction with the nonhandicapped
6. Motivation

WRITTEN DESCRIPTION OF COMPONENTS

Any program that has developed a model for working with individuals with developmental disabilities would do well to have available in written form its component parts including: a) a description of the resources available, b) a description of the program and activities, c) a written philosophy, d) a set of clearly defined goals, e) a set of written procedures for carrying out the necessary activities, f) an organizational flow chart and description of staff responsibilities, g) an evaluation process for assessing child progress, h) a description of initial intake and placement procedures, and i) a breakdown of the methods and procedures used that will provide the necessary information for efficient staff training and replication of the model.

The purpose of describing in written form the various components of the model (e.g., the demonstration classrooms, curriculum, procedures for developing IEPs and behavior management techniques) is to provide the administrator, teacher, teacher trainee, professional, parent, and paraprofessional with one source of proven methods for serving individuals with developmental disabilities. The information included in this book is the result of more than 8 years of research, field testing, revisions, and further research, and as more field testing is conducted, no doubt new ideas and changes will be generated.

ONE-SERVICE PHILOSOPHY

The major philosophy of any special education program should be to provide services of *exemplary quality* in the least restrictive environment, in conjunction with providing a free and appropriate education. Exemplary programs are succinctly defined as those deserving replication elsewhere. In addition, the importance of interdisciplinary team and parental involvement in decisions concerning individual children should be continuously emphasized as a part of that service philosophy (Markel & Greenbaum, 1979). The program for each child must be determined on an individualized basis, dependent on the needs of the child. In cases where the appropriate resources are not available, every effort should be made to obtain or develop the necessary resources, or to refer the child and family to a source that can provide them.

Fredericks, Baldwin, Grove, Hanson, McDonnell, Riggs, Furey, Jordan, Gage, Lebac, Alrich, and Wadlow (1975) have outlined additional components of a philosophy underlying a model educational program. This philosophy can be used to set up educational programs outside the self-contained classroom whenever the needs of the special child are being considered. A modification of this philosophy proposed by Fredericks, Baldwin, Grove, Hanson, McDonnell, Riggs, Furey, Jordan, Gage, Lebac, Alrich, and Wadlow (1975) follows.

1. Every child with a developmental disability can learn. If a child is not learning, the problem has to do with the programming and the staff implementing the programs, not with the child.
2. Children with developmental disabilities learn at a slower rate than normal children, usually using the same learning principles. Thus, they require more intensive instruction to compensate for this difference in rate and have a greater need for careful programming of consequences following behavior.
3. Other than by teaching, there is no way to determine the extent to which a child will progress (Baer, 1981a; Noonan, Brown, Mulligan, & Rettig, 1982). Therefore, no ceiling is placed on the curriculum. The teacher must be prepared to take the child as far and as fast as he or she can go.
4. The range of individual abilities among a population with developmental disabilities is usually more varied than among a normal population. The team working with individuals with moderate and severe handicaps must set up individualized programs. (PL 94-142 and many state laws require it.)
5. The population with developmental disabilities is extremely heterogeneous and oftentimes difficult to control due to previous ineffective training. Thus, effective instruction, especially for those with severe or profound handicaps, may require one-to-one and small group training in addition to large group training. Therefore, the utilization of paraprofessionals to provide individualized instruction in the classroom is considered mandatory.
6. No child should be denied special education services because he or she is not toilet-trained. In fact, toilet training should be considered an essential part of the education program of children with moderate and severe developmental disabilities.

7. No child should be denied admittance into a program because she or he is nonambulatory. The development of fine and gross motor skills, including the ability to creep, crawl, or walk, is an integral part of the special education curriculum.

8. No child should be denied admittance because he or she cannot communicate. Instruction in communication skills is emphasized.

9. No child should be denied admittance to a special education program because of the presence of inappropriate or bizarre behaviors. Such behaviors can be modified and efforts to do so are an integral part of any special education program.

10. A lower age limit for admission into a special education program (i.e., a younger child's age would not preclude admission) should be avoided, thus allowing greater flexibility in admission of children to programs.

11. No lower IQ limit should be set, since IQ measures at the lower levels and with young children are not reliable estimates of capability (Fredericks, Baldwin, Grove, Hanson, McDonnell, Riggs, Furey, Jordan, Gage, Lebac, Alrich, & Wadlow 1975). In addition, IQ has little if any relevance when individualized programs are used.

MODEL PROGRAM GOALS

Realistic goals for a model program are as follows:

1. Exemplary programs provided for educating students with developmental disabilities should focus on six main objectives:
   a. To encourage each child's development toward his or her fullest potential
   b. To base the educational goals for each child on the long term needs of the student while working on short term and intermediate objectives
   c. To identify the individualized special needs of each student in order to complete long term, short term, and intermediate objectives
   d. To determine the next potential placement for each student in the program and the entry level necessary for such placement
   e. To train functional and age appropriate skills
   f. To program for generalization of acquired skills across people, situations, and locations, and to assure that the skills are maintained over time

2. Parental involvement in selecting and achieving the objectives necessary for each individual student should be actively solicited using several methods:
   a. Frequent informal communication with parents via written notes or phone calls
   b. Ensuring that parents are invited to their child's IEP staffing
   c. Providing parents with information on their role and encouraging parent involvement when they attend IEP staffings

d. Sending a copy of the child's proposed goals, and then, following the staffing, sending a copy of each child's individualized education program (IEP) to the parents and updating it at least semi-annually

e. Providing parent-team or parent-teacher conferences, as needed

f. Inviting parents to observe and participate in classroom activities

g. Making *no* major decisions concerning a child without obtaining parental input

h. Providing parent training workshops

i. Helping parents locate external resources (e.g., medical and legal aid)

3. Interdisciplinary inservice training should be provided for staff and para-professionals, and state-of-the-art techniques for intervention with the developmentally disabled student should be taught.

4. Interaction with local and state education, health, and social service agencies should be used to improve and develop new resources for serving persons with developmental disabilities.

5. Periodic evaluation for purposes of revising and updating program goals, staff training, and intervention strategies and techniques is necessary.

MODEL PROGRAM DESCRIPTION

The description of a model education program for children in special education should include a balanced, individualized program based on the particular needs of each child, with built-in recurring evaluation procedures. A comprehensive interdisciplinary educational assessment should be completed for each child entering the program, and his or her individualized education program (IEP) should be designed on the basis of that assessment in combination with other informal assessments, background information, and observational data collected. The program must be flexible enough so that new services or training can be added as the need becomes apparent, or new approaches are developed. The model must be in constant flux with activities being carried out and data collected to determine the impact of the activities. These data must be analyzed and fed back into the system so that staff performance and procedures and materials used may be changed as needed. The effective procedures and materials need to be made available to professionals in other locations for replication and field testing. Again, data must be collected to allow for needed changes. Staff should be trained to think in terms of individuals *with* developmental disabilities rather than in terms of individuals *who are* developmentally disabled. This book will attempt to use the terminology appropriate to individuals with developmental disabilities.

ASSESSMENT AND PROGRAMMING

Comprehensive assessment and subsequent programming based on individual need and administrative constraints often include:

1. Standardized assessment. Most states require intelligence testing for classification purposes. In addition, criterion-referenced testing and direct observation of children should be used to assess individual needs and progress made.
2. Self-help and home-living skills. The self-help skills taught may include dressing, eating, grooming, and toilet training. Home-living skills taught may include washing, drying, and folding clothes; setting tables; cooking; cleaning sinks, toilets, and floors; dusting furniture; vacuuming; and making beds.
3. Speech and language acquisition. Individual speech and language training should be provided to all students who require it. Expressive, receptive, and social language may be emphasized as well as nonverbal communication using augmentative communication devices and approaches such as sign language, communication boards, or even computer-synthesized speech and articulation training.
4. Physical and motor development. Training in physical and motor development should be provided for all students. In addition, physical and occupational therapy should be provided where it is prescribed, and physical education should be provided daily for students.
5. Pre-academic and academic skills. Pre-academic skills, such as matching, sorting, recognition, identification, categorization, and conceptualization should be provided for students when appropriate for their annual goals or short term objectives. The basic fundamentals of reading, arithmetic, writing, and spelling are taught when the child is ready for such instruction. The focus for students with developmental disabilities should be on the functional aspects of these more traditional school subjects (e.g., in math—time telling, money skills, etc.). Many diverse commercial and teacher-constructed programs and materials should be utilized.
6. Social skills. Training in and opportunities for interaction with others in a socially appropriate manner is essential.
7. Behavior management. When personal behavior is a problem, individualized behavior programs should be designed and implemented. For example, if a child cries excessively, a program to reduce crying and to teach more appropriate ways of coping with the environment should be designed and implemented. Programs should be designed to develop behaviors appropriate to the child's developmental level.
8. Medical assessment and consultation. A registered school nurse or family physician should be used both in assessment and in providing services to children in need. A child with seizures may require ongoing medical monitoring, and interaction and consultation between the teacher and the physician is necessary to ensure that the child's seizures are controlled without side effects such as drowsiness.

INSTRUCTION AND MANAGEMENT IN THE CLASSROOM

In accordance with the philosophy set forth earlier, instruction is provided on an individual, small or large group basis. Almost all instruction must be individualized, although this may be accomplished within both small and large group activities provided for the children. Instruction should be provided by highly trained, certified special education teachers, other professionals, and paraprofessionals such as classroom aides, volunteers, parents, and trainees. Educating children with developmental disabilities necessitates an ongoing interdisciplinary team effort that includes parents, and that is functional in terms of assessment, program implementation, and monitoring (Markel & Greenbaum, 1979). All volunteers, students and trainees should work under the direct supervision of the appropriate staff, e.g., speech therapy trainees should work under the direct supervision of certified speech pathologists.

The most effective teaching methods and materials available should be used and new programs should be developed, reviewed, and tested (guidelines for evaluating materials are presented in Chapter 8). Children's performance data from these programs must be recorded consistently in order to evaluate individual progress. Progress should be discussed with the parents a minimum of twice during the school year. If progress is not adequate, changes and comparisons should be made to determine if more effective procedures can be employed.

The behavioral model of instruction has received the most support in published literature as the approach that results in the greatest change in student progress. It can be employed in both the behavior management and instructional components of the classroom. In using this approach, it is assumed that behavior is affected by what immediately follows it (its consequences). Thus, in order to modify a behavior, the behavior must first be clearly defined in measurable terms. This means the behavior must be observable and measurable. In essence, two people must be able to readily agree on when the behavior has occurred. After clearly defining a behavior, one rearranges the consequences of a behavior to be very desirable or undesirable, depending on whether one wishes to increase or decrease the behavior. Behavior management is not easy to implement, but efforts to acquire behavior management skills will repeatedly pay off in terms of child progress.

Behavior Management

Many individuals with developmental disabilities must be taught to discriminate between the specific environmental cues that lead to a reward, and those that do not. To do this, the teacher or other staff must change the environment in such a way that there is:

1. An increase in the probability of occurrence and recurrence of desirable and appropriate behaviors, and
2. A concomitant decrease in the probability of occurrence and recurrence of undesirable or maladaptive behaviors.

The use of behavioral techniques is outlined in detail in Chapter 6.

Instructional Management

When instruction is effective, the learner has acquired a new behavior, specifically, what the teacher/therapist wants him or her to learn. To obtain maximum effectiveness, it is recommended that programs use an instructional strategy that is composed of three parts: a) a task analysis approach to instructional development, b) programmed tutoring to ensure that learning occurs, and c) a sequence for programming for the occurrence of generalization of skills learned to other people, places, and times (Howell, Kaplan, & O'Connell, 1979; Whitney & Striefel, 1981).

Task Analysis   Task analysis is the first step in designing an instructional program. By analyzing the task or breaking it down into component subtasks or steps, the instructor can easily determine both *what* to teach and in what *sequence* the subtasks will be presented (McCormack, 1976; Semmel & Thiagarajan, 1973). Task analysis also provides a method for determining the essential prerequisite skills that the student should have before beginning the sequence of sub-tasks or steps. For example, imitating sounds is a prerequisite to imitating words (Frank, 1973; Howell et al., 1979).

Programmed Tutoring   Programmed instruction consists of "a series of combined teaching/testing tasks that are designed to carry the student gradually through the material to be learned" (McCormack, 1976, p. 9), and has been used successfully in various situations to assist students with handicaps to acquire new skills in a variety of educational settings (Wunderlich, 1972). Behavioral techniques used in both management and instructional situations are discussed at a later point in this book. Howell et al. (1979) discuss personalized programming that also takes into account how a child learns, and they use that method, whether it be print, auditory, or visual, to program for the student.

Programming for Generalization   Another aspect of instructional management, in addition to using the behavioral techniques of task analysis and programmed tutoring, is ensuring that the skill being taught will be demonstrable across locations, people, and times. When the student is able to demonstrate a behavior, regardless of the location or person requesting it and at any time of day, he or she is said to have generalized the behavior. In the past, programming to achieve generalization was not a primary concern of educators (Whitney & Striefel, 1981), but it is now essential to emphasize the necessity of including procedures in developing IEPs that will test for generalization. Generalization within IEPs is discussed in detail in Chapter 5, Developing, Implementing, and Evaluating Functional Individualized Education Programs.

PARENT INVOLVEMENT

Because parental involvement is considered a necessary component in the child's education, staff/parent involvement should be integrated through several channels. The classroom teachers and various other staff (e.g., speech therapists, coordinators, special project staff), should communicate directly with the parents through home visits, telephone calls, and parent contact in school. All parents whose children are involved in a special education program should be involved in parent/teacher meetings (known as staffings). They should occur once every 10 to 12 weeks. Special interest parent meetings can and should be arranged on an informal schedule throughout the year by the teacher or other staff as needed. Working individually with each parent on programs that are beneficial for home and school is an aim of both the preschool and school-age classrooms. Chapter 10 deals more extensively with the parenting component.

SUMMARY

This chapter has provided information fundamental to the development of a comprehensive special education program, including: the impact of PL 94-142; the importance of program implementation occurring in both the classroom and community; the significance of generalization and parent involvement, and of having the components of the comprehensive special education program available in written form; the philosophy of a model service program along with its goals and a description of the program; and information on assessment and behavior management. The information presented provides the basis for the chapters that follow.

2

Services
Staff and
Personnel
Procedures

After reading this chapter, you should have an understanding of:

1. The disciplines needed to operate a comprehensive special education program
2. The importance of staff comprehending the program's goals and recognizing the rights and responsibilities of other team members
3. The components needed in written personnel policies
4. How the dimensions of a job affect the psychological state of staff
5. The function of well developed job descriptions and their relationship to staff evaluation
6. The impact of job enlargement and job enrichment, including the relationship of staff motivation and participation to child progress and program success
7. The function and services of the therapy consultant, as well as implementation of the therapy consultant model

THIS CHAPTER DEALS with the most critical component of any special education program: the staff and the personnel policies that affect them. This chapter also covers the role of the consultant in the classroom, since school districts in rural areas often do not have on their staff representatives of the many disciplines needed to provide the services required by the district's students with developmental disabilities. For the reader requiring more extensive coverage of personnel policies than is possible in this chapter, a variety of published resources (e.g., Kerr, 1979; Kolb, Rubin, & McIntyre, 1979; Sciarra & Dorsey, 1979; Van Beck, 1982a, 1982b) is available.

DISCIPLINES AND COMPREHENSION
OF GOALS AND RESPONSIBILITIES

The staff involved in a comprehensive special education program may include individuals in the following roles: program director (e.g., superintendent or pupil personnel director), program coordinator (e.g., principal or special education director), special education teacher, speech and language pathologist, behavioral or school psychologist, occupational therapist, physical therapist, nurse, parent trainer, nutritionist, music therapist, and classroom instructional aide, at minimum. When each team member understands the program goals and the rights and responsibilities of each person, the quality of services is increased, communication is increased, friction reduced, and negotiation between members can occur. Role clarity is of the utmost importance and is cited in Shaw et al. (1981) as the most significant variable for stress reduction in the management of stress for employees. To clarify rights and responsibilities for employees, written personnel policies should be developed.

WRITTEN PERSONNEL POLICIES

Personnel policies make clear to each individual what is expected of him or her so that confusion and misdirected energy are minimized. Such policies also reduce errors in procedure, free administrators from unnecessary involvement in problem resolution, and help reduce staff frustration by making staff members aware of individual and team expectations (Sciarra & Dorsey, 1979).

Ultimately, personnel policies should define each team member's role within the broad context of program goals. This in turn should provide for better services to clients by directing energy toward their needs rather than into continually defining staff roles. It is important that personnel policies be available in written form and that all staff have direct access to them. The policies should be specific, comprehensive, easy to read, and take into account the needs of the organization, the staff, and the children served. Where written personnel policies need to be developed, the program director may have ultimate responsibility for doing so. It is helpful to have input into development of new policies, and periodic review and revision of existing policies. Such input can be obtained from all or a representative sample of staff and from parents of children served via questionnaires and face-to-face meetings. It is useful for personnel policies to be reviewed and updated annually with the express purpose of better meeting the needs of the organization, the staff, and the children served. Personnel policies should include at a minimum the following items:

1. Program goals and philosophy
2. Job descriptions for each position that outline the qualifications and responsibilities for each job

3. Contract samples that specify employment conditions
4. Standard operating procedures that specify how program operations are to be carried out
5. Daily schedule of when staff are expected to be on the job, as well as free time for breaks (lunch, coffee, etc.)
6. Fringe benefits available to staff in terms of retirement plans, health insurance, educational opportunities, social security, workman's compensation, liability coverage, holidays, vacation leave, sick leave, and maternity leave
7. Staff evaluation and grievance procedures, including sample forms
8. An organization chart indicating the chain of authority and specifying who reports to whom
9. Probationary policy specifying length and conditions of the probationary period, and procedures for dismissal
10. Termination procedures (e.g., 30 days notice when leaving) should be spelled out
11. Procedures for changing and amending personnel policies

It may also be useful to include policies, if the agency has any, on items such as salary ranges, meeting schedules, career ladders, health exams, transportation, security, and communication.

PSYCHOLOGICAL STATE OF STAFF

Interdisciplinary teams are being used more frequently to provide special education and related services to children with handicaps in education settings. In addition to the teacher and an aide, any of the following staff and others may at one time or another be involved in developing, implementing, and monitoring education programs for the student with a handicap: program director, program coordinator, speech and language pathologist, behavioral psychologist, occupational therapist, physical therapist, nurse, parent trainer, nutritionist, music therapist, recreation therapist, and adaptive physical educator. With this many people involved, it becomes essential to clearly specify roles and responsibilities. The organizational chart in Figure 2.1 provides an example of lines of authority for an agency. The configuration of relationships on an organizational chart may vary from agency to agency, but, regardless of the configuration, it should be useful to staff in knowing how each position fits into the service network and what lines of authority are to be recognized.

The positions of program director and program coordinator are considered to be primarily administrative ones while the remainder of the positions on the organizational chart are direct service positions. In reality, the distinction between administrative and direct service positions is an overlapping one. Direct service providers may work with students directly and also supervise

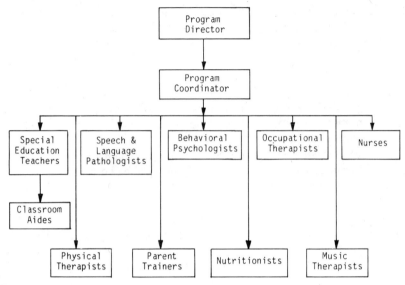

Figure 2.1. A sample organization chart.

others who work with students who have handicaps. Direct service providers are supervised by the administrative staff for program planning, implementation, and evaluation. Often, the responsibilities within a special education service unit are shared among the various staff members. However, each staff member is responsible for specific activities and duties.

Hackman and Oldham (1975) indicated that any job can be described in terms of five dimensions, including:

1. Skill variety, the extent to which a job involves a variety of different skills and talents
2. Task identity, the extent to which a job involves completion of a task from the beginning to the end, including a visible end product
3. Task significance, the extent to which a job has an impact on the work or lives of other people (e.g., other staff or children served)
4. Autonomy, the extent to which a job allows an individual freedom to decide when and how to complete the tasks related to the job
5. Task feedback, the extent to which job performance results in direct and clear feedback on the effectiveness of task completion

These dimensions influence three psychological states of workers (Kerr, 1979); experienced meaningfulness of work, experienced responsibility for work outcomes, and knowledge of results of work activities. The meaningfulness of work is likely to be high when skill variety, task identity and task significance are included in the job. Increased autonomy on the job influences the experienced responsibility for work outcome, and feedback affects knowledge of results of work activity. The higher the level of these three psychological states, the more favorable the personal and work outcomes obtained.

Each professional position in a special education program can be designed to include high levels of each of the five job dimensions so that the three psychological states are satisfied, thus motivating professionals to do their best. As many of these aspects as possible should be included in developing the job description of aides and other paraprofessionals so that these positions are also meaningful and desirable. There is a direct relationship between well-developed job descriptions and staff evaluations. The more specific the job description, the easier it is for the supervisor to evaluate the performance of the activities listed in the job description.

JOB DESCRIPTIONS

Five sample job descriptions and a listing of the major responsibilities or functions, minimum qualifications, and desired capabilities for all of the major positions within most special services units serving individuals with handicaps are included in this chapter. Responsibilities or functions refer to those activities that staff must be able to carry out effectively in order to function adequately in the role. Minimum qualifications refer to the abilities, education, and/or experience that a person *must* have to be minimally acceptable in the various roles. Desired abilities refer to the abilities, education and/or experiences that, although they are not strictly required, are desirable in obtaining the highest quality of service possible.

Job Description for Program Director

Responsibilities (Functions):

1. Overall responsibility for development and supervision of entire program
2. Overall responsibility for development and supervision of a program of pre- and inservice training for program staff
3. Overall responsibility for providing technical direction for program goals and objectives
4. Overall responsibility for management of the financial aspects of the program including budget preparation, authorization of purchases, contract negotiations, grant writing and administration, salaries, and annual raises
5. Overall responsibility to serve as a liaison and public relations manager for the program in interactions with state and local agencies and other institutions
6. Overall responsibility for providing administrative support to the program coordinator and staff, and for providing consultation on problems with children being served
7. Monitoring and evaluating program effectiveness

8. Overall responsibility for hiring staff, evaluating staff performance, and terminating staff
9. Overall responsibility for development and maintenance of personnel policies
10. Overall responsibility for resolving staff or program conflicts
11. Overall responsibility for assuring that services are delivered in accordance with local, state, and federal laws and regulations governing services to persons with developmental disabilities

Minimum Qualifications

1. A doctoral degree in psychology, special education or a related field or a master's degree and 5 years of relevant experience (in many states, an administrative or supervisory certificate or specialized degree is required)
2. Three or more years experience in working with individuals with developmental disabilities
3. Three or more years experience in administration and staff supervision
4. Three or more years experience in program development, implementation and evaluation
5. Training or experience in contract and grant writing, budget preparation and management
6. Demonstrated public relations skills
7. Familiarity with state and federal laws and regulations governing programs for individuals with developmental disabilities
8. Experience in working with interdisciplinary teams

Desired Abilities, Experience, and/or Knowledge:

1. One or more years of successful administrative experience with special education teachers and parents of children with developmental disabilities
2. Demonstrated ability in developing educational contracts and/or grants
3. Professional experience in developing, monitoring, and controlling accessible finances
4. Familiarity with the operating procedures of the state board of education and local school districts

Job Description for Program Coordinator

Responsibilities (Functions):

1. Coordinate the activities of the special education services unit with the program director, state and regional programs, the state's social service office, the state education agency, and school districts
2. Coordinate the management and design of treatment programs and progress of students with developmental disabilities
3. Manage daily tasks involved in educating the children served

4. Supervise interdisciplinary teams in service delivery
5. Coordinate the annual evaluation of the program and staff
6. Assist the program director in annual contract review and negotiations
7. Coordinate the activities of special programs and grants
8. Coordinate the implementation of due process procedures if necessary
9. Assist in the screening and evaluation of students for inclusion in various programs
10. Properly organize the review and evaluation of student records and obtain all necessary releases and required forms
11. Coordinate the monitoring of the budget and assist in budget preparation
12. Coordinate staff meetings and staff inservice training
13. Supervise parent training
14. Coordinate public relations activities

Minimum Qualifications:

1. A master's degree in special education, psychology or related field
2. Three or more years of experience training children with developmental disabilities
3. Certification in special education with the appropriate supervisory and teaching endorsements
4. Demonstrated ability in developing individualized education programs and curriculum management
5. Demonstrated ability in establishing and maintaining effective working relationships with staff and other agency personnel
6. Familiarity with federal and state laws and regulations governing programs for individuals with developmental disabilities
7. Demonstrated ability to function as a member of an interdisciplinary team

Desired Abilities, Experience, and/or Knowledge:

1. One or more years of administrative experience in an educational setting
2. Demonstrated ability in developing educational contracts and/or grants
3. Experience in developing, monitoring, and controlling accessible finances
4. Familiarity with the functions of the state board of education and local school districts

Job Description for Special Education Teacher

Responsibilities (Functions):

1. Coordinate and manage a classroom for children with developmental disabilities including the provision of direct services to the children
2. Conduct and coordinate individual staffings for each client served

3. Communicate and cooperate with other program staff
4. Schedule, monitor, and manage paraprofessional help in the classroom
5. Provide supervision to paraprofessionals through instruction, demonstration, and formal and informal feedback
6. Administer the criterion and adaptive behavior instruments necessary to appropriately place students in an educational program
7. Monitor the collection and analysis of data in the classroom
8. Physically care for students
9. Establish and maintain a comprehensive services program for each child
10. Locate and/or develop appropriate curriculum materials and instructional programs
11. Ensure that parents have an opportunity to review their child's program and file annually
12. Attend staff meetings and staff inservice and training functions
13. Prepare or supervise preparation of progress reports on students
14. Evaluate each child's progress and skills in terms of the student's IEP and recommend placement at the end of each school year in a written report
15. Maintain special education teaching certification with the appropriate endorsements as required by state law
16. Inventory all equipment and materials at the beginning and end of the school year
17. Provide coverage for other teachers in case of absence
18. Maintain contact with parents regarding progress of children

Minimum Qualifications:

1. A bachelor's degree in special education
2. Special education teaching certificate with the appropriate endorsements

Desired Abilities, Experience, and/or Knowledge:

1. A master's degree or equivalent in special education
2. Experience in teaching children with developmental disabilities
3. Experience on an interdisciplinary diagnostic or instructional team
4. Experience in data collection and analysis relative to instructional programs
5. Demonstrated ability to develop and implement IEPs
6. Demonstrated ability to write and edit comprehensive reports
7. Experience in parent training
8. Ability to use behavior management techniques with children with developmental disabilities

Job Description for Classroom Instructional Aide

Responsibilities (Functions):

1. Provide program support to the teacher

2. Assist in conducting basic instructional activities
3. Assist in monitoring data collected on student performance
4. Monitor and maintain classroom supplies
5. Supervise student activities
6. Attend to students' physical needs
7. Facilitate communication between the school and parents
8. Assist in monitoring student attendance

Minimum Qualifications:

1. Desire to work with students with developmental disabilities
2. Ability to follow directions
3. Ability to get along with other people

Desired Abilities, Experience, and/or Knowledge:

1. Experience in working with children with developmental disabilities
2. Experience in directing group activities
3. Experience in making teaching materials for children
4. Experience using behavior management techniques

Summary of Job Description for Other Positions

To avoid redundancy and yet provide the reader with information to complete job descriptions for the disciplines of speech and language pathology, psychology, occupational therapy, physical therapy, nutrition, music therapy and parent training, job descriptions are summarized in one list. With minor changes, one could use this basic job description for any single discipline.

Responsibilities (Functions):

1. Conduct comprehensive assessments of students in the areas appropriate to the specific discipline (e.g., speech and language) using standardized and criterion-referenced tests, annually or as needed
2. Write and edit comprehensive assessment reports for students
3. Train and supervise professionals, paraprofessionals, and parents in conducting treatment programs
4. Serve as a member of interdisciplinary teams for students enrolled in the program
5. Design, write, implement, and monitor individualized programs for students, and provide direct services within the specific discipline
6. Provide case consultation to staff members or professionals from other agencies
7. Provide inservice training for professionals and paraprofessionals as needed
8. Keep daily progress records and write complete semi-annual summary reports on each client

9. Utilize behavior modification techniques as needed to ensure client progress
10. Evaluate and revise programs, and obtain or make equipment to meet individual client needs
11. Attend client staffings with parents or guardians to interpret test results and review progress made during treatment
12. Attend professional staff meetings and inservice or training workshops

Minimum Qualifications:

1. A bachelor's or master's degree in the appropriate discipline
2. Certification or licensure in the particular discipline if appropriate (e.g., certificate of clinical competence in speech and language pathology)
3. Demonstrated ability in assessing students' skills and deficits in areas related to the specific discipline and in writing an appropriate assessment report
4. Demonstrated ability to cooperatively work with other staff

Desired Abilities, Experience, and/or Knowledge:

1. Experience in functioning as a team member on a interdisciplinary team
2. Experience in supervising students or volunteers
3. Experience in working with children with developmental disabilities and their families
4. Experience in using behavior modification principles and techniques
5. Experience in conducting professional inservice and parent training
6. Experience in locating or making curriculum materials, resources, and adaptive equipment
7. Experience in writing individualized programs and using data collection systems

JOB ENLARGEMENT AND JOB ENRICHMENT

Job enlargement and job enrichment are two areas that are receiving increasing emphasis in many agencies and organizations. Job enlargement can be defined as an increase in the number and variety of activities an individual performs on the job, and job enrichment can be defined as an increase in the degree to which an employee controls the planning and performance of the job as well as his or her involvement in the setting of agency policy (Lawler, 1969). Although the various studies in these two areas have design problems (Kerr, 1979), they generally report increased job satisfaction, productivity, and motivation, and decreased turnover and "burnout." To enlarge and enrich jobs, several activities can be completed by administrators. These include being open to and encouraging input from staff on decisions that affect their jobs, encouraging and reinforcing creativity in accomplishing the job, providing individuals with more freedom to make decisions regarding their job based on their performance and demonstration that they can handle such freedom, providing staff with new but not overwhelming challenges and activities, encouraging and/or re-assigning staff to work with different children every second or third year (e.g., assigning a teacher who has been working with autistic children to work with the trainable educatably retarded), promoting staff to new positions within the system when such positions become available, and offering incentives such as trips to conferences and new equipment for the classroom (Shaw et al., 1981). A staff member who is not regularly challenged by a routine job is likely to become a nonproductive staff member because the number and quality of reinforcers obtained from the job decrease. It is important that each staff member remain productive if the children served are to receive the quality services and the staff are to receive the job satisfaction they deserve.

Participation and Staff Motivation

Motivated staff are productive and fun to work with, whereas unmotivated staff are not. One of the best methods for motivating staff is to have them participate in decisions that affect their jobs. A variety of methods exist for eliciting their participation. One good method is to conduct an annual group retreat for planning goals and objectives. Topics such as how to accomplish goals and objectives, time lines, resources needed, methods for evaluating achievement, inservice activities, changes in policies, how each individual's effort contributes to the group's success, and any other activities needed for a productive and efficient year may be discussed. During the year, regular staff meetings can focus on follow-through of retreat activities and on current business. In staff meetings, staff members should be encouraged to participate, and be provided with positive comments for their participation. They should have their ideas considered, no matter how good or undeveloped, and should be involved in decision making. These are ''group maintenance functions,'' (activities concerned with the wellbeing of group members). In addition to these maintenance functions, it is important that task functions be taken care of; that is, functions such as getting the job accomplished and meeting time lines. Administrators must make it clear to staff that the administrator is ultimately responsible for final decisions but that decisions are best made after collecting information from all sources and that staff input can affect most decisions. In order to maintain credibility, an administrator should not present an issue to the staff, as if seeking their input, if the decision has already been made or if it is an issue where existing constraints (e.g., money or state rules and regulations) dictate the only acceptable solution. By being honest with staff so they know when their input can and will be used and when it won't, staff will more likely be responsive to administrative needs while simultaneously feeling they have some control over their professional future. An administrator must also follow through on commitments made to staff. Additional information on participative management can be found in almost any organizational management text (Kerr, 1979).

The staff working in a special education setting are motivated by the same things that motivate others: the consequences of their own behavior. Each staff member's performance is motivated by the occurrence of activities that have meaning to them. These may include, among other things, seeing a child make progress as a function of their efforts, having a supervisor make positive comments about their performance, having a child become attached to them as demonstrated by the giving of a hug, a touch, a smile or a greeting, having parents respond positively to them, having others in the team seek their advice, hearing their name mentioned in a positive way or seeing a positive written statement about themselves, getting a pay raise or promotion, having someone bring a visitor to meet them, having some freedom to try their own ideas, and having the support of their supervisor. It is important that supervisors realize that staff are motivated to take care of some of their own needs, some of which are inherent in a special education setting (e.g., success evidenced by a child's progress), but many motivators are still directly or indirectly controlled by the supervisor. If a supervisor ignores good performance that should be noticed, it may disappear because it seems unimportant to the staff member who sees others get attention for lack of performance. To correct this, the administrator can positively control components of the work environment such as physical surroundings, leadership style, and goal directions; task design components such as variety, decision autonomy, job challenge and job scope; and job consequences such as salary, feedback and promotions so as to improve staff motivation and performance (Kerr, 1979). It is recommended that administrators learn to use each of these three components to keep staff motivated.

An important part of program efficiency is the evaluation of staff performance and the provision of feedback on such performance. The literature, particularly in the area of organizational development, abounds with information on staff evaluation systems (Kerr, 1979; Kolb et al., 1979). However, many administrators ignore the area of staff performance evaluation, and others see it as a "necessary evil." Yet others appreciate its potential merits. Performance evaluation serves four primary functions: staff motivation, staff development, information dissemination, and control and policy making based on information obtained during the appraisal process (Kerr, 1979).

A good performance appraisal and feedback system will include both an ongoing and a formal component. The ongoing appraisal system provides a means by which a supervisor can provide feedback to staff on a day-to-day basis. It should include feedback in the form of "strokes" for positive performance and skill improvement, and corrective measures for areas in need of change. This combination of feedback is dually effective in that it may provide an individual with both the information needed to improve his or her performance and with an awareness of those areas in which performance is adequate or excellent. The appraisal process may also provide the supervisor with information on areas in which the staff needs additional training. The more closely related rewards or incentives (e.g., pay increase, better position, trip to conference) are to performance, the greater the motivation to perform well. The second type of staff performance appraisal serves many of the same functions as the first, but it consists of a formal evaluation conducted annually or semi-annually. Generally, an evaluation form of some sort is completed. It may be an overall evaluation form on traits, attitudes, and behaviors such as the one included at the end of this chapter on pages 34–37, or it may be a form that evaluates performance on each item listed in the job description, or it may focus on tangible results of staff behavior. A form that evaluates each item on the job description is the best form for several reasons. First, it makes clear to the employee and supervisor what areas will be evaluated. This encourages all concerned to be sure the job description is updated and accurate, which in turn helps assure that each staff member knows what is expected of him or her. Second, it makes explicit the relationship between one's job performance and pay raises, promotions, and renewed contracts. Third, it helps minimize or control the degree to which a supervisor must rely on personalities instead of performance in completing a staff evaluation. Finally, it provides a method of integrating day-to-day staff performance appraisal into the formal evaluation because the areas being evaluated have been specified in advance.

The traditional method of evaluation is one in which a supervisor evaluates the performance of each of his or her subordinates (the individual he or she supervises), and is in turn evaluated by his or her supervisor. Whereas such an evaluation has some advantages, it often lacks useful information. It is recommended that each staff member and supervisor be evaluated by several members of interdisciplinary teams on which the individual serves, or by peers at the same level within the agency, subordinates (e.g., teacher evaluated by aides), parents of children served, and an individual outside of a person's team but within the same organization. These evaluators will have access to overlapping and yet different information. The supervisor can still have the major responsibility for coordinating the integration of all of the evaluation information. A multi-evaluator system such as this is more time consuming than an evaluation by a single individual; however, it is more comprehensive and provides more opportunity for an accurate and finite evaluation in that if two or more individuals can reach a consensus on the positive and deficient aspects of performance, then personality differences are somewhat controlled.

It is not necessary that members of each of the aforementioned groups participate in each formal evaluation, even though doing so would seem ideal. In consideration of time constraints and competing job pressures, an agency may decide to have a supervisor and one or two other individuals from the groups mentioned (e.g., peer and parent) evaluate the staff member one year, and the supervisor and individuals from other groups the next year (e.g., subordinate and staff members from another group in the school).

During the actual appraisal interview between the supervisor and the staff member, certain factors become evident. For instance, subordinate satisfaction with the feedback interview, motivation to improve, and satisfaction with the supervisor are related to the degree of supportive behavior by the supervisor during the interview, the degrees to which the subordinate feels he or she is invited to participate, and the degree to which the subordinate actually participates in goal setting for professional self-improvement (Nemeroff & Wexley, 1977). The latter, professional self-improvement, is one area that may require examination as to how one measures up to the competencies necessary for successful performance on the job. Systematic planning, initiative and self-evaluation are all required for professional growth (Blackhurst & Berdine, 1981).

Staff evaluations should be designed to provide feedback to each team member, pointing out strengths and weaknesses. It is a joint responsibility of the supervisor and the staff member to be aware of weaknesses and to outline appropriate methods for remediation. Since evaluation must be considered as data-oriented decisionmaking (Stevens & King, 1976), such decisions must involve the development of a plan in which specific goals are set, and activities (reading/inservice) for achieving them, time lines and a method for measuring achievement of goals are specified. It is the administrator's responsibility to implement staff evaluations and provide feedback to each professional. It is recommended that formal evaluations occur twice each academic year: once by mid-December and again by mid-April. This process allows evaluators in the educational setting time to become aware of levels of staff performance, and allows staff to obtain formal feedback in the first half of the academic year and gives them 4 months to work on deficiencies before the next evaluation. Improvement efforts should become evident in the second evaluation, and the second evaluation should occur early enough for the supervisor to make appropriate recommendations for salary adjustments and contract renewals and to continue efforts for staff improvement.

THE ROLE OF THE CONSULTANT IN THE CLASSROOM

So far, this chapter has focused on staff working together in a program as full- or part-time contract employees serving individuals with developmental disabilities. The focus now shifts to rural and remote geographical locations where needed staff may not be available, and thus, must be hired on a consultancy basis.

The Education for All Handicapped Children Act (Public Law 94-142) states that "a free appropriate public education emphasizes special education and *related services for handicapped children.*" This concept of "related services" for handicapped children has been open to some heated debate in many school districts where school officials see the extension and additional costs of related services as being a "Pandora's box" of sorts. Most, however, have attempted to live within the letter of the law by providing at least a minimum to moderate level of related services through various service delivery patterns. Related services in many areas include, but are not limited to, physical therapy, occupational therapy, audiology, psychology, recreation therapy, speech and language therapy, adaptive physical education, dietetics, and medicine. However, many school and agency officials have failed to look at the most logical and economically feasible role for the specialist delivering related services to take—that of a therapy consultant. The therapy consultant serves as a consultant and trainer to classroom staff rather than as a direct service provider to children. This allows the therapist to see a larger number of students requiring his or her services and assures that programs will receive follow-through, appropriate practice, and integration into other skill areas even in his or her absence.

This "consultant model" of service delivery is especially beneficial and cost-effective in rural and remote geographical areas where the lack of specialists is most pronounced due to a) the small number of clients in need of the service, b) expense per se, c) the small program tax base, and d) the remoteness of some rural areas, discouraging some specialists from moving to these locations (Striefel, 1982).

This type of model does require a specialist who is secure in his or her profession and level of technical skills. The specialist must be concerned with service delivery and convinced that the integration of skills and therapy across programs provides the student with developmental disabilities with the best possible services pattern. The model requires that the specialist think through each skill to be taught in a functional manner so that he or she is able to teach others to be trainers. It also requires that the specialist set up the program utilizing a behavioral format so that each new skill can easily be measured as it is taught. When carefully established and running smoothly, the therapy consultant model allows a therapist to cover a large population and geographic area within a limited amount of time.

Components of Therapy Consultant Model

The following items are components of the therapy consultant model within the public school system. The model addresses all special related services and covers seven basic topics:

1. Assessment
2. Programming
3. Program Standards
4. Implementation
5. Indirect Services
6. Facilities
7. Forms

(See Tables 2.1, 2.2, and 2.3.)

Assessment The therapy consultant must first obtain parental permission and, if necessary, a physician's written prescription to formally

Table 2.1.
_____

Parent/Guardian Notification of Assessment

Date _____

Dear Parent/Guardian:

Your child's school district and child study team indicated a need for a(n) _____ _____ therapy evaluation.

This evaluation process will assist us in maximizing your child's school performance evaluation by identifying his or her assets and problem areas.

Please sign the attached sheet in order for us to administer the necessary assessments.

Sincerely,

(Signature)
(Title)

Encl.
_____

evaluate the child's level of functioning. The entire evaluation process should include an assessment of the developmental level, as well as the functional abilities and deficits of the pupil. The first step is for the consultant to review all of the client's existing records. In addition, it may be necessary to have the classroom teacher or another staff member conduct some additional assessments using consultant-developed forms, criterion-referenced tests (e.g., Basic School Skills Inventory, Brigance) or checklists such as the one developed by Dever and Knapczyk (1980) to screen for physical problems in the classroom. Ratings on these screening instruments are completed by direct observation. After reviewing available information, the consultant may choose to conduct additional assessments to collect information needed to develop appropriate individualized programs for clients. This evaluation process may include, but is not limited to, test areas according to the specific therapy discipline (Table 2.4).

The names of specific assessment instruments are presented in Chapter 4, Identifying and Assessing the Child in Need of Special Education Services. In addition, Swanson and Watson (1982) provide extensive coverage of available assessment devices and their use.

Programming After the initial assessment is completed, the necessary data collected, and the findings interpreted, a decision is made by the child study team on the type and frequency of related services needed by the student. Documentation of the test results are placed in the student's file, and the development of appropriate goals and objectives is made with the child study team (see Chapter 5). Following this, individual programs are written and classroom personnel are trained in their use. In addition to the design and implementation of programs for individuals or groups, the therapy consultant may also provide additional consultant services to staff, parents, and other

Table 2.2.

_____ Therapy Referral Form
(specify type of therapy required)

Child's name:_____ /_____

Age:_____   Date of birth: _____

School:_____   Grade: _____

Teacher:_____

Special programming (resource room):

_____

_____

Date of referral: _____

Diagnosis (if known):_____

I. Presenting problems: (Be as specific as possible—list in priorities)

_____

_____

_____

_____

II. The areas in which the problems are observed to interfere with level of pupil's performance:

_____

_____

_____

_____

III. Any special equipment or materials used by the pupil presently:

_____

_____

_____

_____

IV. Type of assistance required from the therapist:
Specific therapy programming ☐
Inservice training ☐
Suggested activities ☐   Individual ☐   or   Group ☐
Specialized equipment or materials ☐
Other _____

Signature _____

Title _____

Date _____

professionals or paraprofessionals associated with the student's program. These additional consulting services may include providing specific suggestions to teachers for supplemental exercises or activities that can be incor-

Table 2.3.

Therapy Consultancy Record

School —————— Month —————— Year ——————

| Date | Time | | Total Hours | Pupil/teacher parent seen | Contact information | Signature |
	In	Out				

Table 2.4.   Evaluation test areas

Physical Therapy

Gait assessment
Reflex assessment
Posture assessment
Mobility assessment
Developmental level of gross motor
  abilities

Muscle strength
Range of motion testing
Observational evaluation:
  Use of adaptive equipment, positioning,
  lifting, and transfer techniques and
  mode of mobility.

Occupational Therapy

Eye-hand coordination
Hand function
Muscle strength
Developmental level of fine motor abilities
Oral/feeding assessment
Sensory assessment

Visual perception testing
Range of motion testing
Observational evaluation:
  Use of adaptive equipment, positioning,
  lifting and transfer techniques, and
  mode of mobility.

Audiology

Tympanometry
Pure tone testing

Impedance testing
Brain stem evoked response testing

Psychology

Standardized intellectual assessment
Adaptive behavior assessment

Behavioral assessment
Achievement testing

Recreation Therapy

Recreational interests

Recreational skill level

Speech and Language

Developmental receptive language level
Developmental expressive language level

Articulation testing
Oral exam

Dietetics

Growth charting and monitoring
Anthropometric measurements

Analysis of nutritional intake

Adaptive P.E.

Strength testing
Endurance testing

Basic physical skill assessment

porated into other classroom programs, or making recommendations and/or designing and making special adaptive equipment and devices for use in the classroom or at home.

Standards   It is essential to outline specific program standards to be used on a regular basis in order for the therapy consultant to consistently produce an organized and accurate method of reporting and writing goals, objectives, and pupil programs. The important program standards to be considered by a therapy consultant within the classroom setting include the following:

1. Treatment goals will address the pupil's most immediate problem areas that affect their performance level within the school setting.
2. Specific programs and methods to achieve the above goals will be written along appropriate developmental guidelines.
3. The therapy program plan will be written in specific data-based terminology consisting of a statement of achievable goals, the methods and

materials to attain the goals, teaching frequency of the program, and person(s) responsible for program implementation and monitoring.

4. A record of appropriate data and annual progress records will be kept by trainers for each pupil receiving services and monitored regularly by the therapy consultant.

5. The therapist will document and make appropriate program changes consistent with changes in the pupil's performance and level of achievement. The therapist will carefully demonstrate any program changes made.

6. The therapist will re-evaluate on a yearly basis and document in written form the changes in the pupil's performance and developmental level.

7. The therapist will terminate services when the pupil has attained all short and long term goals or when the student has achieved maximum benefit from therapy programming, as determined by the therapy evaluation and child study team that includes the parents.

Implementation   It is essential for the consultant to thoroughly train teachers and additional classroom staff in the specific therapy programs since the therapy consultant visits the program only on a periodic basis. Training of teachers and support staff (aides, volunteers, and students) assigned to direct the programming of individual students involves all of the following areas:

1. Understanding the specific program objectives and what is expected in regards to student performance

2. Being able to comprehend and utilize the written program format (see Chapter 8)

3. Knowing how to operate and obtain special equipment or materials required for program implementation

4. Being able to carry out program implementation such as what to do with the materials/equipment, what the trainer does and says to the pupil during the program, what the pupil's response should be, what are the number of program trials required per session, and what criteria are to be attained before advancing the student to the next program step

5. Being able to collect data accurately using the methods and forms with each written program

6. Ensuring that classroom staff understand their roles (role clarity), as well as the role of the therapy consultant, and know when and how to seek the services of the therapy consultant

It is the therapy consultant's responsibility to monitor and supervise each trainer. How often the therapy consultant observes the trainer and monitors the program is adjusted according to the type of handicapping condition, the extent and specificity of the treatment program, and the need for consistent program change and adjustment. The therapy consultant is also responsible for the summation of program data and written and verbal progress reporting.

The time allotment for a therapy consultant is important. The therapist's *total role* within the system must be considered. The total role of a therapy consultant involves:

1. Scheduled time for meetings and phone contacts with parents, teachers, physicians, and other therapists
2. Evaluation and re-evaluation process time
3. Preparation of programs, reports, and data summaries
4. Designing and making equipment and special materials
5. Professional and workshop development and inservice training

Indirect Services The therapy consultant can also provide indirect support services to the center or school in which he or she works by:

1. Assisting the staff and parents in the knowledge and understanding of various handicaps in relationship to self-help, motor development and control, or speech and language problems to optimize their teaching strategies
2. Providing consultation to teachers, supportive staff, and parents on general and specific activities to maximize the pupil's performance levels and use of any specialized equipment (wedge, rolls, chairs, communication boards, etc.)
3. Providing teachers, support staff, and parents with specific management techniques for the child with multiple handicaps that would improve the pupil's school peformance level
4. Providing inservice training, demonstrations, and workshops to all staff as needed

Standard Forms In addition to the described guidelines for a therapy consultant within the public school system, it is beneficial to use standard forms while compiling referral and release information, therapy consultant evaluation records, and therapy consultant time schedules. Examples of some forms have been included in other chapters of this book (e.g., Chapter 8). Others, such as release of information forms (Table 2.1) are available in almost every school district office and others, like Tables 2.2 and 2.3, are easily designed.

SAMPLE EVALUATION FORM

As with all evaluation forms, this form is not perfect. Some terms may seem vague to you. If necessary, write in beside the word your definition in terms of how you are rating the particular item. Please read all of the instructions that follow and then complete one evaluation form on each staff member which you are assigned to rate. That list of staff members is attached to this packet of evaluation forms.[1]

General Instructions:

1. For each of your peers, complete Sections I through III on the white sheets and Section IV on the green sheet.[2]
2. If you are a supervisor rating people on your staff, complete Sections I through III on the white sheets and Secton IV on the green sheet.
3. If you are rating your supervisor or if you are a supervisor rating another supervisor, fill out Sections I through III on the white sheets and Section V on the pink sheet.
4. Each statement will be rated using the rating scale that follows:

    > SA = I strongly agree with this statement.
    > A = I generally agree with this statement.
    > U = I am undecided as to how this individual should be rated on this behavior
    > D = I generally disagree with this statement.
    > SD = I strongly disagree with this statement.
    > DK = I do not know enough about the performance of this individual in this area to rate him or her.
    > NA = This statement does not apply to this individual's job.

5. Read each statement and in the space provided to the left of each item place the letter from the rating scale that most closely corresponds to your ranking for the designated individual.

Evaluation Form

Name of person being rated: _____

Rater-ratee relationship (check one):

Person is member of my unit: _____

Person is member of another unit: _____

DATE: _____

Section I: Professional Competency

_____ 1. I would seek out this person's help with problems falling within his or her area of expertise.

_____ 2. This person seems to be aware of current developments in his or her field.

_____ 3. This person is generally able to develop successful programs to deal with clients referred to him or her.

_____ 4. This person generally is able to provide objective documentation of clients' progress in their treatment programs.

_____ 5. This person appears to effectively utilize resources (pre-existing programs, other members of his or her discipline) available on this campus in developing and implementing treatment programs.

_____ 6. This person is able to develop a job description (or work within a pre-existing one) to effectively carry out duties falling within his or her area of expertise so as to maximally meet the needs of the unit he or she is assigned to.

---

[1]The list of staff members is not reproduced here, but should be provided for anyone actually using this evaluation system.

[2]Each evaluator should receive a copy of this evaluation form, printed on the following colored sheets if possible: white (for Sections I–III), green (for Section IV), and pink (for Section V).

Section II: Ability to Work with Other Staff

_____ 1. This person is accessible to other staff.

_____ 2. This person appears sensitive to the needs of the unit as a whole.

_____ 3. This person is responsive to the needs of his or her co-workers.

_____ 4. This person is able to deal with crisis situations in a calm, constructive manner.

_____ 5. This person is able to deal with disagreements in a constructive, not petty or vengeful, manner.

_____ 6. This person is honest in his or her dealings with others.

_____ 7. This person completes assignments within set time lines.

_____ 8. This person appears to be motivated to carry out his or her duties efficiently.

_____ 9. This person generally attempts to use social praise and constructive criticism to help others perform their duties efficiently.

_____ 10. I would not hesitate to give this person constructive criticism.

_____ 11. I generally enjoy working with this person.

_____ 12. This person attends staff meetings pertaining to the function of his or her unit, and/or the center as a whole.

_____ 13. This person appears to put the interests of his or her clients, his or her unit, and those of the center in general above personal desires for power, authority, dominance, etc.

_____ 14. This person cooperates willingly with other discipline members rather than operating as a "lone wolf".

_____ 15. This person accepts input from members of other disciplines who can help him or her in carrying out his or her duties.

_____ 16. This person seeks advice and information from members of other disciplines when needed.

_____ 17. This person fosters and accepts interdisciplinary cooperative programs within his or her unit.

_____ 18. In an interdisciplinary program, this person "does his or her share" as a member of the team carrying out that program.

_____ 19. This person appears to try to carry out his or her assigned duties without procrastination or buck passing.

_____ 20. This person keeps his or her supervisor up to date on progress and problems in his or her job.

_____ 21. In supervising this person, I feel that I can give him or her direction and that he or she will respond appropriately to this.

Section III: Personal Attributes

_____ 1. This person is punctual.

_____ 2. This person appears well organized.

_____ 3. This person is enjoyable to interact with (on the job).

_____ 4. This person conducts him- or herself in a professional manner so as to inspire confidence in others in their own professional competency.

_____ 5. This person is relatively free of annoying habits/mannerisms.

_____ 6. This person is willing to schedule his or her activities so as not to conflict with those of other staff.

_____ 7. This person does not seem to be unfairly or unreasonably critical of other people, motivated by no other reason than simply wanting to put them down.

_____ 8. I would feel comfortable bringing personnel and job-related problems to this person.

_____ 9. I trust this person to treat me in a fair and considerate manner.

_____ 10. This person is willing to accept other staff as true peers with equal competencies, albeit in different areas.

Section IV: Dealing with Clients

_____ 1. This person's major interest appears to be the progress of his or her clients.

_____ 2. This person deals ethically with his or her clients.

_____ 3. This person can be relied upon to provide programming for clients referred to him or her.

_____ 4. This person can be relied on to provide coverage for his or her clients if unable to meet with them.

_____ 5. When disagreements arise with other staff as to the proper treatment of clients, this individual resolves these differences in a data-based, nonarbitrary manner.

_____ 6. When applying treatments that are experimental in nature, this person obtains proper clearance and monitors his or her program carefully.

_____ 7. When dealing with clients, this person seems to plan ahead in terms of long term effects, possible side effects, and the general goals of the referring party (teacher, parent, or the client himself).

_____ 8. In devising programs, the person plans for the generalization and maintenance of treatment gains.

_____ 9. This person does not allow his or her personal moods to adversely affect his relations with clients.

Section V: Leadership

_____ 1. This person is a good leader.

_____ 2. The criticisms made by this individual of other's job appointments are constructive.

_____ 3. The criticism made by this person about other person's job performance is fair.

_____ 4. This person has reasonable expectations of staff member's job performance.

_____ 5. This person lets staff know what is expected of them in terms of job performance.

_____ 6. This person is receptive to the needs of staff members.

_____ 7. This person supports the position of his or her staff members on issues.

_____ 8. This person filters information from above before it is submitted to the staff.

_____ 9. This person filters information from below before it is given to the supervisor.

_____ 10. This person schedules the appropriate meetings.

_____ 11. This person strives for fairness and objectivity in the allocation of resources among staff.

_____ 12. This person tries to use objective criteria in making decisions concerning salary allocations and other matters relating to staff advancement.

_____ 13. This person tries to foster a spirit of cooperation and teamwork among the disciplines in the center.

_____ 14. This person makes staff members aware of and gives them an opportunity to contribute to the development of operational policies.

_____ 15. This person consults with staff members, considers their advice, and attempts to have unit policies represent a consensus.

_____ 16. This person assembles and analyzes facts before making decisions.

_____ 17. This person makes decisions without unnecessary delay.

_____ 18. This person provides adequate information to staff either directly or through other staff.

_____ 19. This person does not pass on his or her own job responsibilities to other staff members.

_____ 20. This person develops adequate long and short range goals toward which administrative efforts are directed.

_____ 21. This person administers the affairs of the unit in a businesslike, efficient manner.

_____ 22. This supervisor makes his or her staff aware of policies that affect the performance of their jobs.

_____ 23. If in disagreement with a staff member, this supervisor does not carry a grudge affecting the constructiveness of future dealings with this staff member.

_____ 24. This supervisor provides reasonable time lines in assigning duties.

_____ 25. In supervising the unit, the supervisor attempts to be aware of the needs of clients within that unit.

_____ 26. The supervisor is willing to trust the expertise of staff members.

_____ 27. In making administrative decisions regarding unit policies, this person always bears the short and long term interests of that unit's clients in mind.

_____ 28. I feel I can disagree with this supervisor without being dealt with in a punitive fashion.

3

Classroom Organization and Operation

After reading this chapter, you should have an understanding of:

1. The importance of organizing and managing for stimulus control, including how stimulus control can be established and enhanced by rearrangement of the physical environment
2. Organization of classrooms and factors to consider in rearranging the environment
3. How time can be used to enhance child progress
4. Methods for keeping track of staff and students and for organizing children's programs, including the role of planning in program success

PREPARING FOR THE DIFFICULT TASK of organizing the classroom so that efficiency and instruction are maximized is the subject of this chapter. Stimulus control and manipulation of the physical environment are discussed in detail, and recommendations for equipment, materials, and supplies are provided.

ORGANIZING AND MANAGING FOR STIMULUS CONTROL

The basic goal of special education is twofold:

1. To establish new behaviors
2. To bring these behaviors under stimulus control

Stimulus control exists when there is a high probability that certain responses or behaviors will occur in the presence of particular events (antecedent stimuli), but not in their absence (Spradlin, Karlan & Wetherby, 1976; Sulzer-Azaroff & Mayer, 1977). This means that children's behavior can be predicted and controlled via the arrangement for the presence of certain stimuli and the absence of others. The stimuli that can be manipulated to control behavior include the physical environment, instructional materials, the behavior of others, and program scheduling.

The most effective way for stimulus control to enhance behavior is through rearrangement of the physical setting. A basic philosophy underlying the physical organization of the classroom is to arrange the environment so that the probability of children making desirable responses is maximized, while potentially disruptive elements are minimized. Classrooms should be set up to include specific physical areas for storage of instructional materials, individual and small group training, play, feeding, and toileting. Such a classroom setting promotes a structure in which children are trained to respond in predictable ways. In essence, specific settings predict that children, when in that structured setting, will sit quietly and attend without being distracted so that training can take place, and when in play settings, they will run, jump, play and conduct themselves in a manner appropriate to that less structured setting.

Some of the variables that need to be considered in the physical arrangement of a classroom are color, sound, space-time, ambiguity and consistency, and usability (Bednar & Haviland, 1969). Color, if a choice is available, should match the activity that will be conducted in the area (e.g., bright orange in play areas and more subtle colors in instructional areas). Sound level in an instructional area should be kept to a minimum since students with handicaps are often easily distracted by noise. Careful arrangement of furnishings and partitions can also help absorb sound. The variable of space-time refers to the arrangement of the space so that it gives the student a sense of where he or she is and the type of activity that will occur there via well placed landmarks. Once an appropriate classroom arrangement is found, it is best to leave the room arranged in this manner for several months or the year so that consistency is established for the student and ambiguity is minimized, especially for visually impaired and mentally retarded students. The last variable, usability, relates directly to the problems of architectural barriers for handicapped individuals. Careful attention to details in the classroom, the school, and the playground will prevent frustrating barriers (stairs for the wheelchair-bound student) and annoyances so the physical space is totally usable. Figures on space allowances for standard wheelchairs, use of textured surfaces for the blind and visually impaired, and possible safety hazards are available from the American National Standard Institute's publication, *Specifications for Making Buildings and Facilities Accessible to and Usable by the Physically Handicapped* (1961). Most alterations, if given careful thought, are neither time consuming nor, in most instances, costly.

Every classroom should and probably will be different and will reflect the teacher's taste and personality. It should also reflect the children and the tasks to be taught in the physical environment. Different tasks generally require varying physical arrangements and often these arrangements must coexist in one classroom. Careful planning for the best utilization of the existing environmental space is most easily accomplished by drawing or obtaining a floor plan (diagram of room size drawn to scale) of the room. A floor plan helps one visualize room space accurately without wasting time and energy physically rearranging furnishings. In some cases, several rooms may be used, each of which reflects a different set of physical elements (e.g., teaching self-help and housekeeping skills might occur in a classroom arranged like an apartment, or teaching academic skills might take place in a highly structured instructional setting. Most schools or centers unfortunately do not have the luxury of available extra space.

The importance of establishing physical settings and training children to discriminate what behavior is expected in each setting should not be discounted. When an instructional environment has been created so that potentially disruptive elements such as noise, lighting, and visual interferences are removed, it is essential that staff also react appropriately when in that environment. Staff should expect and encourage on-task, disruption-free behavior from all children and adults in this environment. Diverse activities such as searching for instructional materials, using timeout with another child, assessing another child's skills, or working in the presence of multiple ongoing instructional groups can all occur smoothly and simultaneously in a carefully planned classroom environment. Other environments such as free play areas should be busy and inviting and differ dramatically from the instructional environment. This will enable children to associate appropriate behaviors with the setting. Staff expectations of child behavior should match the setting.

Another factor of extreme importance in creating a classroom environment is the need for establishing environments that are similar to what children might find in other situations. For example, teaching children social skills within a highly structured teaching environment may initially be desirable. However, children must also be taught to use these skills in more realistic situations. Therefore, it is important to have such realistic or typical environmental situations accessible to staff in providing training. These environments for generalization of skills taught may actually be extensions of classrooms, but should be identified prior to the beginning of the school year and should include the child's home, the playground, the lunchroom, and whenever possible, other settings in the community (e.g., a grocery store, restaurant).

ORGANIZATION OF CLASSROOMS

"Classroom" is used to refer to any room in which instruction occurs. Planning classroom space based on the instructional and practical needs of the students to be served in that space can initially be time consuming, but will pay off in the long run. Each school serving children with handicaps should attempt to organize varying classroom or instructional environments so they are appropriate for conducting extensive training. The room may look like an apartment, a kitchen, an open space or a work place, and may or may not have classroom-type furniture, but it is still a classroom. Some sample floor plans with varying types of focus for different students are presented as examples (see Figures 3.1 through 3.8).

The preschool classrooms (Figures 3.1 and 3.2) are organized to facilitate individual and small group instruction while eliminating distractions both visually and, to some extent, audibly through the use of fabric or carpet-covered partitions. School-age classrooms (Figures 3.3 and 3.4) are organized much the same as the preschool classrooms; however, more space has been allocated for individual instructional activities. Some specialty instructional areas are also set up, such as laundry, kitchen, and work skill areas. The physical and occupational therapy room (Figure 3.5) is set up to maximize the

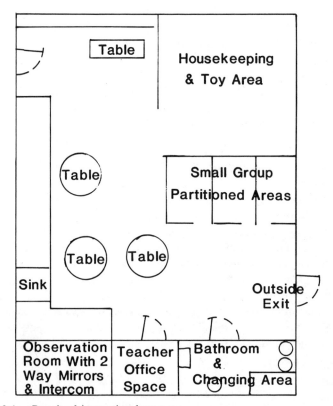

Figure 3.1.   Preschool instructional areas.

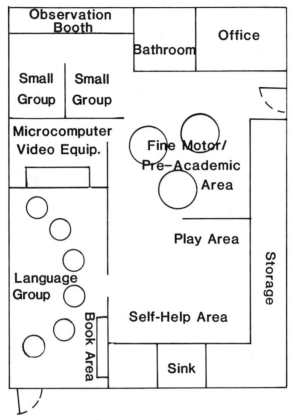

Figure 3.2. Preschool learning centers.

space and to allow several ongoing activities to occur without distractions at any one time and also to keep more active and, hence, potentially dangerous activities away from the less active, more sedentary activities. A wide variety of specialized equipment and materials are located in this room. Access to the room is controlled and only those children accompanied by a therapist should be permitted to enter.

The activity room (Figure 3.6) contains equipment that is located around the perimeter of the room and easily returned to the storage area so that the flexibility of the room is maintained and staff desiring to use the room for their students can set it up the way they wish. The activity room is useful for free play, recess, and other noisy and semi-structured activity and has an adjoining locker/shower and bathroom. It is also frequently used for large group activities such as movies, music, and special programs. The outside play areas (Figures 3.7 and 3.8) are different from each other. One area (Figure 3.7) is designed to strengthen existing motor, balance, and coordination skills, and to urge the

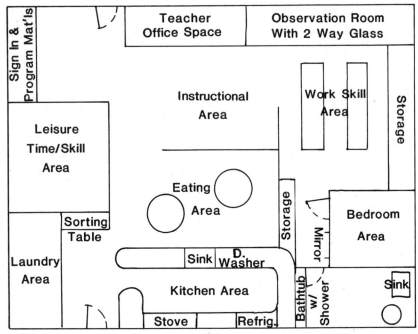

Figure 3.3.   Prevocational area.

student with developmental disabilities to achieve his or her full ability. The second outside play area (Figure 3.8) is designed for use by smaller and more involved children, and includes wheelchair ramps, grassy mounds, a slide without steps, elevated sand tables for wheelchair use, and adapted climbers and swings. Play areas should be extensions of the classroom environment and should be planned with as much care and foresight (Moore, Cohen, Oertel, & Van Ryzin, 1979) as the interior environment.

Considerations in Organizing Classrooms

As can be seen from Figures 3.1–3.8, organizing space to maximize stimulus control is rather straightforward. In organizing a classroom, the following considerations should be made:

1. Space should be arranged specifically for each different activity. A teacher should consider the activity that will occur (e.g., large group teaching vs. individual instruction) and arrange the space accordingly. Instructional areas should be noticeably different from those that accomodate noisy activities. Dividers and the materials available in an area are useful for accomplishing this.
2. The arrangement of tables, chairs, and mats in individual and group work areas should reduce, as much as possible, the distractions caused by

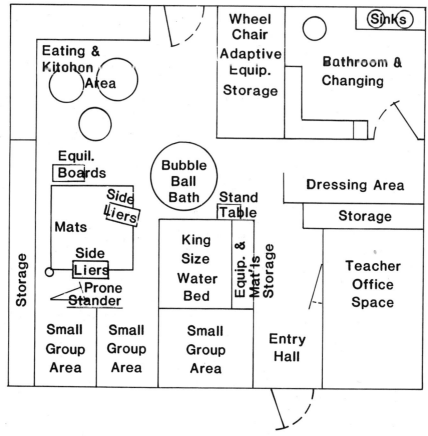

Figure 3.4. Multihandicapped classroom.

children and staff moving from one area to another. By using dividers and partitions, and facing children toward nearby walls and away from walkways where traffic may be heavy, distractions will be reduced. At times, corners are even more effective in eliminating distractions than are walls.

3. Acoustics play a very important role in the stimulus control in a classroom. Too much noise will distract children. It is helpful to locate areas and arrange spaces where noise levels are controlled and discourage children from engaging in noisy activities while others are performing tasks that require concentration and quiet surroundings.

4. Facilities for clothing storage should be located in each classroom. Swimming suits, sweaters, extra pants, and diapers should be stored close to the bathroom and diaper area. Hats and other articles of clothing may be stored in a plastic bin for each child that, in turn, is stored in a cupboard or closet.

5. If self-help skills such as showering and personal hygiene are to be taught,

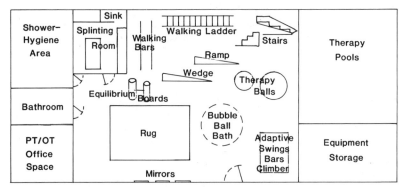

Figure 3.5. Physical and occupational therapy area.

bathing facilities such as a bathtub or shower are desirable. These facilities are also useful in toileting children when accidents occur and should be adjacent to the classroom whenever possible.

6. If instruction is to be conducted on the floor, rugs, mats, individual carpet squares, or other space markers should be provided to help minimize physical contact between the children when they are on the floor. They also help prevent body heat from flowing quickly into concrete and other stone-like surfaces. Many children with handicaps have pre-existing health-related problems that should not be compounded by colds and/or pneumonia. In addition, rugs are more comfortable for both children and staff during work periods.

7. All fire exits must be clear and free of obstacles. Furniture and work areas should be arranged so that they facilitate a rapid evacuation if necessary. Clearly marking areas to be checked for missing children during emergencies is also helpful. Fire departments will often provide decals or stickers to identify rooms where children might be located.

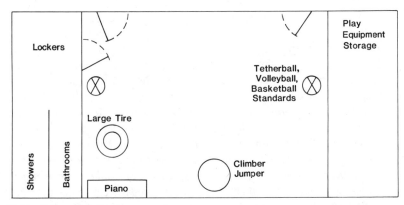

Figure 3.6. Activity area.

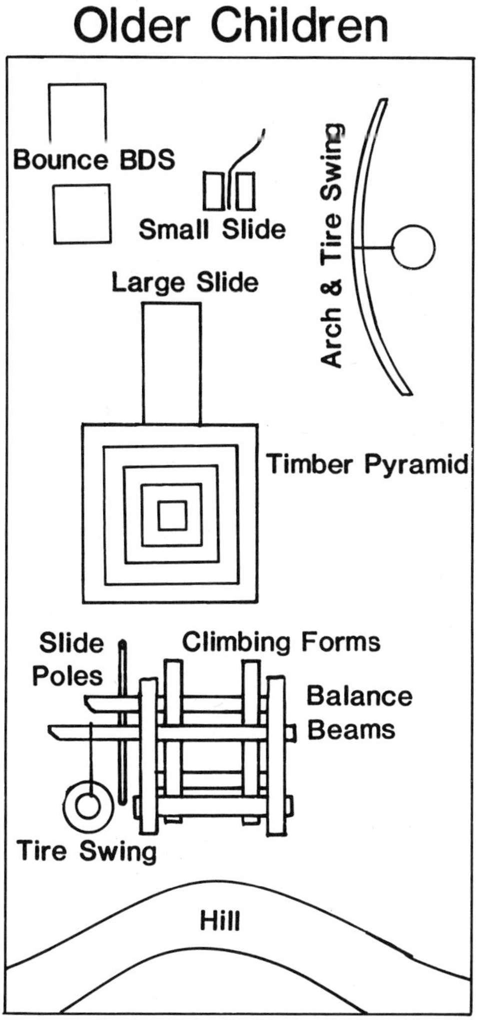

Older Children

Figure 3.7. Outside motor development and play area.

8. Instructional materials should be clearly labeled and kept in an easily accessible area close in proximity to where they will be utilized. They should always be ready in advance for teaching sessions. Often, materials can be adapted for mobility, allowing for easy transfer from their storage area.

9. Wall decorations are strongly suggested, and where children are often on the floor or in seating arrangements that cause them to look up, ceiling decoration may be in order. Decorations liven up a classroom and provide added visual stimulation for children. They can be used for educational

Non-Ambulatory & Small Children

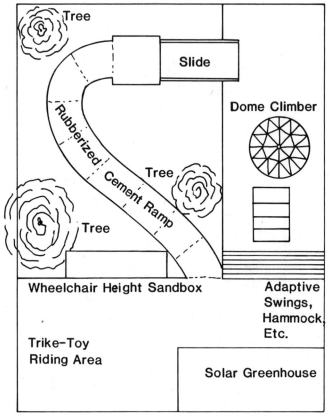

Figure 3.8. Therapeutic preschool play area.

purposes (calendar, maps, etc.) or to enhance play areas (textures to feel, familiar pictures, mirrors). They should be used judiciously, however, in areas where instruction will occur. They can be powerful distractions for children.

Once the various instructional settings have been organized within a classroom, teaching may begin. The settings in which instruction is conducted will be influential in determining a child's response. This is a desirable situation, particularly in the initial stages of training when minimizing novel stimuli and distractions is advantageous. Too many extraneous stimuli can overload a training session and produce distractions and other problems.

As behavior and skills are acquired in limited teaching settings, other instructional settings should be introduced to facilitate generalization of train-

Students / Times	Amy	Bill	Joe	Sam	Teri	Ann	Dick	Jason	Pete	Robert	Jane
9–9:30	▨	▨									
9:30–10	▨	▨									
10–10:30	▨	▨									
10:30–11	▨	▨									
11–11:30	▨	▨									
11:30–12	▨	▨									
12–12:30	▨										
12:30–1											
1–1:30											
1:30–2											
2–2:30											
2:30–3											

9–9:30	9:30–10	10–10:30	10:30–11	11–11:30	11:30–12

12–12:30	12:30–1

Card

Program Location	Where Session is Taught
	Individual's Name Session Title Time
Area Taught In	Who Will Teach Program

Card

IPB	Small Group Cubicle in Room
	Amy Speech 9:00
Group Lang. Area	Clinician Steve Jones

Figure 3.9. Sign-in board.

ing and to enable the child to use newly acquired skills in more functional settings. These potential instructional settings may include other classrooms, the gym, or the lunchroom. Arrangements should also be made for these skills to occur within other community settings and the home. Additionally, the most functional settings for a particular child should be probed periodically to determine whether the newly acquired skills are being demonstrated there. For example, in training a child to set a table, the most functional settings for this skill to ultimately occur are the home, a kitchen area, or the lunchroom. Throughout training, these settings should be periodically probed to determine whether the child is demonstrating the skill in these settings. Complete mastery of a skill may only be assumed when a child demonstrates a skill in various functional settings.

Just as important as training behavior so that it occurs in other locations is the need to have the behavior occur in the presence and/or under the control of people other than the person who originally trained the skill. To accomplish this, the child must regularly receive exposure to other people who probe for and/or retrain behaviors trained by someone else. The classroom aide, other teachers, and family members can serve this function. For more details concerning generalization, see Chapter 6.

USING TIME TO ENHANCE PROGRESS

Once the content of student instructional programs has been decided, it translates easily into a series of program sessions. It is important when scheduling the program sessions to maintain a balance between the type of sessions and the amount of bodily activity and movement allowed by the student in each session. Maintaining a balance helps eliminate behavior problems, especially restlessness while sitting. Scheduling a speech session, then a motor session, then a pre-academic session is a much better balance than planning two language sessions to be followed by a pre-academic session. Lunch, play periods, rest periods, and leisure activities can also be interspersed throughout the day to help achieve a balance. It is also useful to consider that when scheduling students, sessions can be conducted by different staff members in differing locations to promote the generalization of the skill across settings and trainers and to help maintain balance between the types of program sessions.

The greatest difficulty with the session approach to scheduling students is that, often, especially for students with severe handicaps, training programs become disjointed and lack continuity. For instance, language training may occur only once each day, or cleaning up after oneself may only take place during the self-help session. For the more involved student, this is not functional.

Another method of session scheduling that has been used effectively (Striefel & Hofmeister, 1980) is to have each of the student's daily programs conducted several times per day as mini-sessions within longer, one-hour blocks of time rather than the 15–30 minute sessions. In this way, the child will receive training in each of his or her programs during each hour of the instructional day. The child's instructional day can be divided into time blocks as follows:

1. 9:00 – 9:20   Toileting (arrival at school)
2. 9:20 –10:30   Instructional block #1
3. 10:30 –11:30 Instructional block #2
4. 11:30 –12:00 Music/other large group activities

5. 12:00 –12:30   Lunch
6. 12:30 – 1:30   Instructional block #3
7. 1:30 – 2:40   Instructional block #4
8. 2:40 – 3:00   Toileting (prepare to leave school)

Once the integrated training session has been designed, it can be reviewed with each of the staff that will be responsible for the child during each of the instructional blocks. Implementation of the integrated training sessions can then begin.

Each integrated training session by necessity allows for fewer training trials on each of the child's training programs. However, over the entire instructional day, the child may actually receive more trials on each program than with the previously mentioned teaching sessions. Built into each of the training sessions of the instructional day are times for toileting (if appropriate), rest periods, and play. Because so many training sessions take place within the instructional day, staff members must become familiar with a wider range of training content, as well as the differing data collection strategies employed for each training session.

The benefits of integrated training sessions are clear. First, each child receives training in specific skills at various times during the day by a variety of persons. This enhances the potential for the skills that are being trained to generalize across trainers and times (Whitney & Striefel, 1981; Williams, Brown, & Certo, 1975). Additionally, staff frequently alter the instructional settings in which sessions are conducted, thus providing for further generalization across settings. This is an important factor in providing maximally efficient, appropriate instruction.

Second, the design of the integrated training sessions requires staff to become familiar with the child's entire training program, rather than just one aspect of it. Therefore, they are better prepared to reinforce occurrences of behaviors that were previously only reinforced in limited training sessions. This also facilitates the child's generalization of his or her newly acquired skills. The biggest drawback of this technique is that it requires the availability of enough staff and/or volunteers to be able to repeat all of the programs several times per day and to work a complete hour each time. In some settings, this may not be realistic; however, paraprofessionals can easily help with sessions. Further research is needed to determine the ideal staff-to-student ratio, the types of children such a procedure is most useful and/or necessary for, and the essential components of the procedure.

METHODS OF ORGANIZATION OF INSTRUCTIONAL PROGRAMS

Vitally important to classroom operation is the development of methods for monitoring staff and students and for organizing children's instructional activities and programs.

Sign-In Board The sign-in board is a helpful tool in implementing instructional programs such as the integrated training sessions. It enables the teacher to visually monitor the programs for each child in the classroom. It also aids in monitoring staff by providing feedback to them on how they conducted their sessions. The sign-in board is placed on a bulletin board or wall near the classroom's main entrance. It consists of a matrix of children's names and time blocks (see Figure 3.9). Cards (2" × 2") are placed within the body of the matrix. These sign-in cards on the schedule board carry useful information for the classroom staff, including client name, subject, time of session, where the program is located, who works with the client, where the session is being taught, and a description of the activity. One card is placed on each time block for each child and may be color coded to facilitate identification of certain activities, e.g., toileting (red card), instructional blocks (blue card), group activities (yellow card), lunch (orange card).

At the beginning of any time block, the staff member responsible for a particular child removes the card for that time block and puts the card into an envelope labeled with the correct time that is attached to the bottom of the bulletin board. In this way, the teacher is able to glance at the sign-in board from any location in the classroom and determine immediately whether all children are being served. This is done by glancing across the column representing the time block. If any cards remain on the sign-in board, this indicates that some children are not being worked with and the teacher may immediately take steps to get children into sessions.

Another useful aspect of the sign-in board is that the teacher may communicate with particular staff members, volunteers or clinicians regarding a certain program by pinning written messages on the card (e.g., "see me about this session," or "review data collection procedures for this session"). These messages may be written at the end of the day while the teacher is reviewing data for each of the children. Staff, upon entering the classroom the following day, check the session card and make the necessary changes or meet with the teacher.

The sign-in board is not necessary or useful in classrooms where there are no staff other than the teacher. Such classrooms for handicapped children should be few, based on the requirements of Public Law 94-142 (Education for All Handicapped Children Act of 1975).

Individual Program Books (IPBs) All of the training programs for each child served are included in a three-ring binder called the Individual Program Book or IPB. In each IPB, the following materials are included:

1. General information on the child, including his or her picture, specific health information related to types of food to be eaten, seizure information, toileting skills and language level
2. A list of reinforcers available for use with the child, including both tangible and intangible items

3. Training programs, materials, and data collection sheets for each teaching session in the day. These are organized in a sequential order for each time block in the day (e.g., under 9:30 A.M., one might find a motor training program followed by an appropriate data collection sheet, followed by a divider for 10:00 A.M.).

Upon entering a classroom, staff or paraprofessionals will follow the procedures previously outlined for the sign-in board, pick up the child's IPB, and take the child to the designated training setting. When the training session is completed, the IPB will be returned to a central location where it is available to other staff working with the child. Data on child progress is easily monitored by the supervisor in this fashion. The reader is referred to Chapter 8 for additional information on the IPB.

Program Materials and Resources   Any materials that are necessary for conducting a training session will be noted within a child's IPB for that session. In one area of the classroom, a box with each child's name on it will have all necessary materials and resources for conducting the training sessions that are unique to each child. The materials in the box will be materials not generally available in the training setting; thus, the staff member will take the necessary materials from the child's box and use them. Other materials in the classroom are stored in labeled storage cabinets available for easy access. The materials and items of equipment that are required in operating a classroom are dependent on the handicapping conditions and other specific characteristics of the children to be served. A list of these materials and items of equipment is included at the end of this chapter on pages 54–55.

Planning Ahead   An integral part of the organization and operation of any special education classroom is planning activities throughout the school year. Special activities, vacation days, and other important dates must be anticipated. To facilitate this, a planning calendar to note these dates, as well as proposed IEP review dates and staffing meetings, is used. The planning calendar should be posted in a central location for all staff to inspect and should be updated, as necessary, during planning meetings. Sound advice for staff involved in service delivery to children with developmental disabilities is: "Plan your work and work your plan."

RECOMMENDED EQUIPMENT, MATERIALS, AND SUPPLIES

Basic Furnishings

Tables (adjustable, formica topped)
Chairs (student size)
Storage cabinets and/or shelves (may be built in)
Teacher desk and chair
Cassette tape recorder, earphones, and earphone jack
Chairs (adult size)—rocker, straight
Chalkboards (portable, stationary, hand held)
Bulletin boards
Chart holder
Punches (3 hole, single hand-held)
Paper cutter (access to)
Wall clock (preferably with plain clear numerals for teaching purposes)
Copies (access to photocopier)
U.S. flag
Dry mount press (access to)
Full length mirror
Yardstick
Sink
Record player
Partitions, room dividers

Wastebaskets (covered garbage can for food disposal)
Stove (for cooking and food preparation)
Refrigerator (for food storage)
Dishwasher (optional health standards may require)
Laundry unit (washer, dryer, clothesline, iron, ironing board)
Easels
Stapler
Scissors (adult size)
Tape dispenser
Opaque projector (access to)
Television (access to)
Movie projector (access to)
Filmstrip projector (access to)
Film screen (access to)
Maps—U.S., world
Pencil sharpener
Microcomputer or other programmable teaching devices
Flannel board
Typewriter (access to)
Coat and boot rack or individual lockers

Health, First Aid Equipment

Tweezers
Cotton balls
Medicated soap
Sterile gauze (roll)
Assorted adhesive bandages

Blanket
Kleenex
Thermometer (oral and rectal)
Vaseline
Disinfectant

Language Arts

Alphabet cards
Photo library picture cards
Assorted books
Assorted puzzles
Easy-to-play table games

Assorted toys and role play materials
Mounted drawings
Actual assorted objects
Flannel board materials
Musical instruments

Motor Equipment

Manipulative toys and puzzles
  Bolsters
  Therapy balls (large, small)
Walkers
Equilibrium boards (large, small)
Balance beams
Beanbags
Full length mirror
Walking bars
Stairs (with rail, without rail)
Mobility devices (rowcar, bicycles with or without training wheels, tricycles— regular or adapted)

Balls (nerf, soccer, softballs, fabric, cage, beach, basketball)
Climbing apparatus
Scooter boards
Jump ropes (individual length or group)
Tumbling mats
Wedge (large, small)
Ramp
Prone boards
Specialized seating devices (corner chair, box chair, kindergarten chair, sling chair, etc.)

RECOMMENDED EQUIPMENT, MATERIALS, AND SUPPLIES
(continued)

Arts and Crafts

Paint brushes
Crayons
Colored chalk
Clay
Clear contact paper
Adhesives (glue, rubber cement, paste
  containers; plastic, various sizes)
Needles (various sizes and types)
Paint (acrylic and tempera)
Crepe paper
Finger paint paper

Butcher paper (assorted colors)
Scissors (student size) left and right hand
Wheat powder
Liquid laundry starch
White flour
Salt
Sponges
Construction paper
String
Foil
Waxed paper
Art smocks

Academic Supplies (Consumable)

Pencils
Chalk
Chalkboard erasers
Erasers (pencil)
Chart tablets
Paper clips (large, small)
Gummed labels
Markers (broad tip, narrow tip,
  waterbased, permanent)
Pens (preferably black as it is easier to
  read)

Paper (copy, letterhead, plain bond,
  construction, oak tag, oak tag strips,
  newsprint, drawing, primary lined or
  lined theme paper, manila, note pads)
Rubber bands (assorted sizes)
String
Tape (strapping, masking, transparent)
Pushpins
Pins (safety, straight)
Staples
Paper reinforcers

Housekeeping Supplies (Consumable)
(Note: Hazardous materials should be kept in a securely locked cabinet)

Liquid soap
Laundry detergent
Fabric softener
Carpet shampoo for minor accidents
Distilled water (iron)
Window cleaner
Hand soap
Furniture polish
Floor wax
Dishwasher soap (optional)

Oven cleaner
Rubber gloves (several pair)
Scouring pads
Dishcloths
Towels
Paper towels
Disinfectant
Cleanser
Sponges
Bibs

Housekeeping Equipment

Brooms (lightweight, straight, push—long
  handle)
Brushes (nail, flat—scrub)
Bucket
Sponge mop

Dust pan
Sink strainers
Drain tray
Dish rack

Miscellaneous Tools

Screwdriver
Hammer
Can opener

Sharp knife
Various utensils

4

Identifying and Assessing the Child in Need of Special Education Services

After reading this chapter, you should have an understanding of:

1. The intake procedures for conducting the evaluations necessary to determine if a child is in need of special education and related services, including screening and obtaining information from referrals prior to the scheduling of an evaluation
2. The types of assessment instruments available and commonly used tests that may be of use in the evaluation process
3. The steps involved in assessment and diagnosis and the role of various staff members in the evaluation process
4. The placement decision

TIMELY IDENTIFICATION AND ASSESSMENT of children and youth are prerequisite steps to the process of placement of an individual in a special education program. This chapter addresses the tasks an interdisciplinary team should undertake once a child has been identified as a possible candidate for special education services. The traditional screening and placement methods for entry of a "normal" student into a public school classroom are often not appropriate when a student with moderate to profound handicapping conditions is assessed for classroom entry.

INTAKE PROCEDURES

An *intake* refers to the procedures conducted in identifying, assessing, and placing a child with developmental disabilities in a special program. The following procedures are applicable for determining eligibility, and assessing and diagnosing normal children or children with developmental delays. In determining need for special education services, attention is focused on referral and screening procedures. In assessment and diagnosis, attention is given to testing procedures, testing methods, and tests to be used with a specific child.

Referrals

Each state has its own child find plan that must be adhered to, thus, providers should become familiar with their state master plan. A copy of this plan can usually be obtained from the state board of education. It may, in some cases, be available in the local school district office. The Utah and Idaho plans are referred to in the process that follows. In accordance with the Utah and Idaho child find plans, all children and youth with developmental disabilities are to be referred to appropriate individuals and agencies to ensure rapid attention to their special needs, as those needs are identified. In some school districts, the child would be referred to the school psychologist for assessment and for determination of eligibility for special education and related services. In other school districts, school psychologists are not available; however, community resources may be able to respond to some of the service needs. Various agencies maintain a service unit to respond to such requests. Most commonly, this might be a community mental health center or other specialized agency. The agency component that responds to such referrals is often entitled the *Clinical Services* or *Diagnostic Unit*.

Referrals to specialized centers or classrooms where children with handicaps are served may come from several sources: a) school districts, b) parents, c) state or county agencies, d) preschool projects, and e) other private sources. School districts may contract with specialized facilities to provide educational programming for pupils with handicaps that reside in their catchment area. The majority of referrals for school-age children to specialized facilities are made by school districts that lack the capability for providing specialized assessment and programming or that have such a small population that to operate a program requiring so many related services is not economically feasible. These difficulties are more common in rural and remote areas.

Preschool children may be referred privately, through family physicians or pediatricians, or through a state social service or health agency. Such agencies may contract for the provision of educational and therapy services for preschool children with developmental disabilities. The state agency responsible for services to preschoolers with developmental disabilities varies from state to state, but commonly it is the state board of education, the state health department, or the state social services department.

Most assessment agencies and school psychologists have a requisite form for recording referral information. The purpose of the referral form is to collect some basic information, such as: a) student's name and address, b) parent or guardian's name, address and telephone number, c) name of school and teacher making referral (if applicable), d) statement of problem for which referral was made, e) statement of diagnostic services requested, f) previous assessments conducted, and g) where additional information may be obtained. Completion and return of the form is usually required before services are initiated. After the completed form is returned, information-gathering and screening processes are initiated by the agency's school psychologist or the intake coordinator. Some agencies may also require a verification of disability form to be filled out by a physician prior to the initial evaluation. Informed consent for testing and other ethical guidelines should be adhered to in all the services offered. Informed consent consists of explaining to the parents and child, if appropriate, the purpose of the tests, and having the parents sign a form indicating that they understand the purposes and give their permission to have their child tested.

Screening

Each referral to an agency outside the school district results in the assignment of a person to be the coordinator for that case throughout the intake process. This person is often called the *case coordinator* or *case manager*. The case coordinator or manager facilitates and follows through to completion the information-gathering activities before an intake is conducted. An initial contact sheet may be used that requests information that was not provided or not clear on the referral information form. Information collection may require additional telephone calls or written communications. The coordinator collects any other relevant information, including previous educational or medical evaluations and hospital records, which may be needed by the clinical evaluation team.

This available information should then be evaluated to determine whether an intake at the center is appropriate or if referral to another source is warranted. If intake is deemed appropriate, an initial interview with the parents or guardian is scheduled, a "client file" is established, and an assessment specialist and essential members of a multidisciplinary team, selected on the basis of client-identified preliminary needs, are assigned to conduct the intake. This team may include any or all of the following disciplines: psychology, special education, regular education, speech pathology, audiology, physical therapy, occupational therapy, medicine, and social work. Parents, legal guardians, the client and other family members are often involved in all levels of the assessment procedures. Table 4.1 describes how these professionals function.

COMMONLY USED TESTS

Pages 66–67 at the end of this chapter provide a list of both criterion-referenced and norm-referenced assessment instruments that may be used to

Table 4.1. Function of professionals in assessment procedures

Type of assessment	Professionals involved	Functions
Medical	Family physician, medical specialist, nurse	1. Determine current physical condition 2. Identify specific systematic deficits or liabilities 3. Specify organic limitations for classification 4. Prescribe possible medical treatment 5. Referral
Psychological	School psychologist, licensed psychologist	1. Identify cognitive, affective, and psycho-motor performance levels for classification purposes according to state regulations 2. Identify developmental and behavioral assets and deficits 3. Prescribe behavioral and/or other psychological therapy or counseling
Social/family	Psychologist, social worker	1. Identify typical behavior and critical interpersonal behaviors at school, home, and elsewhere 2. Prescribe environmental modifications for treatment
Behavioral	Psychologist, teacher, parent trainer	1. Observe behaviors in context of environment 2. Prescribe behavioral programs
Vision/hearing	Medical specialist, ophthalmologist, audiologist	1. Identify sensory limitations 2. Prescribe medical or prosthetic devices 3. Classify handicapping conditions
Language	Speech pathologist, teacher	1. Identify language status, deficits, and quality 2. Prescribe language development or remediation programs

(continued)

Table 4.1. *(continued)*

Type of assessment	Professionals involved	Functions
Educational	Educational diagnostician, special educator, school psychologist	1. Identify current level of performance 2. Identify specific skills, strengths, and deficits 3. Prescribe educational/ training programs

evaluate the performance of handicapped children. It is a select rather than comprehensive list. Swanson and Watson (1982) provide brief descriptions of most of these assessment instruments. In addition, the *Mental Measurement Yearbook* (Buros, 1978) provides extensive coverage of these and other tests.

Testing and evaluation materials and procedures should be appropriate for the individual student and his or her handicapping condition(s). In addition, they should consider the possible impact of race, national origin, or sex. Some tests were standardized with students of a specific race, national origin, or sex; thus their usefulness with other populations is questionable. Therefore, wherever possible, materials and procedures should be substituted to minimize the adverse impact of such biases on the assessment outcome due to the norms on which tests were standardized. Usually, several standardized instruments need to be given in order to meet state guidelines for programs for individuals with handicaps. Such instruments may include one or more tests of general ability, achievement tests, and tests of language functioning, perceptual-motor ability, and emotional development. State guidelines are usually quite specific in identifying the type of test information needed for classification purposes.

ASSESSMENT AND DIAGNOSIS

In dealing with parents, emphasis should be placed on conducting a comprehensive assessment for the purpose of determining what services are needed and appropriate. When the intake interview is scheduled, the parents or guardian should be informed that at least one of them is to accompany the child to the center for the intake interview. Parental input is *critical* to the completion of a comprehensive and accurate assessment. The parents or guardians should be asked to bring only the child being referred so that valuable staff time and space are not needed for ''babysitting'' and so parents are free to deal with only the child of concern. It is helpful to ascertain whether parents prefer to talk in the presence or absence of their child at the onset of the interview.

The efficiency of any intake is greatly enhanced by establishing and following procedures entailing responsibilities such as those listed below:

1. *Parent arrival.* The parent(s) (or legal guardian) and the child meet with the records secretary upon arrival at the center. The records secretary obtains demographic information needed for billing purposes (the school district is charged for school referrals) (see sample Table 4.2) and parent/legal guardian signature(s) on the release form permitting the evaluation to occur and the release of records to the referral source (if other than the parent(s) or legal guardian). If it is a private referral, the records secretary will also explain the fee schedule. The records secretary completes all appropriate insurance forms and answers questions relative to procedures for insurance payment of fees. The records secretary is also responsible for providing the parent(s) or legal guardian with a parking permit (if needed).

Table 4.2.

Financial information

_____ / _____ / _____
Month   Day   Year   Client no. _____

Client name _____ Date of birth _____

Address _____ Phone _____

Responsible for payment _____

Address _____

Total yearly family income
(Circle appropriate level.)

0–3,999	10–10,999	No. family members at home _____
4–4,999	11–11,999	Insurance company _____
5–5,999	12–12,999	Med. card no. _____
6–6,999	13–13,999	Med. card exp. date _____
7–7,999	14–14,999	
8–8,999	15–15,999	
9–9,999	16–19,999	
20,000 or above		

Guardianship

____ Bio-parents   ____ Public agency

____ Bio-father   ____ Maternal/paternal relatives

____ Bio-mother   ____ Other family members

____ Adoptive   ____ None currently established

Father   **Mother**

Birth year _____   Birth year _____

Last grade of education _____   Last grade of education _____

Occupation _____   Occupation _____

Employer _____   Employer _____

I hereby declare that the above information is correct, and I will assume financial responsibility for the evaluation and treatment rendered to my child, _____ , by the
(First/Last)
Clinical Services staff of _____ .

_____   _____
Witness   Parent/Guardian

2. *Intake room.* The records secretary then escorts the parent(s) or other adult(s) and the child to the interview room (except in instances where arrangements have been made to exclude the child from the initial interview), and notifies the case coordinator or manager.

3. *Intake appointment.* The case coordinator or manager is responsible for the following aspects of the intake appointment:

   a. He or she should arrange for child care when the child is not to be present during the initial interview.

   b. He or she should take the major responsibility for the interview unless a team member has been specifically designated for this role. Some guidelines for the general intake interview that may be of use in assisting an agency in the development of its own guidelines are provided on pages 68–70 at the end of this chapter. The major advantage of using such a form is that it ensures a certain degree of consistency in terms of the information available for all clients served. The form should be completed and remain in the client's file.

   c. A brief staffing should be conducted with all team members after the initial interview and prior to the evaluation to determine which assessments will be given, to schedule the assessments, and to discuss how the case is to proceed.

   d. Specific evaluations that are to be conducted by the team members are assigned and conducted. (When clinical practicum students are assigned as team members, the director of clinical services should be consulted before assignments are made.)

   e. A preliminary wrap-up meeting is held with the entire team to discuss evaluation findings and recommendations and to determine when the verbal summary of the evaluation and recommendations is to be presented to the parent(s) or legal guardian. In cases with special problems, the case coordinator or manager may wish to consult with his or her supervisor on items such as the assessment instruments used, interpretation of test results, possible treatment to be provided, possible parental assignments, follow-up plans, and special problems.

   f. The case coordinator or manager should conduct a verbal summation of the evaluation and discuss recommendations with the parent(s) or guardians and in some cases, the client. Team members may or may not be present at this meeting, depending on arrangements made with the case coordinator.

   g. The case coordinator or manager should complete the billing form and contact notes and place them in the client's file, then return the client file to the records secretary following the intake appointment.

   h. Preparation of the comprehensive written report is the responsibility of the case coordinator or manager. This report is to be prepared according to the report-writing outline and procedures of the particular agency (see sample outline on pages 71–73 at the end of the chapter) and is to be submitted to the clinical services supervisor for approval. Although such a process takes additional time, it ensures a level of quality control in all reports leaving the agency. Such a quality control can focus on the increased communicative value of the reports, realistic recommendations, and avoidance of statements that could later prove embarrassing to the agency.

  i. Parent's or legal guardian's signatures must be secured on required forms to obtain or release information to or from other relevant parties or agencies. This is the responsibility of the records secretary.

  j. Appointments should be scheduled with the client for follow-up contacts where applicable, and are the responsibility of the case coordinator or, if applicable, a member of the multidisciplinary assessment team.

4. *Team responsibility.* Each team member is responsible for the following aspects of the intake appointment:

  a. Review of the client file prior to the intake interview.

  b. Meeting with the case coordinator or manager prior to the intake interview.

  c. Participation in the wrap-up interview staffing with the case coordinator or manager.

  d. Evaluations conducted in his or her specialty areas and/or completion of assignments that have been agreed upon with the case coordinator or manager.

  e. Participation in the staff evaluation summary conducted by the case coordinator or manager and, wherever possible, the verbal summation and recommendation session with the parent(s) or legal guardian and, if appropriate, the client.

  f. Quick preparation of specific assigned sections of the clinical report or the entire clinical report (in accordance with the sample report-writing outline and procedures) and adherence to time lines designated by the case coordinator and the supervisor of clinical services.

It may be desirable for the director of special education from the referring school district to be included in the intake process through observation and/or participation in the evaluation process. Such involvement will provide the special education director with a sound basis for making recommendations about the eventual placement of the child.

PLACEMENT

Upon receipt of the recommendation for placement, the district special education director reviews the assessment report to determine if special education placement is appropriate. If appropriate services are available in the regular classroom of the home school district, no pupil should be considered for placement in a more restrictive environment such as a self-contained special education classroom, special school for individuals with handicaps, or residential institution. If the special education director decides that special education might be an appropriate placement, a meeting is scheduled with a committee responsible for such activities, the child study team (CST) (Meyen, Gautt, & Howard, 1976). Complete coverage of the composition and function of the CST is included in the next chapter.

SUMMARY

The process of special education is initiated when someone suspects or becomes aware that a child does not seem to be functioning at a level consistent with his or her age (identification). A referral is then made to an appropriate professional or agency, and after the necessary information has been collected, an intake and assessment is conducted. After the assessment information has been summarized, a decision is made concerning whether or not the child will be referred for special education and related services.

CRITERION-REFERENCED AND NORM-REFERENCED ASSESSMENT INSTRUMENTS

Individually Administered Tests of Mental Ability

Basic Concept Inventory
Bayley Scales for Infant Development
California Abbreviated WISC (CAW)
Cattell Infant Intelligence Scale
Columbia Mental Maturity Scale
Detroit Test of Learning Aptitude
Leiter International Performance Scale
McCarthy Scales of Children's Abilities
Minnesota Preschool Scale

Nebraska Test of Learning Aptitude
Peabody Picture Vocabulary Test
Slosson Intelligence Test
Stanford-Binet Intelligence Scale
Test of Concept Utilization
Wechsler Intelligence Scale for Children (revised 1974)
Wechsler Preschool and Primary Scale of Intelligence
Woodcock-Johnson Psychoeducation Battery

Group Tests of General Abilities

Analysis of Learning Potential
Boehm Test of Basic Concepts
California Short Form Test of Mental Maturity
Cognitive Abilities Test

Culture Fair Intelligence Tests
Kuhlmann-Anderson Intelligence Tests
Lorge-Thorndike Intelligence Test
Primary Mental Abilities Test

Individually Administered Tests of Specific Areas

Ammons Quick Test
Embedded Figure Test
Goodenough-Harris Drawing Test
Memory for Designs

Ohwaki-Kohs Tactile Block Design Intelligence Test for the Blind
Raven Progressive Matrices Test
Spatial Orientation Memory Test
Torrance Tests of Creative Thinking

Achievement Tests

Basic Schools Skills Inventory

Peabody Individual Achievement Test
Wide Range Achievement Test

Diagnostic Tests

Brigance Inventory of Basic Skills
Diagnostic Reading Scales (Revised)
Key Math Diagnostic Arithmetic Test

Prescriptive Math Inventory
Stanford Diagnostic Mathematics Test
Stanford Diagnostic Reading Test
Woodcock Reading Mastery Test

Tests for Processing Visual and Auditory Information

Assessment of Children's Language Comprehension
Auditory Discrimination Test
Carrow Elicited Language Inventory
Developmental Sentence Analysis
Fisher-Longemann Test of Articulation
Functional Voice Evaluation
Goldman-Fristoe-Woodcock Auditory Skills Test Battery
Goldman-Fristoe Test of Articulation
Illinois Test of Psycholinguistic Abilities
Northwest Syntax Screening Test

Receptive-Expressive Emergent Language Scale
Screening Test for Auditory Comprehension
Southern California Sensory Integration Test
Speech Mechanism Evaluation
Stuttering Standard Interview Procedure & Recording Form
Templin-Darly Tests of Articulation
Test for Auditory Comprehension of Language
Test of Language Development
Utah Test of Language Development
Verbal Language Development Scale

(continued)

CRITERION-REFERENCED AND NORM-REFERENCED
ASSESSMENT INSTRUMENTS
(continued)

Tests for Perceptual Motor Skills

Auditory Discrimination Test
Bender Visual-Motor Gestalt Test
Cratey's Perceptual & Motor
  Development of Infants &
  Children
Developmental Test of Visual-
  Motor Integration
Frostig Developmental Test of
  Visual Perception

Memory for Designs Test
Minnesota Percepto-Diagnostic
  Test
Motor-Free Visual Perception Test
Bruininks-Oseretsky Tests of
  Motor Proficiency
Subtest of the Illinois Psycho-
  linguistic Abilities

Emotional Development Assessment

Anxiety Scale Questionnaire
Bender Visual-Motor Gestalt Test
California Psychological Inventory
Children's Apperception Test
Education Apperception Test
Graham-Kendall Memory for Designs
  Test
Inferred Self-Concept Scale
Minnesota Multiphasic Personality
  Inventory

Nowicki-Strickland Locus of Control
Perceived Competence Scale for Children
Process for In-School Screening
  of Children with Emotional
  Handicaps
Rohde Sentence Completion Test
Tennessee Self-Concept Scale
Thematic Apperception Test
Weschler Intelligence Scales

Behavioral Scales

Behavioral Rating Instrument for
  Atypical Children
Burk's Behavior Rating Scales
Child Behavior Rating Scale

The Autism Screening Instrument for
  Educational Planning
Walker Problem Behavior Identifica-
  tion Checklist

Adaptive and Social Assessment

Adapative Behavior Scale
Alpern-Boll Developmental
  Profile
Anecdotal Reports and
  Records

Behavioral Observation in the
  Classroom and at Home
California Preschool Social Competency
  Scale
Camelot
Callier-Azusa Scale

Vocational Assessment

McCarron-Dial Work Evaluation System
Singer Vocational System
Talent Assessment Programs

Vocational Information and Evaluation
  Work Samples
Wide Range Employment Sample Test

GUIDELINES FOR GENERAL INTAKE INTERVIEW

Interviewer: _____ Client: _____
Supervisor: _____ Client age: _____ Date: _____
Parents' names _____

Developmental history and background:

Pregnancy: Normal ____ Complications: _____

Child delivery: Normal ____ Complications: _____

Adopted: _____ Age: _____

Walking age: _____ Talking age: _____

Speech or language problems: _____
_____

Unusual illnesses: _____
_____

Language patterns: _____

Medications: _____

Current family physician: _____

Approximate date of last medical exam: _____

Visual examination: _____ Date _____ Results _____

Hearing examination: _____ Date _____ Results _____

Unusual accidents/injuries: _____

Eating patterns: _____

Coordination problems: _____ Gross: _____ Fine: _____

Comments: _____

Toilet training: _____ Day _____ Night (Comments) _____
_____

Sleeping patterns: _____

Family situation (adults living in home, i.e., grandparents, single parent family, foster children in home, etc.): _____
_____

List any previous psychological testing or treatment (including where, when, the purpose and results)._____
_____
_____

Nursery/preschool experience and where: _____

   Problems: _____

   Strengths: _____

Public school experience and where: _____

   Problems: _____

   Strengths: _____

Social interactions (individual and group, peers and adults):

   School? _____

   Neighborhood? _____

   Family? _____

Home situation:

Problems: _____

_____

Strengths: _____

_____

Independent skills? (What can child do with minimal or no assistance?)

_____

_____

Problems:

Parental description of the problem (if behavioral problem, frequency? In what situations? Other related information?)

_____

_____

_____

_____

_____

_____

_____

_____

_____

_____

How long has problem(s) existed and how has problem(s) been handled?

_____

_____

_____

Summarize and prioritize problems:

1. _____
2. _____
3. _____

Referral question: (What do parents and/or school want from this evaluation?)

_____

Behavioral observations (child/parent): _____

_____

_____

Assessment: (Check and initial if completed.)

1. Describe tests to be administered to parent(s) and child: ☐ _____
2. Invite parent(s) to observe testing: ☐ _____
3. Advise parent that summary of test results will be given orally at the end of session(s) and follow-up written report to be sent: ☐ _____
4. Provide parent with summary of test results: ☐ _____

Treatment/recommendations:

1. Discuss rationale for home/school observations if applicable to situation.
   When _____ Where _____

2. Advise parent if additional assessment or team consultation is needed (eye exam, medical, psychological testing, speech, etc.).

   Type of assessment: _____

   When: _____

   Who is responsible for arrangements? _____

3. Recommendations: _____

   _____

   _____

   _____

   _____

4. Parent assignments: (Make clear and explicit. Provide data collection sheets and written instructions where necessary.)

   _____

   _____

5. Obtain parent feedback on service provided and an understanding of procedure.

   ☐ _____

6. Schedule next appointment time: _____

OUTLINE FOR COMPREHENSIVE EVALUATION REPORTS

Client:
Name:
Age (years and months):
Birthdate:
Grade (if school-age child):
Parent(s):
Address:

Date(s) of evaluation: Include all dates pertinent to evaluation.

Test(s) administered: Provide complete titles of tests administered.

Referral question:
Include:
A. Who referred the child and is responsible for payment? Provide name, title or relationship to child and/or agency. For example: Mr. Jones, Pupil Personnel Director, Washington School District, or John's mother, Mrs. Booth.
B. Why was the child referred to the center? This should be a brief statement informing the reader of the purpose for evaluation (e.g., "Johnny was referred for an academic evaluation because he has not been achieving at grade level during the current school year").

Background information:
A. Include a summary of information relevant to the referral question that is provided during the interview by those present at the interview. Also provide developmental history where pertinent (particularly applicable for child under 6 years of age or for developmentally disabled individuals). For school-aged children, provide name of school student is attending.
B. The information provided in this section of the report should convey to the readers a concise description of past and current events and situations relating to the referral question. Be specific in terms of dates, sequence of events, where previous significant events occurred (i.e., John was evaluated in September, 1980 at Primary Children's Hospital in Salt Lake City), but do not use specific names of physicians or teachers in the report. Information gathered by all team members should be integrated or incorporated into this section.
Use a separate paragraph for the information provided by each source (e.g., one paragraph for parents' information, another for teacher's information). Identify the sources for all information provided in the report, e.g., Mrs. X reported that. . . . Direct quotes are infrequently acceptable; therefore, the report writer generally should summarize comments made.

Behavioral observations:
Identify what child behaviors were observed during the interview and/or testing. Information provided should be specific to each child; avoid trite phrases such as, "the child attended adequately." It is acceptable to include the examiner's opinion regarding a specific behavior described if the opinion statement is designated as such. Observations made by all team members should be integrated or incorporated into this section.

Test or assessment results:
A. A separate paragraph should be written for each test administered. Provide the name of the test and a brief description of what the test purports to assess and how the information is obtained (e.g., what the child is asked to do or who gives the information required by the test). Indicate test results and report the child's strengths and weaknesses, e.g., John demonstrated a high degree of fine motor control when reproducing the simple geometric figures on this test.
B. Provide a rationale if two tests are given in the same area of functioning (e.g., the Slosson and the WISC-R). Informal testing procedures such as counting or naming the letters of the alphabet should be classified as such. Do not include the child's I.Q. score in the report unless it was specifically requested. Instead, indicate the range of

OUTLINE FOR COMPREHENSIVE EVALUATION REPORTS
(continued)

intellectual functioning. On school referrals, the IQ score is typically used for purposes of placement to meet state board of education guidelines. If the child falls in one of the ranges of mental retardation, it is appropriate to note that in the report, indicating that this designation is made from the state board of education guidelines.

C. In reporting projective test results, preface your interpretation with a statement indicating that such results may be interpreted in different ways and the interpretation to follow is that of the examiner. Try to support your interpretations with observable behavior noted. *Avoid ambiguous terms and professional jargon.*

Speech and language evaluation:
When extensive evaluation is conducted in this area, it may be appropriate to include this section in the report. If so, tests used should be described and results reported in this section rather than in the assessment or test results section of the report.

Motor skills evaluation (gross, fine, visual/motor):
When extensive evaluation is conducted in this area, it may be appropriate to include this section in the report. If so, tests used should be described and results reported in this section rather than in the assessment or test results section of the report.

Medical evaluation:
The individual writing the comprehensive evaluation report will need to write a one- or two-paragraph summary of the medical report that is included in the child's file. Medical terms should be defined for the reader if needed. The report writer should adhere to the words used by the medical director, particularly those relating to the general impressions section of the medical report.

School contacts:
This section of the report should be included whenever a contact (telephone call, school visit) is made on behalf of the child. The section should include a summary of information obtained during this contact that is relevant to the referral question. Identify the date of contact, type of contact, and the individuals contacted by name and title. If several individuals have been contacted (i.e., regular classroom teacher, resource room specialist), use separate paragraphs for summarizing their input.

Home visits:
If a home visit is conducted as part of the intake evaluation, this section of the report should be included. Provide a summary of that visit, describing specific observations made, areas discussed, etc. Identify date and time of visit, those present, and the situation in which the visit occurred (i.e., during dinner hour).

Summary:
This section is probably the most difficult for the report writer. If the report reader were to read this section of the report only, he or she should be able to determine why the child was referred, general evaluation findings, and what is suggested for resolution of the referral question. All information you have obtained about the child, i.e., test and evaluation results, parent and other's input, behavior observed at the center, etc., should be integrated and summarized in this section, but should not be a reiteration of previously stated information. Do *not* repeat all of the specific test results. Briefly state the child's strengths and weaknesses. Be certain that you respond to the referral question. Provide a prognosis statement where appropriate. In this section, also discuss all information relevant to recommendations that are to be made. After writing this section, review and reflect on how it will sound to parents, administrators, teachers and others who will read it.

Recommendations:
Recommendations should be brief and statements specific. If more than one recommendation is to be provided, number recommendations (i.e., 1, 2, 3), prioritizing recommendations in order of relevance to referral question. Recommendations included in reports from other team members should be integrated into recommendations or included separately as written in team member's reports. This is left to the discretion of the report

OUTLINE FOR COMPREHENSIVE EVALUATION REPORTS
(continued)

writer; however, recommendations written by various team members may not be consistent in format and may need to be revised. Identify who will be expected to take responsibility for carrying out the recommendations and when or under what circumstances the recommendations are to be carried out. Do *not* include a recommendation unless there has been a reference to the problem or area leading to the recommendation in the summary section of the report. Be sure to include all recommendations that are appropriate to the referral questions, as well as recommendations that may have resulted from the evaluations, e.g., visual examination needed.

Team members: (Signature)
(Name, title, and/or discipline)   Case Coordinator

                                                          (Signature)
                                                          Director of Clinical Services

5

Developing, Implementing, and Evaluating Functional Individualized Education Programs

After reading this chapter, you should have an understanding of:

1. The intent and rationale of PL 94-142, including the concepts of least restrictive environment and accountability, and the rights of students and their families
2. The components of an individualized education program (IEP)
3. The composition, functions, and responsibilities of child study teams
4. Development of an IEP, including the selection and use of appropriate IEP forms
5. The steps in completing an IEP
6. The procedures for evaluating the quality, functionality, and generality of IEPs, as well as the methods for monitoring and revising the IEP
7. The concept of staffing procedures

THIS CHAPTER PROVIDES a systematic method for complying with the intent of the law, while simultaneously simplifying what is considered by many to be a complex process. The materials and procedures that follow were developed and refined over a 7-year period, and have been used successfully in a variety of educational settings located in both urban and rural areas. Children with all levels of handicapping conditions, both preschool and school age, were involved in the development of the procedures and materials. While recommended procedures are provided, options are also discussed to allow individual readers the flexibility that may be needed to function effectively in individual situations.

AN OVERVIEW OF PUBLIC LAW 94-142

Rationale

PL 94-142, the Education for All Handicapped Children Act of 1975 (1976), mandates that handicapped students receive the special education programming and related services they need. Special education is defined by the law as "specially designed instruction, at no cost to parents or guardians, to meet the unique needs of a handicapped child, including classroom instruction, instruction in physical education, home instruction, and instruction in hospitals and institutions" (Education for All Handicapped Children Act of 1975, 1976, p. 3). In order "to meet the unique needs of a handicapped child" with "specially designed instruction," *planning* and *individualization of education programs* are required.

Providing an *individualized education program* (IEP) requires understanding of the concepts involved in the term IEP (Morgan, 1981). "Individualized" means that programs must be designed to meet the unique needs of each child rather than those of a group of children. "Education" means that the child's program is limited to those aspects that are specifically defined by the law as special education and related services. "Program" means the IEP is a statement of what will be actively provided to the child, as distinct from a *plan* that provides guidelines from which a program will subsequently be developed. The IEP represents a clear description of the special education and related services that a particular child with a handicap will actually receive rather than a plan of "proposed" services.

Least Restrictive Environment

The law mandates that educational services be delivered in the least restrictive environment, as described below.

> ... to the maximum extent appropriate, handicapped children...are educated with children who are not handicapped, and that special classes, separate schooling, or other removal of handicapped children from the regular educational environment occurs only when the nature or severity of the handicap is such that education in regular classes with the use of supplementary aids and services cannot be achieved satisfactorily. (Education for All Handicapped Children Act of 1975, 1976, p. 7).

This definition *does not* require that all children be educated in the regular classroom, but rather that placement be determined on the basis of individual need. For example, the least restrictive environment for a nonambulatory blind child may well be a special rather than regular classroom because of the severity of the handicap. Placing such a child in a regular classroom could well be placing him or her in a *more* restrictive environment because the structure in a regular classroom could preclude the conditions necessary for that child to learn. The decision on what the least restrictive environment is should be made for each child based on the nature and severity of his or her handicap. The child study team (defined later), including the parents, should make the decision by reviewing all possible alternative placements available to the specific child and then deciding which of these alternatives will most enhance the child's educational possibilities.

Accountability

Educators should develop IEPs so that child progress can be evaluated to determine the appropriateness of the established goals and objectives and so that program changes can be made on the basis of objective facts. The goals and objectives written in an IEP must be clearly stated in measurable terms so that systematic performance data can be collected for each goal and objective written for a particular child (Whitney & Striefel, 1981). Evaluation of child progress in achieving the goals and objectives specified on the IEP via standardized tests (e.g., Stanford-Binet) or criterion-referenced tests (e.g., the Adaptive Behavior Scale) is usually not sufficient. Most of these testing instruments are not sensitive to the types of gains made by children with handicaps in an academic year. Criterion-referenced systems may detect some changes for higher functioning children; however, individual evaluation data on child performance are best (Anastasiow, 1979). Such evaluation data can be tailored to the programs of individual children so that programming decisions can be made on an "individualized" basis. Individual data also provide for the accountability that is central to the intent of the law.

COMPONENTS OF AN IEP

Required Components

An IEP is defined by law as:

> . . . a written statement for each handicapped child developed in any meeting by a representative of the local educational agency or an intermediate education unit who shall be qualified to provide, or supervise the provision of, specially designed instruction to meet the unique needs of handicapped children, the teacher, the parents or guardian of such child, and, whenever appropriate, such child which statement shall include (a) a statement of the present levels of educational performance of such child, (b) a statement of annual goals, including short-term instructional objectives, (c) a statement of the specific educational services to be provided such child, and the extent to which such child will be able to participate in regular education programs, and (d) the projected dates for initiation and antici-

pated duration of such services, and appropriate objective criteria and evaluation procedures and schedules for determining, on at least an annual basis, whether instructional objectives are being achieved. (Education for All Handicapped Children Act of 1975, 1976, p. 3).

The IEP requirement of PL 94–142, the Education for All Handicapped Children Act of 1975 (1976), is important because it requires teachers, administrators, and other relevant staff to focus on the individualization of instruction for each handicapped child served. A fundamental premise of both individualized instructional theory and special education practices is that no two learners are alike (Morgan, 1981). IEPs emphasize that children with handicaps differ from one another in terms of their needs, capabilities, and receptivity to alternate instructional methods.

Optional Components

In addition to the minimum requirements, many education agencies include additional components to increase the comprehensiveness of IEPs. One almost universal addition to IEPs is the inclusion of a signature block for parent permission for placement. This is not a required component of an IEP but it is a required component of the law; therefore, to eliminate the need for an additional form, it is frequently included on the IEP.

A number of other components such as statements of alternative placements, recommendations for specific materials, procedures or techniques, identification of responsible persons for each goal or objective, or specific testing information may be included at the discretion of the educational agency. One important factor that should be considered is the consistency with which the IEP forms are used by staff. This is discussed in more detail in a later section of this chapter.

THE CHILD STUDY TEAM

Team Composition

A multidisciplinary team that herein will be referred to as the child study team (CST) is responsible for development of the IEP. Selection of individuals to serve on a CST may determine the comprehensiveness of the IEP. PL 94-142 provides a general outline of the membership of a CST. At minimum, each CST must include a representative of the school or public agency, the child's teacher, one or both of the child's parents or guardians, the child where appropriate, and other individuals at the discretion of the agency or the parents. On an individual need basis, CSTs frequently include specialists from such fields as regular education, special education, psychology, physical therapy, occupational therapy, adaptive physical education, and speech pathology.

When the CST is developing a child's initial IEP, it is essential that a member of the initial evaluation team be present on the CST or that some member of the team is knowledgeable of the evaluation procedures and instruments used and capable of interpreting and explaining the results of the evaluation. This requirement ensures that the evaluation information obtained is translated accurately into programs for the child. In addition to evaluation and administrative personnel, CSTs should also include staff who will be responsible for the implementation of the completed IEP. This is seen as essential to ensure the successful implementation of procedures outlined in an IEP by local staff. Educational agencies should always attempt to limit membership on CSTs to only those individuals who have direct bearing on the child in question. Doing so will help keep the number of people present small enough so that the parent(s) will not feel overwhelmed and will help protect the time of the professional staff so they can accomplish their other responsibilities, e.g., implementing the IEPs.

Competencies Required of CST Members

Individuals selected to participate on CSTs should have specific information concerning: 1) PL 94-142 (Education for All Handicapped Children Act of 1975, 1976) and 2) the child in question. It would be desirable for each CST member to be knowledgeable in both areas. Realistically, it is satisfactory if the CST as a group has the required knowledge. The basic knowledge requirements for CSTs are:

1. Knowledge of due process as related to the development and implementation of IEPs
2. Knowledge of the individual needs of the child in question and potential goals that may be appropriate
3. Knowledge of alternative service delivery possibilities that may be available
4. Knowledge of ways to ensure that procedures and services will be implemented to maximize accountability

Knowledge of due process is essential to ensure that all parent and child rights are met throughout the development and implementation stages of the IEP process. Failure to understand due process may result in serious problems for the education agency. Some parents of handicapped children are quite knowledgeable of the nuances of the law and will demand that all of the rights and services guaranteed them by the law be delivered. Therefore, to enable a child to begin receiving services sooner and to save time and effort, knowledge of due process is highly desirable.

The other areas of knowledge required of a CST may be greatly facilitated by the involvement of staff who will actually implement the developed IEP. As previously mentioned, involvement of implementers tends to ensure that the program specified by the IEP is actually feasible and practical. CSTs without representation by implementers frequently end up with IEPs that may be negatively received by those staff who are charged with their implementation.

Responsibilities of the CST

The responsibilities of the CST begin with the referral of a child for special education and continue throughout all phases of the child's participation in such services. Only at the point at which a child returns to regular education on a full-time basis is a CST released of its responsibility.

In developing an IEP the CST should ensure that:

1. Services identified and provided are of high quality
2. The completed IEP is both practical as well as feasible from the standpoint of the implementers
3. Compliance with the letter and intent of the law is maintained

An overview of the major activities in which CSTs engage during the development and implementation of an IEP is provided in Table 5.1. Each of these activities is discussed in the material that follows. These activities can be divided into the following three areas: a) preplanning, b) planning/evaluation, and c) implementation/evaluation. Each area is discussed in detail in a later section.

DEVELOPING AN IEP

Structuring the CST Process

The importance of ensuring that the IEP is a group rather than individual effort and that the parents (guardians) and, where appropriate, the child have considerable impact in the process has already been pointed out. In many cases, however, it is extremely difficult to bring all CST members together several times to discuss and develop a single IEP. Moreover, requiring multiple meetings is extremely inefficient. Practical alternatives to these problems must be identified that will be acceptable, realistic, and yet meet the requirements of the law.

Optimally, the entire content of the IEP should be developed during formal CST meetings; however, this is extremely time consuming and can generally not be completed in one meeting. One reasonable alternative is to combine formal CST meetings with separate work sessions where individual CST members identify program components. Tentative areas of need, based upon evaluation information and potential goals, may be identified prior to conducting the initial CST meeting. By doing so, the initial CST meeting may be spent by: a) reviewing the evaluation information, b) developing a statement of current levels of performance, and c) developing the proposed goals for the child in question. The information assembled prior to the initial CST meeting can be used to facilitate the development of the IEP.

Once the IEP goals have been identified and agreed upon by the CST in a formal meeting, the short term instructional objectives and services required

Table 5.1.

Child Study Team Sequential Activities Checklist

Client _____ Referral date _____

Note: Phase I and II should be completed within 30 days.

Phase	Task	Responsible person(s)	Scheduled for (date and time)	Completion date
I. Preplanning activities	Members of CST assigned Team chairperson assigned Information reviewed Needed services identified Proposed goals established Proposed goals sent to parents/ guardians Formal CST meeting scheduled			
II. Planning activities	Basic information summarized Present level of client perfor- mance summarized Annual goals written Short term objectives written Placement decision finalized IEP implemented			
III. Evaluation activities	Client progress monitoring Daily Quarterly Semi-annually Annual Annual client review held Comprehensive client re- evaluation (minimum every 3 years)			

may be discussed in general. Then, upon concurrence by all CST members, individual CST members may be assigned the responsibility of outlining tentative short term objectives for particular goal statements. The CST meeting is adjourned and the members begin this development task. When the objectives and related services (speech, psychology, audiology, physical and occupational therapy, recreation, medical services, counseling, and transportation services) have been developed, a draft IEP is written and forwarded to the parents or guardians for their inspection. If the parents or guardian agree to the written IEP, permission for placement is granted and the IEP is implemented. If any questions arise, a second CST meeting is scheduled to complete the development process. This CST meeting arrangement is preferable because it allows all members of the team to have maximal input without monopolizing the time of professionals involved. Other alternatives may be patterned after the above format.

Selection of Forms

Selection and/or development of a set of forms to be used in writing IEPs is a very important task for an education agency. Forms that have been used to write IEPs vary widely in their format and content. An education agency should require that all IEPs be written in a standard format to ensure both comprehensiveness as well as consistency. This eliminates the difficulty faced by readers in reviewing IEPs. In adopting a standard format, an education agency also ensures that each IEP will have all of the components required by the agency and by law.

Figures 5.1, 5.2, and 5.3 show IEP[1] forms that are recommended for use by education agencies. They have been designed to include all of the information required by PL 94-142 and portray this information in a logical and organized fashion. Figure 5.1 represents a Summary Information Form that is used as the face sheet for the IEP. Included on this form are: a) basic demographic information about the child, b) a statement of the child's present levels of educational performance, c) the child's extent of participation in regular educational programs, d) names of the CST members, e) an annual review summary, and f) space for parents or guardians to sign, indicating approval of the IEP.

The Annual Goals Form, Figure 5.2, provides space for: a) the writing of annual goals, b) the delineation of needed services, c) the frequency with which services will be provided, and d) time lines associated with initiation and duration of these services. Also, to ensure that forms are not inadvertently misplaced or misfiled, space is provided at the top of the Annual Goals Form for filling out basic identification information about each child.

---

[1]The IEP forms in this chapter are reproduced herein with the permission of the authors and are available from the authors.

Individualized Education Program

SUMMARY and ANNUAL GOALS

name Jeffrey Brown

address 400 East 1200 North - Logan, Utah 84321

school U.S.U. Exceptional Child Center/Edith Bowen School

present placement Self-Contained/Resource Classroom

handicapping condition Intellectually Hand.

birthdate May 24, 1976

telephone 753-1000

initial placement date month 9 day 1 year 82

review date month___ day___ year___

present levels of educational performance: Jeff follows simple directions and has verbal and motor imitation skills. He is easily distracted and is unable to work in small groups. Though he follows directions, he complies with instructions appropriately only 20% of the time. He can communicate his basic needs by making verbal requests, consisting of single word utterances. Jeff has age appropriate fine motor coordination but is unable to toilet himself. He demonstrates physical aggression toward others in school settings.

extent of participation in regular educational program: Attends music, P.E., lunch and recess with regular school children.

CHILD STUDY TEAM:
Mr. Steve Radcliff, Principal -
Ms. Cheryl Stevens, Psychologist -
Ms. Ann Jeffreys, Resource Teacher -
Mr. Clayton Jones, Self-Contained Class Teacher -
Ms. Susan Cummings, Educational Diagnostician -
Mr. Doyle Brown, Parent -

I/we have participated in the development of this program and approve of the placement.

Parent signature _____ Date _____

Parent signature _____

© Exceptional Child Center
Utah State University 1978

REVIEW SUMMARY

Team _____

date _____

ES 12

Figure 5.1. Summary information form.

83

ANNUAL GOALS & OBJECTIVES

YEAR: 1979-1980
TEACHER: Handley
CLIENT: J. Brown

SERVICES NEEDED
1. Speech/Language
2. Occupational Ther.
3. Work Experience
4. Social Services
5. Transportation
6. Physical Therapy
7. Recreation Ther.
8. Medical Services
9. Psychologist
10. Special Ed.

	ENTER NUMBER	TEACHING FREQUENCY	STARTING DATE	PROGRESS NOTE	FINAL REPORT
1.0 During all instructional play activities at school, Jeff will not physically aggress toward others on five consecutive days.	9,10	M-F (all day)	10/2		
2.0 Jeff will independently demonstrate the ability to toilet himself without an accident on five consecutive days.	10	M-F (all day)	10/2		
3.0 During a social skills training session with 3-5 children, Jeff will comply with each of the trainer's instructions within five seconds of their delivery 90% of the time on five consecutive days.	10	M-F (all day)	10/15		
4.0 During a social skills training session with 3-5 children, Jeff will demonstrate the ability to work for thirty minutes with less than three disruptions on 10 consecutive days.	10	M-F (30 min./day)	10/15		
5.0 When presented with pictures or objects or actions, Jeff will identify the objects or actions using phrases or sentences of noun-verb-noun format in 100% of trials on five consecutive days.	1,10	M-F (30 min/day)	10/2		

ES 13

Figure 5.2. Annual goals form.

The Short Term Instructional Objectives Form is shown in Figure 5.3. Short term instructional objectives are written on this form. At the top of each copy of this form, the annual goal pertaining to the short term instructional objectives is listed, along with basic identification information and other program implementation guidelines. The short term instructional objectives are written in the columns provided on this form. Objectives are broken down into the following components: a) objective number (step), b) materials necessary to perform the skill or behavior indicated, c) what the trainer does and says, d) what the child does, e) the number of trials conducted per session, f) the criteria established for mastery, and g) the start and completion dates for the objective. Objectives should be listed in a developmental sequence with the terminal objective being identical in content to the referenced annual goals. These three IEP forms (Summary Information Form, Annual Goals Form, and Short Term Instructional Objectives Form) are used in the following discussion on the development of an IEP.

STEPS IN COMPLETING AN IEP

Preplanning Stage

The primary purpose of the preplanning stage is to assemble all necessary information for planning and to ensure that due process is met with regard to parent notification and involvement. Principal activities include: a) assigning membership to specific CSTs, b) outlining the assessment and evaluation information needed and collecting such information, c) reviewing the information collected for comprehensiveness (additional information will be obtained as necessary), d) beginning to identify the types of programs and services needed, and e) scheduling the formal CST meetings that are part of planning.

Additionally, other activities may be conducted to facilitate the planning process. Individual CST members may review the assessment and evaluation information and begin to develop tentative statements of present levels of educational performance. The purpose of these preplanning activities is not to circumvent the interdisciplinary process, but rather to facilitate it. Care should be taken to maintain the letter and intent of the interdisciplinary process. Individual CST members should not make decisions concerning goals and objectives for a child, but leave that task for the formal planning meetings. Correctly conducted, preplanning activities may greatly assist the planning process.

Pretesting   Emphasis should be placed on developing an individualized prescriptive education/training program for each child and youth served. Once a child is admitted to a special education program, the formulation of an individualized education program (IEP) is initiated. The formal responsibility for the development of the program belongs to the teacher and other CST

Learner J. Brown
Date St.
Date Mast.
Supervisor R. Handley
Implementor

Program Name Toilet Training
Term. Obj. 2.0 Jeff will independently demonstrate the ability to toilet himself without an accident for five consecutive days.

Reinforcement Tangible and social praise
Correction Verbal and Motor Prompts

STEP	MATERIAL	WHAT YOU DO WITH THE MATERIAL	WHAT YOU DO AND SAY	WHAT THE LEARNER DOES	TRIALS	CRIT.
2.1	-none-		Stand Jeff in front of the toilet Say "Jeff, pants down" and point to his pants.	Jeff will unsnap and unzip his pants and pull them to his knees.	10	90% on 3 days
2.2	-none-		With Jeff standing with his pants at his knees, say "Jeff, pants up" and point to his pants.	Jeff will pull up pants and zip and snap them.	"	"
2.3	-none-		With Jeff standing with his pants at his knees, say "Jeff, sit down" and point to the toilet.	Jeff will sit down on the toilet and remain seated 10 minutes without moving.	1	100% on 3 days
2.4	-none-		Based on toileting schedule, seat Jeff on toilet.	Jeff will urinate/defecate within 10 minutes.	1	100% on 3 days
				When he needs to use the toilet Jeff will make verbalizations indicating his need.	1	100% on 10 occas
2.5	toilet paper	Hand Jeff the toilet paper.	Immediately following toileting, say, "Jeff, use toilet paper."	Jeff will appropriately use the toilet paper.	"	"
2.6	-none-			Jeff will use toilet appropriately without prompts in three settings other than training setting.	1	100% on 20 occas

ES 14 © McCormack 1975   © Revisions: USU ECC Education Staff 1978

Figure 5.3. Short term instructional objectives form.

members. However, all individuals who are working with that student are involved in both the development and approval of the IEP during the staffing (more details are given later in this chapter). Preparation for the formulation of the program is begun by evaluating prior data, such as: a) test results, b) health records, c) anecdotal teacher reports, and d) the report developed by the diagnostic intake team. At this point, additional diagnostic information may also be collected in the form of pretesting through teacher observations of the type of errors made by the student during a task, the way the student approaches tasks, what motivates or reinforces the student, and what teaching strategies seem to be effective for this individual.

Pretesting and informal assessments should be conducted in the classroom in a flexible, relaxed environment, rather than in the formal atmosphere typically associated with standardized testing. Informal assessments usually include criterion-referenced tests (CRTs) or checklists of a diagnostic rather than survey nature, or teacher-designed criterion checklists or matrices (Mc-Cormack, 1975). A major purpose of these informal assessments is to establish a baseline of the child's current level of functioning. The baseline may include initial observations of the child at home and at school, diagnostic teaching probes, completion of developmental scales if they have not been previously completed, the recording of behavior through the use of media such as videotape, and will also include the completion of an instrument such as the Program Assessment and Planning Guide (Striefel & Cadez, 1983) for clarification of the student's strengths and deficits (more information follows later in this chapter).

Planning Stage

Planning responsibilities of the CST involve: a) actually developing an IEP, b) conducting formal CST meetings, and c) making a decision concerning the most appropriate placement for the child. The planning stage of developing the IEP includes five basic components:

1. Summarizing basic information on the child
2. Summarizing present levels of educational performance
3. Writing annual goals and indicating necessary services and time lines
4. Writing short term instructional objectives for each annual goal
5. Indicating placement options based upon the services required

Summarizing Information The first task of the CST in the initial planning meeting is to summarize all of the basic information obtained from parents or guardians, school records, or other CST members. The following information is generally required on an IEP: a) name, b) address, c) school, d) present placement, e) birthdate, f) telephone, g) primary handicapping condition (spelled out), and h) the names of the CST members. An example of such information is included on the Summary Information Form in Figure 5.1.

It is essential that all of this information be provided. A good general practice is to *never leave a blank space where information is requested.*

Statement of Present Levels of Educational Performance This is the first substantive task that must be addressed by the CST in the planning stage. Adequate preplanning will greatly facilitate the development of this statement. Several steps are involved in writing a statement of present levels of educational performance. An example of each step of the procedure is provided at the end of the chapter on pages 110–111. The steps involved in writing a statement of present levels of educational performance are:

1. Assemble all of the assessment and evaluation information on the child to document his or her strengths and weaknesses. This information should clarify the concerns that resulted in the referral of the child for special education services.

2. The assembled information should be reviewed by the CST and a list of the child's strengths and weaknesses should be developed as in part (a) of the example. Along with each strength and weakness, the source of the information should be included to facilitate any necessary cross-referencing.

3. Any discrepancies noted with regard to strengths and weaknesses should be resolved by the CST before proceeding. If discrepancies exist, the sources of the discrepant information should be reviewed and the necessary corrections made.

4. Once all the strengths and weaknesses for a child have been listed, these statements should be organized into categories as in part (b) of the example. These categories will vary according to the types of strengths and weaknesses displayed by the child. For children who are mildly handicapped, academic categories may be emphasized. Categories for a child with more severe handicaps may lean toward vocational, social, and motor development skills. For each category listed, a summary statement may be prepared that describes the relevant strengths and weaknesses.

5. The statement of present levels of educational performance is then simply a summarization of the individual summary statements. This statement is provided in part (c) of the example. Once developed, the statement is written into the IEP on the Summary Information Form (Figure 5.1).

Developing a PAPG-IEP Interface Once information has been summarized and a statement of present levels of educational performance has been formulated, the most immediate and important responsibility of the CST, developing an IEP, can take place. This can be accomplished by using, where appropriate, the performance objectives recorded for a new student on an instrument such as the Program Assessment and Planning Guide (PAPG) (Striefel & Cadez, 1983). The IEP for each student must be appropriate (Bender, Valletutti, & Bender, 1976; Houts & Scott, 1975) to:

1. The developmental levels of the child
2. The family situation
3. The environmental setting
4. The child's handicapping condition
5. The prerequisite skills required
6. The student's interests, strengths, and needs
7. The materials and resources needed to teach the child
8. The medical and paramedical consultative and treatment services needed
9. Parental concerns and priorities
10. The future placement goals for the student
11. Fostering of appropriate values and attitudes
12. The demands of a changing society

Once the functioning level of the student has been established, the child study team prepares a proposed set of annual goals in accordance with the aforementioned criteria and the best interests of the total child. The proposed goals are sent to the parents who are given 7–10 days to study the proposed goals and to add to, delete, or revise these goals prior to the child study team meeting that has been scheduled to finalize the individualized educational program. The IEP is a working document that is placed in each student's working file. It is recommended that a three-ring binder be used and labeled the *Individual Program Book*. The Individual Program Book containing the IEP and working programs should be made available to all staff and paraprofessionals working with the child in accordance with confidentiality guidelines. It serves as a means of organizing the activities of the staff so that the student receives the identified services on the frequency schedule established by the CST. Teachers have the major responsibility for developing and keeping the IEP current. In addition, other staff should assist the teacher in the development and regular monitoring of student progress on the IEP.

A copy of the IEP should be included in each student's main file. This main file should consist of pertinent test data, test protocols, treatment information, progress and evaluation reports, information from other agencies, and other background information. For identification purposes, the student's name should be placed on the outside of the cover of the main file. Information received from other agencies should be marked as such so it is not sent out to others requesting information on the client. Only information generated at the current facility may be sent out upon request (requiring the signing of the release of information form).

Inside the file, the student's full name, the name of his or her parents or guardians, the student's address and telephone number, emergency phone numbers, instructions on medication, special dietary restrictions and recommendations, physical restrictions, seizure potential, or other critical information are all recorded in an obvious place. This information is collected during intakes and is updated at the beginning of each school year. Following this, there can be a section containing the initial diagnostic information. This includes the report of the intake team, containing, at a minimum, the names of the team members, a summary of previous diagnostic evaluations and educational training, a summary of the team's findings, any prescriptive recommendations made, information on eligibility decisions, current level of functioning, and projections about future child performance. Other sections in the main file include: a) records of all staffings held, noting who attended and what decisions were made, b) records of meetings held by the CST and its decisions, c) the student's education, health, and social service program, d) information concerning progress or lack of progress in each of these areas, and e) background information.

When the CST is ready to begin developing and preparing an IEP for each student, it may consider the objectives of an instrument such as the PAPG (Striefel & Cadez, 1983). The PAPG is a planning instrument that can be used for several different purposes by those working with handicapped students. First, the PAPG can be used as an assessment tool for determining the specific behavioral skills and deficits of the handicapped students. The results can then be used for planning the student's program or as a curriculum guide or resource for planning programs for individual children whose skills and deficit behaviors have already been determined by the PAPG assessment or other assessment instruments. The PAPG can also be used for planning training programs for students and volunteers working with individuals with handicaps.

The PAPG consists of 1,400-plus objectives, developmental ages for most objectives, a list of resources, student profile sheets, and a student profile graph. The objectives in each of the skill areas are presented, when possible, in a developmental sequence. Within many of the objectives, the user is referred to a program or programs that may be used to teach the skills associated with the specific objective. The PAPG can also be used by teachers to establish annual goals and short term objectives for inclusion in the IEP of handicapped students. Whenever practical, a developmental age for each behavioral objective has been included. The developmental ages may be used primarily as a guideline and as a basis for comparison with nonhandicapped students. For each behavioral objective in each area, an attempt was made to list one or more resource materials that provide information on how to teach the objective.

Included in the PAPG are student profile sheets used to record a child's level of performance on behaviors contained therein. The student profile sheet is divided into individual sections that correspond to the sections of the PAPG such as receptive language, expressive language, etc. The student profile graph provides a visual summary of the student's performance in each of 26 skill areas:

1. Gross motor—e.g., sitting, standing, walking and running
2. Fine motor—e.g., picking up small objects and drawing geometric figures

3. Receptive language—e.g., following one- and two-step commands and selecting opposites
4. Expressive language—e.g., verbal imitation of sounds and words, and verbal responses to questions
5. Social—e.g., making eye contact and smiling at others, and playing with others cooperatively
6. Social language—e.g., initiating conversation with others and saying "please" and "thank you"
7. Eating—e.g., drinking from cup with assistance and eating with spoon without assistance
8. Dressing—e.g., cooperating when being dressed and tying shoes correctly
9. Toileting—e.g., using toilet unassisted and asking for toilet location if in new location
10. Personal hygiene—e.g., cooperating when nose is wiped and can wash own hair unassisted
11. Safety—e.g., moving away when told "hot" and obeying traffic rules when on bicycle
12. Music—e.g., moving in rhythm to music and singing songs
13. Writing—e.g., scribbling, drawing lines, and writing own name
14. Reading—e.g., telling story about pictures and reading words
15. Math/numeration and operations—e.g., counting objects and adding and subtracting numbers
16. Seasons and time—e.g., naming four seasons of year and telling time correctly to the minute
17. Money—e.g., naming coins, counting out amounts of money correctly
18. Calendar—e.g., naming days of week and months of year
19. Volume—e.g., pointing to measurement units named and pouring liquid in cup to designated amount (1/2 cup)
20. Linear—e.g., measuring items by inches and knowing which of three items is longer
21. Housecleaning—e.g., dusting furniture and fixing bed correctly
22. Clothing care—e.g., hanging up clothing and sewing on button
23. Kitchen and cooking—e.g., setting table and cooking simple foods
24. Survival and security—e.g., answering telephone and locking doors
25. Appliance operation—e.g., using toaster, electric stove, and lawn mower.
26. Travel—e.g., using bus and public restrooms unassisted

As a short or long term monitoring or assessment tool, the PAPG can help a teacher maintain a specific record of quarterly or annual progress for each individual child.

As a training tool, the PAPG provides the trainee, classroom aide, or volunteer with an overall plan for use with children, an appropriate developmental sequence for most subject areas, and the information needed to set up a supplementary resource file containing appropriate educational programs and suggestions for teaching each objective. For further details on using the PAPG to aid in the writing and development of the IEP, see Chapter 8.

Writing Annual Goals Writing annual goals may be simplified by following the steps outlined in the example on pages 110–111 for developing a statement of present levels of educational performance. For the sake of objectivity and accountability, it is recommended that goals be written to reflect a child's potential annual attainments rather than indefinite long range attainments. Additionally, annual goals should be stated with the same amount of precision that short term instructional objectives are stated. The view of some educators is that annual goals may be general statements of attainment while short term instructional objectives should represent more measurable skills and behaviors. This attitude contrasts with the need for accountability. Without precision, evaluation of general annual goals is difficult at best, and subject to considerable variance depending upon who is performing the evaluation.

It is recommended that annual goals be written technically and represent skills and behaviors that are functional for the child as well as generalizable. Annual goals with these characteristics will be easier to interpret by others and will be directly amenable to objective evaluation. The following steps are involved in writing annual goals:

1. Refer to the categories outlined in the development of the statement of present levels of educational performance (see page 110 of the example). The CST should identify from these categories specific areas of need that represent weaknesses that the child exhibits. The identification of these areas of need provides the basis for the development of annual goals for the child. The areas of need are shown in Table 5.2(a). Once the areas of need have been identified by the CST, potential annual goals are written. It can be seen from this table that multiple annual goals may be developed from a single area of need. These potential annual goals should not represent a finished product but rather a basic delineation of what the CST would like to see the child learn within a year's time.

2. The potential annual goal statements are then developed into measurable and objective statements of desired attainment. The CST should evaluate the quality of each of the annual goals that are written. This may be accomplished using the quality evaluation procedures for assessing technical adequacy, functionality, and generalizability that are described in a later section (Evaluating IEP Content). The CST should ensure that annual goals contain a clear description of exactly what the child will do and under what conditions. Also, the skill should enable the child to realize more independence in his or her environment and should be generalizable to other situations. Drafts of these annual goals for the example provided are shown in Table 5.2(b).

Table 5.2.   Writing annual goals

Areas in need and potential annual goals (a)

Area of Need	Potential Annual Goals
Pre-instructional skills	
Easily distracted and unable to work in groups of 3–5 children without disruptions. Complies with instructions 20% of the time.	Will demonstrate ability to work in groups of 3–5 children for 30 minutes without disruptions. Will comply with instructions within 5 seconds
Self-help skills	
Not toilet-trained	Will demonstrate ability to independently toilet himself
Social skills	
Physical aggression toward others	Physical aggression will not occur during school activities
Language skills	
Does not speak in phrases and sentences	Will identify objects and actions using phrases and sentences

Drafts of annual goals (b)

1.0   During a social skills training session with 3–5 children, Jeff will demonstrate the ability to work for 30 minutes without disruptions.

2.0   During a social skills training session with 3–5 children, Jeff will comply with each of the trainer's instructions within 5 seconds of delivery 90% of the time.

3.0   Jeff will independently demonstrate the ability to toilet himself without an accident for 5 consecutive days.

4.0   During all school activities, Jeff will not physically aggress toward others for 5 consecutive days.

5.0   When presented with pictures of objects or actions, Jeff will identify the objects or actions using phrases or sentences of a noun-verb-noun format in 100% of trials on 5 consecutive days.

Prioritized annual goals (c)

1.0   During all instructional and play activities at school, Jeff will not physically aggress toward others on 5 consecutive days.

2.0   Jeff will independently demonstrate the ability to toilet himself without an accident on 5 consecutive days.

3.0   During a social skills training session with 3–5 children, Jeff will comply with each of the trainer's instructions within 5 seconds of delivery 90% of the time on 5 consecutive days.

4.0   During a social skills training session with 3–5 children, Jeff will demonstrate the ability to work for 30 minutes with less than 3 disruptions on 10 consecutive days.

5.0   When presented with pictures of objects or actions, Jeff will identify the objects or actions using phrases or sentences of noun-verb-noun format in 100% of trials on 5 consecutive days.

---

3.   Through quality evaluation of the annual goals drafted by the CST, revisions may be suggested. The purpose of these revisions is to make the annual goals more easily understandable and measurable. After revision,

the annual goals should be prioritized by the CST in terms of their importance for the child, and they should be realistically attainable. Realistic attainment means restricting the number of annual goals that are placed on an IEP to the number that can be achieved. Four to six have been found in field testing by teachers to be realistic. It is important for the user to realize that a child's complete daily/weekly program can consist of more activities than are listed on the child's IEP. Table 5.2(c) shows the prioritized annual goals for the example. Note that in this case, the CST has placed a high priority on intervening with the child's aggressive behavior. CSTs make decisions concerning priorities based upon their perceptions. This is a principal reason why the CST should be a multidisciplinary team.

4. Once the annual goals have been written and meet the satisfaction of the entire CST, they are transferred to the Annual Goals Form (Figure 5.2). At this time the CST indicates the services necessary for each annual goal, the frequency with which these services will be delivered, and the expected implementation date and duration of services. This information is written on the Annual Goals Form for each annual goal (Figure 5.2). The dates associated with the actual start and completion of services are entered as they occur. In this way, the CST may evaluate potential discrepancies that occur in the delivery of services during the annual review process.

Writing Short Term Instructional Objectives The identification of functional short term instructional objectives can be the most time consuming task faced by the CST. The delineation of short term instructional objectives determines the training activities that will be implemented for the child. These objectives are developed from each of the annual goal statements through the use of task and concept analysis procedures that consist of breaking a task (behavior) or concept into small steps. These procedures may be used by the CST to divide annual goals into their component parts. These component parts are subsequently written into short term instructional objectives. A discussion of task and concept analysis is beyond the scope of this manuscript. The reader is referred to texts by Becker (1971), Striefel (1974), and Thiagarajan, Semmel, and Semmel (1974) for excellent treatments of these topics.

The steps taken in writing short term instructional objectives are:

1. Each annual goal should be evaluated to ensure its technical adequacy, functionality, and generalizability. Revision of any improperly stated annual goals is strongly suggested. For the purpose of example, the annual goal in Table 5.3(a) will be used as a basis for developing short term instructional objectives.

2. The annual goal should be task and concept analyzed as necessary to identify the heirarchy of steps needed to train the child to demonstrate the skill or behavior referenced in the annual goal. Table 5.3(b) provides a brief description of the steps involved in toilet training the child. Note that

Table 5.3. Writing short term instructional objectives

Annual goal (a)

2.0 Jeff will independently demonstrate the ability to toilet himself without an accident for 5 consecutive days.

Task analysis of annual goal (b)

Ability to sit independently on a toilet for 10 minutes
Ability to raise and lower pants upon request
Ability to urinate/defecate within 10 minutes of scheduled time (determined through base-line observation)
Ability to verbally indicate need to go to the toilet
Ability to use toilet paper correctly following use of toilet
Ability to use toilet independently in training settings and other locations

Drafts of short term instructional objectives (c)

2.1 Jeff will demonstrate the ability to lower and raise his pants upon request, correctly using zippers and snaps in 90% of trials in three consecutive sessions.
2.2 Jeff will demonstrate the ability to sit independently on the toilet for 10 minutes without excessive movement in 90% of trials in three consecutive sessions.
2.3 Jeff will urinate/defecate within 10 minutes of the scheduled time (determined through baseline observation) on 5 consecutive days.
2.4 When he needs to use the toilet, Jeff will make an appropriate verbal indication of his need on 10 consecutive occasions.
2.5 Jeff will demonstrate the ability to use toilet paper correctly following his use of the toilet on 10 consecutive occasions.
2.6 Jeff will demonstrate the ability to use the toilet independently in training settings and other settings on 20 consecutive occasions.

---

the extent of the task analysis is dependent upon the child's noted strength and his or her general level of ability. For a more severely handicapped child, a larger number of steps will be involved in toilet training and the behavior will be broken into smaller components.

3. Once the hierarchy of steps leading to the attainment of an annual goal have been identified, each is written into a separate short term instructional objective statement. These statements are shown in Table 5.3(c). Again, as was the case in the development of annual goals, short term instructional objectives must be technically adequate, functional, and generalizable for the child. The quality of these statements should be evaluated using the procedures identified in the *Conducting a Quality Check of IEP Content* section of this chapter.

4. The completed short term instructional objectives should be organized in a sequence from initial to terminal behaviors. *The terminal short term instructional objective should be identical to the stated annual goal.* These statements are then written on the Short Term Instructional Objectives Form in the indicated spaces (Figure 5.3). Note on this form that the annual goal appears at the top of the form and that each of the short term instructional objectives is broken into the following components:

a) materials needed, b) what the trainer does and says, c) what the student does, d) the number of trials to be conducted on the objective during each session, e) the criteria for mastery, and f) the start and completion dates. One convention has been used in the writing of short term instructional objectives that may be helpful. Each annual goal is associated with a reference number indicating its priority ranking (e.g., 2.0 on Figure 5.3). Short term instructional objectives receive a reference number that indicates the annual goal that it is related to as well as its position in the hierarchy of steps identified through the task or concept analysis (e.g., 2.1 through 2.6 on Figure 5.3). This allows for the quick reference of any objective to an annual goal and provides a rough estimation of accomplishment toward the attainment of the annual goal.

As mentioned, the delineation of short term instructional objectives can be extremely time consuming. Many times it is advantageous for individual CST members to identify tentative short term instructional objectives during pre-planning activities and to refine them during the planning stage. It is also helpful to adjourn the meeting and allow individual members to develop objectives to show to each of the CST members for approval, instead of trying to write all of the statements in formal meetings. Predeveloped skill sequences such as those found in the Program Assessment and Planning Guide (Striefel & Cadez, 1982) can also be used. Both of these approaches may save a considerable amount of time in the planning process.

Determining Placement Alternatives The final step in the planning stage of IEP development is the determination of the most appropriate placement for the child to receive the necessary services. The most appropriate educational placement for a child should be based upon: a) the child's *right* to be educated with normal children as much as possible, and b) the concerns of the parent(s) about available placements. It is essential to indicate the extent of a child's participation with nonhandicapped students. Each CST must determine the placement and the extent of participation in regular educational programs for a child on an individual basis. The Summary Information Form (Figure 5.1) contains space for this information.

The last activity that must occur prior to implementing a child's IEP is the parents' or guardians' indication of their approval of their child's IEP and their permission for placement. If parents have been involved as equal partners on the CST in developing an IEP, they will readily agree to the placement decision. If parents do not agree with placement, the team must determine the reasons and negotiate a solution agreeable to everyone on the CST. If no agreed-upon solution can be achieved, parents can request a due process hearing in which a hearing officer will make the decision. A space for a parent's signature is included on the Summary Information Form. After parents agree to placement by signing the IEP, they normally receive a copy of the completed IEP document and the child's program is implemented.

EVALUATING AND MONITORING AN IEP

PL 94-142 (Education for All Handicapped Children Act of 1975, 1976) requires, *on at least an annual basis,* a review of each IEP to evaluate the appropriateness of the programs and placement of the handicapped child. This review constitutes a formal evaluation of the IEP.

Once an IEP has been developed and approved by the CST, it is normally implemented immediately. It is at this stage that the CST becomes responsible for monitoring the IEP's implementation and for evaluating the progress made by the child as a function of the programs and services provided.

Evaluation procedures advocated by educational agencies have generally focused on determining the child's progress toward attainment of stated annual goals and short term instructional objectives (Lilly, 1977; Turnbull, Strickland, & Brantley, 1978). Typically, this progress is expressed in terms of annual goals or objectives achieved or the amount of special education services provided to the child. These quantitative measures mean little if the document upon which they are based, the IEP, is poorly written and does not facilitate objective evaluation of annual goals or short term instructional objectives. Therefore, two levels of evaluation are recommended for determining the appropriateness of IEPs and their resulting programs: 1) an internal evaluation of the content of the IEP focusing on the annual goals and short term instructional objectives, and 2) an ongoing evaluation or monitoring of the implementation of the IEP. It is the CST's responsibility to see that both of these evaluation components are implemented in evaluating and monitoring an IEP. A correctly implemented content evaluation will ensure the clarity and conciseness needed to do an outcome evaluation.

The evaluation of the content of the IEP is conducted by the CST during the development process. This evaluation may be referred to as a quality check and ensures that completed IEPs are relatively free from ambiguities and dubious annual goals and short term instructional objectives. The importance of such a quality check has been previously noted.

Ongoing evaluation or monitoring of the IEP begins as soon as the IEP is implemented. It involves the monitoring of the child's IEP and resulting program to determine his or her progress and the appropriateness of the recommended placement. This monitoring is frequently conducted as an annual review of the IEP by the CST. However, one proven method suggests that 1) quality IEPs be developed, 2) supporting data collection strategies be in place within the educational agency (see Chapter 7), and 3) continual monitoring occur. Only then can timely and objective decisions be made on a child's program on a regular basis. Within the continuum presented by annual review and continuous monitoring lies a realistic level of monitoring. This is further discussed later in this section.

Conducting a Quality Check of IEP Content

A written IEP should be a comprehensive description of the services that a handicapped child will receive and should specify objectively what behaviors and skills the child will learn as well as the level of required mastery. Writing annual goals and short term instructional objectives correctly is critical to objectivity and clarity in IEPs. Three factors must be evaluated to determine the quality of the content of written IEPs (Whitney & Striefel, 1981):

1. The degree of functionality that annual goals and short term instructional objectives have for a given child
2. The technical adequacy of the annual goals and short term instructional objectives
3. The generality of the annual goals and short term instructional objectives for a given child

These three factors apply equally to annual goals and short term instructional objectives. Annual goals are frequently dealt with as general levels of attainment with short term instructional objectives being more finite and specific. However, without clarity and specificity, annual goals and short term instructional objectives cannot be objectively evaluated. Therefore, child progress may be difficult to interpret. Thus, the following procedures apply to both annual goals and short term instructional objectives.

Quality Check Form   A form for use in performing a quality check on functionality, technical adequacy, and generality of annual goals and short term instructional objectives is pictured in Figure 5.4.[2] (Reading the information on the form may be of use to the reader in understanding the discussion that follows.) The form is used by writing a goal or objective in the space for Annual Goal/Objective and then evaluating whether or not the goal/objective exhibits the essential characteristics of the three requirements. The details for completing this evaluation and examples will follow. Once completed for all annual goals and short term instructional objectives, the quality check sheet may be attached to the IEP as documentation of the quality check.

Functionality   The first requirement of correctly stated annual goals and short term instructional objectives is that they represent functional skills for the child in question. There is no reason to evaluate other aspects of a goal or objective if the skill to be taught is not functional. Instead, such cases require

---

[2]The IEP quality check form is reproduced herein with the permission of the first author and is available from the author.

DIRECTIONS: Write the annual goal or short-term instructional objective statement and its reference number in the space provided. Indicate whether all of the components required for functionality, technical adequacy and generality are present. Circle "Y" if the component is present, "N" if it is absent. If an "N" is scored for any component, elimination or revision of the goal or objective is strongly suggested. Attach this form(s) to the IEP.

CHILD _____ PAGE ___ OF ___
EVALUATOR _____
DATE _____

ANNUAL GOAL/OBJECTIVE: _____

FUNCTIONALITY					TECHNICAL ADEQUACY			GENERALITY		
NECESSARY	ALTERNATIVES	SIMILARITY	STANDARDS	AGE-APPROPRIATE	CONDITIONS	RESPONSE	CRITERIA	PERSONS	SETTING	TIME
Y N	Y N	Y N	Y N	Y N	Y N	Y N	Y N	Y N	Y N	Y N

ANNUAL GOAL/OBJECTIVE: _____

FUNCTIONALITY					TECHNICAL ADEQUACY			GENERALITY		
NECESSARY	ALTERNATIVES	SIMILARITY	STANDARDS	AGE-APPROPRIATE	CONDITIONS	RESPONSE	CRITERIA	PERSONS	SETTING	TIME
Y N	Y N	Y N	Y N	Y N	Y N	Y N	Y N	Y N	Y N	Y N

ANNUAL GOAL/OBJECTIVE: _____

FUNCTIONALITY					TECHNICAL ADEQUACY			GENERALITY		
NECESSARY	ALTERNATIVES	SIMILARITY	STANDARDS	AGE-APPROPRIATE	CONDITIONS	RESPONSE	CRITERIA	PERSONS	SETTING	TIME
Y N	Y N	Y N	Y N	Y N	Y N	Y N	Y N	Y N	Y N	Y N

ANNUAL GOAL/OBJECTIVE: _____

FUNCTIONALITY					TECHNICAL ADEQUACY			GENERALITY		
NECESSARY	ALTERNATIVES	SIMILARITY	STANDARDS	AGE-APPROPRIATE	CONDITIONS	RESPONSE	CRITERIA	PERSONS	SETTING	TIME
Y N	Y N	Y N	Y N	Y N	Y N	Y N	Y N	Y N	Y N	Y N

ANNUAL GOAL/OBJECTIVE: _____

FUNCTIONALITY					TECHNICAL ADEQUACY			GENERALITY		
NECESSARY	ALTERNATIVES	SIMILARITY	STANDARDS	AGE-APPROPRIATE	CONDITIONS	RESPONSE	CRITERIA	PERSONS	SETTING	TIME
Y N	Y N	Y N	Y N	Y N.	Y N	Y N	Y N	Y N	Y N	Y N

FUNCTIONALITY

NECESSARY—is the skill necessary to prepare the child to function in his or her daily or probable future environment? For example, teaching a child to set a table rather than teaching him or her to stack blocks.

ALTERNATIVES —is this alternative skill the best one for helping the child to reach the desired level of functioning most quickly? For example, teaching a child a general rule for using a skill rather than teaching all of the appropriate instances in which to use the skill.

SIMILAR—are the skills, materials and tasks involved in teaching similar to those that will be encountered in the child's environment? For example, teaching a child to tell time using real clocks instead of clocks made from paper plates.

STANDARDS—are the criteria that have been established for determining mastery of the skill consistent with the standards that will be expected in the child's environment? For example, the child may be taught to dress himself and demonstrate that he can perform all of the components of the skill, but he requires 30, rather than 5, minutes to complete the task.

AGE-APPROPRIATE—does the skill represent a chronologically age-appropriate skill for the child? For example, teaching a 16-year-old moderately handicapped child to ride a bicycle rather than a tricycle.

TECHNICAL ADEQUACY

CONDITIONS—does the statement indicate the situation, setting, required materials or resources necessary for the child to perform the skill?

RESPONSE—does the statement indicate what the child will do to demonstrate the skill or behavior in question?

CRITERIA—does the statement indicate how well or how often the child must demonstrate the skill or behavior to achieve mastery?

GENERALITY

PERSONS—does the goal/objective statement specify that the behavior must occur in the presence of persons other than the original trainer(s)?

SETTINGS—does the goal/objective statement specify that the behavior must occur in a setting other than the one in which it was trained?

TIME—does the goal/objective statement specify that the behavior must occur across time (different days)? It would also include different times of the day.

Figure 5.4.   IEP quality check form.

rewriting of the goal or objective so that it is functional. An evaluation of the functionality of a particular goal or objective depends upon a complete knowledge of the child in question. More importantly, this means a knowledge of his or her probable future needs, not only a knowledge of his or her present condition. This should be addressed by the CST.

Functionality consists of five characteristics (Brown, Branston, Hamre-Nietupski, Pumpian, Certo, & Gruenewald, 1979; Brown, Nietupski, & Hamre-Nietupski, 1976; Whitney & Striefel, 1981). These characteristics may be expressed in the form of questions as follows:

1. Is the skill *necessary* to prepare the child to function in his or her daily or probable future environment? An example would be teaching a child to set a table rather than teaching him or her to stack a set of blocks.

2. Of the *alternative* skills available, will the present skill allow the child to reach the desired level of functioning most efficiently? An example of this would be to teach the child a general rule (do what I do when I do it) for using a skill rather than teaching all of the appropriate instances (each individual imitation) in which to use the skill.

3. Are the skills, materials and tasks involved in teaching *similar* to those that will be encountered in the child's environment? An example of this would be teaching the child to tell time using real clocks instead of paper clocks.

4. Are the criteria that have been established for determining mastery of the skill consistent with the *standards* that will be expected in the child's environment? An example would be to teach a child to cross a busy city street correctly 100% of the time as opposed to 90% of the time. A lower criteria, while perhaps realistic for certain skills and behaviors, would be totally inappropriate for this skill. In fact, ensuring only a 90% level of mastery could result in physical harm to the child.

5. Does the skill represent a chronologically *age-appropriate* skill for the child? An example of this would be to teach a 16-year-old moderately handicapped child to ride a bicycle rather than a tricycle.

Each question can be answered with a yes or no response (marked Y or N) on the Quality Check Form (Figure 5.4). In order for a goal or objective to be considered functional, it must receive ratings of yes (Y) for all five questions. If an annual goal or short term instructional objective scores an N on any of these characteristics, revision of the statement is strongly suggested. Assessment for functionality *should be conducted by the CST as a group,* as should any necessary revisions. The attainment of functional annual goals and short term instructional objectives will benefit a handicapped child far more than attainment of skills and behaviors with questionable functionality.

To evaluate the functionality of annual goals and short term instructional objectives requires considerable information concerning the specific child. The CST should have information concerning the child's capabilities at present, the environments to which he or she is exposed, and the potential environments to which he or she will be exposed in the future. Without this background information, evaluation of a goal or objective from the standpoint of functionality is virtually impossible. To evaluate the functionality of this annual goal, the CST must review some general information concerning Jeff. The following is a summary of relevant information previously provided concerning Jeff:

> Jeff is a student in a classroom serving moderately and severely handicapped children. He is 6 years old and has been in this program for the past 2 years. In addition to his placement in the moderately and severely handicapped classroom, he also attends a regular classroom for 1 hour a day and participates in physical education and social activities with other children. It is the desire of Jeff's parents and the CST to focus his program on the attainment of skills necessary to enable him to function more appropriately in the regular classroom.

With the above information, a determination of the functionality of the annual goal is demonstrated in Table 5.4. The slightly modified annual goal in Table 5.2 and a portion of the quality check form will be used to illustrate the quality check for functionality.

The first characteristic of a functional goal or objective is that it be necessary to prepare the child to function in his or her environment. Jeff is expected to work without disruptions and will be expected to do so in future instructional settings. Therefore, a circle was placed around the Y underneath Necessary.

The next characteristic concerns the possibility of teaching alternative skills. In this situation there are no alternative skills available. Therefore, the present skill will allow Jeff to reach the desired level of functioning most efficiently. A circle was placed around the Y underneath Alternatives.

The third characteristic of functional goals and objectives involves the similarity between the tasks, skills, and materials, if any, in the annual goal and those that would be found in other environments. In the example above, the skill identified in the annual goal represents an expectation that is made of all children in Jeff's classroom. Children participate in sessions for 30-minute periods several times daily. That expectation is also realistic for Jeff. Therefore, a circle was placed around the Y underneath Similar.

The mastery criteria for Jeff are consistent with the standards expected of all the children in the classroom. Therefore, the standards for Jeff are realistic and a circle was placed around the Y underneath Standards.

The final characteristic of a functionally stated goal or objective is that it be chronologically age-appropriate. Since the skill required in the example is similar to that required of all children Jeff's age, it may be considered chronologically age-appropriate for Jeff. A circle was placed around the Y underneath Age-appropriate.

In reviewing our findings concerning the functionality of this annual goal for Jeff, we may conclude that since all Y's have been circled, the annual goal is

Table 5.4. Determination of the functionality of the annual goal

Portion of Quality Check Form

Directions: Write the annual goal or short term instructional objective statement and its reference number in the space provided. Indicate whether all of the components required for functionality are present. Circle Y if the component is present, N if it is absent. If an N is scored for any component, revision of the goal or objective is strongly suggested.

ANNUAL GOAL/OBJECTIVE: During a small group social skills instructional activity with 3–5 children, Jeff will demonstrate the ability to work for 30 minutes with less than 3 disruptions on 10 consecutive days.

FUNCTIONALITY				
NECESSARY	ALTERNATIVES	SIMILARITY	STANDARDS	AGE-APPROPRIATE
Ⓨ N	Ⓨ N	Ⓨ N	Ⓨ N	Ⓨ N

indeed a functional goal for Jeff. It should be clear that the determination of functionality of a particular annual goal for a child is highly individualistic. In fact, different members of the CST may disagree as to a particular annual goal's functionality for a particular child. They must resolve such a disagreement. It is clear that responsibility for determining functionality is granted to the CST by PL 94-142 (Education for All Handicapped Children Act of 1975, 1976). The CST (including the parent or guardian) is solely responsible for the appropriateness of the IEP for a child, and a determination of functionality is clearly within this responsibility.

Technical Adequacy   The second requirement of an appropriately stated annual goal or short term instructional objective is technical adequacy. The goal or objective is written in measurable terms so that different persons can agree on the occurrence or nonoccurrence of the behavior. A technically adequate annual goal or short term instructional objective includes three characteristics in the form of questions (Striefel & Hofmeister, 1979), as follows:

1. Are the *conditions* under which the child will demonstrate or perform the behavior or skill specified? Conditions may include such things as the necessary materials, resources or setting. In many cases, the conditions may be deduced from other parts of the statement (e.g., if a child were expected to write the answers, then paper and pencil would be required). Whenever possible however, it is preferable to explicitly state the conditions.

2. Is the *response* that the child will make to demonstrate the behavior or skill clearly specified in behavioral terms? This means the response must be measurable and will include terms such as "listing" or "pointing." Terms such as "learning" or "recognizing" are too general and require additional clarification before the response can be measured.

3. Are the *criteria* that are required for mastery by the annual goal or short term instructional objective specified (e.g., how often the behavior must occur)? Adequately stated criteria should indicate that the desired behavior or skill occurs across time to insure the durability of the attained behavior. For example, if the criteria stated that the child would only need to demonstrate the desired behavior once, it may be possible that on the second attempt the child would fail. Therefore, could it be said that the child mastered the skill? A more appropriate criteria statement would indicate that the student list all combinations correctly on five consecutive occasions. The requirement of consecutive performances tends to rule out unstable performing on the part of the child. Teachers may then be more assured of a child's mastery when criteria such as this are explicitly stated.

The annual goal stated in Table 5.5 does indicate the conditions under which the behavior will occur. It indicates that Jeff will demonstrate the behavior "during a small group social skills instructional activity with 3–5 children." This is a description of the setting that is sufficient in this case. Therefore, in evaluating this annual goal, the requirement relating to the conditions has been met and was indicated by placing a circle around the Y beneath Conditions as indicated in the rating box.

The second characteristic of technically adequate annual goals and short term instructional objectives is that the response that the child will make to demonstrate the skill or behavior is clearly identified. In Table 5.5, the annual goal says that Jeff "will work for 30 minutes without disruptions." Thus, the response that Jeff will be required to make to demonstrate the skill or behavior has been stated clearly. In evaluating most goals or objectives, one would look for the verb statement that describes *what the child will do*. The primary concern in evaluating the response is "can it be measured?" The above example appears to be capable of being measured. Additional clarification could be provided such as indicating specifically what disruptions were included or what Jeff would do to demonstrate "work." However, the annual

Table 5.5. Determination of technical adequacy of annual goal (For illustration purposes the annual goal in Table 5.2(b) will again be used along with the relevant portion of the quality check form to evaluate technical quality.)

ANNUAL GOAL/OBJECTIVE: During a small group social skills instructional activity with 3–5 children, Jeff will demonstrate the ability to work for 30 minutes without disruptions.

TECHNICAL ADEQUACY		
CONDITIONS	RESPONSE	CRITERIA
Ⓨ N	Ⓨ N	Y Ⓝ

goal appears to meet the minimum requirements. Therefore, in evaluating the annual goal for technical adequacy, a circle was placed around the Y beneath Response.

The final characteristic of technically adequate annual goals and short term instructional objectives is the statement of criteria. In the example, Jeff will demonstrate the behavior, but the requirements for mastery are not clearly delineated. It is implied by their absence that Jeff only needs to demonstrate the skill once for 30 minutes in order to demonstrate mastery. Explicit criteria such as "for 5 consecutive days" should be included. In evaluating this annual goal for technical adequacy concerning the presence of criteria, a circle was placed around the N indicating that the statement lacks appropriately stated criteria. If an N is circled when completing a quality check for an annual goal or short term instructional objective, revision of the statement in question is strongly suggested. Such was the case with the above example. The annual goal was subsequently revised to read as follows: "During a small group social skills instructional activity with 3–5 children, Jeff will demonstrate the ability to work for 30 minutes with less than 3 disruptions on 10 consecutive days." The revised annual goal now includes each of the required components for technical adequacy.

Generality In the past, generalization has been seen as the natural outcome of all training. As a result, few people have concerned themselves with describing the situations or conditions under which it occurs or have attempted to develop procedures to facilitate its occurrence (Stokes & Baer, 1977). One type of generality concerned with the occurrence of behavior over time, more frequently called maintenance of behavior, was already addressed to some degree in evaluating the mastery criteria in the technical adequacy section.

The need for generalization of acquired skills and behaviors is unquestionably one of the major emphases of education (Baer, 1981b; Brown, Nietupski, & Hamre-Nietupski, 1976; Hupp & Mervis, 1981), particularly for severely handicapped children who may not generalize learned behavior as easily as normal children. Generalization must be planned (Anderson & Spradlin, 1980; Baer, 1981b). One way to ensure attention to generalization is through its inclusion in annual goal and objective statements (Striefel & Hofmeister, 1979; Whitney & Striefel, 1981). It is recommended that annual goals and short term objectives address three levels of generality. These three levels of generality in the form of questions follow:

1. Does the goal/objective statement specify that the behavior must occur in the presence of persons other than the original trainer(s)?
2. Does the goal/objective statement specify that the behavior must occur in a setting other than the one in which it was trained?

3. Does the goal/objective statement specify that the behavior must occur across time (different days)? It would also include different times of the day.

The annual goal in Table 5.6 specifies that the behavior will occur in the presence of different teachers and groups of children in different classrooms and across a time span of 10 days. Therefore, in evaluating the annual goal, the requirements of all three levels of generality were met and a circle was placed around the Y for each of the three conditions (as indicated in the rating box).

An option that some individuals may wish to consider is placement of generalization statements within each instructional program. The statements should specify the settings, persons, and/or time across which the skills or behaviors will be expected to generalize before being considered mastered. Another form of generality essential to ensure that a skill has been learned is the generalization of the skill across materials or irrelevant stimulus characteristics of objects (concept generalization). For example, if a child is taught the concept of "ball," he or she should be able to identify balls regardless of their size or color. Concept generalization is most aptly handled in the programming stage rather than in writing the IEP.

Monitoring the IEP

Determining whether a child is progressing toward the accomplishment of the annual goals and short term objectives requires that an IEP be monitored. The purposes of these monitoring activities are to ensure that each child receives all of the services needed to accomplish the IEP goals and objectives and to ensure that needed changes are made in the implementation programs and/or goals and objectives as dictated by each individual child's situation.

Table 5.6. Determination of generality of annual goal (For illustration purposes, an annual goal is provided and will be used, along with the relevant portion of the quality check form, to evaluate for adequacy of programming for generality.)

ANNUAL GOAL/OBJECTIVE: During a small group instructional activity with 3–5 children, Jeff will demonstrate the ability to work for 30 minutes with less than three disruptions on each of 10 consecutive days. Once this behavior is mastered, Jeff will demonstrate the same skill to the same criteria in the regularly scheduled music and art classes, in the music and art classrooms, in the presence of different teachers and small groups consisting of different children.

	Generality	
PERSONS	SETTING	TIME
Ⓨ N	Ⓨ N	Ⓨ N

When appropriate performance data are available, two levels of monitoring occur: 1) daily or weekly monitoring by the teaching staff (see Chapter 7) and 2) an annual review by the CST. In fact, PL 94-142 (Education for All Handicapped Children Act of 1975, 1976) requires a review of every IEP at least once a year. The annual review is a bare minimum and is often insufficient for the operation of an efficient and effective education program. Monitoring should be an ongoing process of daily and, at minimum, weekly collection of performance data. Only through regular collection of performance data can one monitor child progress toward attainment of goals and objectives and thus make timely changes in programs, goals or objectives when lack of progress indicates the need for changes.

Daily/Weekly Monitoring This level of monitoring is generally conducted by the classroom teacher. Performance data for each program for each child served are reviewed, and one of the following decisions may be made: 1) continue the program as written, 2) alter the teaching or reinforcement procedures as necessary, 3) take appropriate steps to be sure that the trainer is reliable and consistent in carrying out the instructional procedures, or 4) recommend to CST that the goal or objective be altered to more adequately meet the child's needs.

Annual Review The annual review is conducted by the CST. In order to avoid overloading the team members, it is helpful to stagger the time schedules for the reviews so that they *do not* all occur at one time during the year. It is easier to schedule several from a classroom each month, thus spreading out the workload but also allowing team members to better prepare for the review.

During the annual review, the CST: 1) reviews child progress, 2) modifies annual goals and/or short term objectives, 3) reviews start and anticipated completion dates, and 4) task analyzes goals and objectives as necessary. Input and consensus is sought from all members of the CST during all phases of the annual review. The annual review may be conducted more often than once per year if necessitated by unusual progress, lack of progress, need for changes in the IEP, or other unusual circumstances. For more information on data collection and monitoring, see Chapter 7.

STAFFING PROCEDURES

Staffings of children should occur soon after a child enters a special education program, preferably the first week a new child enters the program. Parents should be contacted at least 5 working days before their child's staffing. Parents have the legal right to sit in on any staffing being conducted for their child.

Staffings serve many functions. One function is to determine whether continuation in the present placement should occur, or if a different placement should be sought. Another function is to establish long range goals. In essence, life expectancies are described as points on a continuum of personal/social/

economic independence, e.g., living in a group home and working in the community to earn enough money to take care of one's own needs. In addition, intermediate goals are specified. The staffing team determines realistic time lines for each individual goal in the program and specifies who will be responsible for accomplishing each goal, reassigns personnel as necessary, and seeks additional resources. The staffing team can also initiate changes in teaching strategies when necessary and make recommendations to the CST and others.

Staffings also serve as an ongoing monitoring process to ensure that continuous evaluation of a student's program occurs. If progress does not seem to be occurring, the IEP is modified and adjusted to the specific individual in terms of his or her own needs and potential for success (note Chapter 8 for details).

Although difficult to accomplish, it is recommended that at least three staffings per year be held. Doing so helps ensure that staff continue to change programs when programs are in need of change. In addition, regular staffings keep parents *informed* and *involved* in their child's program. If three staffings are not possible, a minimum of two staffings should be held annually. The arrangement of the room in which the staffing is conducted is important (Kroth, 1975). The size of the room should be adequate and comfortable as should the seating arrangement so that everyone can be seen and heard, and the ventilation should be good. Adequate paper, pencils, tissues, etc., should also be at hand. The chairperson of the staffings should be either the child's classroom teacher or the special education director if he or she is familiar with the child's case. The other members of the team will consist of the parents, paraprofessionals, and other professional staff members who are working with the student, or who seem appropriate for working with that student in developing and implementing the IEP.

There are at least four types of staffing models available for use. These are a) in-house staffings, b) formal IEP staffings, c) field staffings, and d) paraprofessional staffings.

1. *In-house staffings* may be held weekly or as needed by the in-house staff (i.e., those who work with the student regularly). These staffings are for the purpose of discussing student progress, and in the event gains are not being made, to modify and revise existing instructional procedures. This type of staffing helps the team understand the student completely and keep up on all the changing variables relative to that student, e.g., family stiuations. Placement decisions are not made at in-house staffings.

2. *Formal staffings* (CSTs) should occur at least twice a year with in-house staff, the student's parent(s), the district representative from the child's school district, other nonschool professionals, and in some cases, the student. The purposes of this type of staffing are the same as in-house

staffings except that placement decisions can be made. An analysis of procedures that can be implemented is listed below.

3. *Field staffings* are conducted periodically in locations other than the school in the presence of one or more staff members and the child's parents. In some cases, a representative from the local school district may be present. Field staffings are most frequently conducted by a home trainer or teacher and are held primarily to discuss child progress, placement, and specific problems.

4. *Paraprofessional staffings* should occur quarterly if the setting serves as a training site for college students. Those present should include the cooperating teacher, practicum students, volunteers who work with the specific student, and possibly the practicum supervisor. The purpose of these staffings is identical to in-house staffings, with the addition of providing a training experience for those paraprofessionals from the special education, psychology, or social work departments.

The following is an analysis of procedures that can be implemented during a formal staffing:

1. The special education director or cooperating teacher serves as the chairperson in the staffing. The following people are contacted at least 5 working days prior to the staffing and informed of the procedures that will be followed during the staffing:
    a. Parents
    b. Teacher
    c. School district representative (in some cases)
    d. Specialists involved with the child
    e. Parent advocate (where appropriate)

2. If the parent cannot attend the staffing on the date that has been set, a second date is set at the parent's convenience.

3. The chairperson chooses a setting for the staffing that is free from interruptions and distractions, is large enough to hold the group, and has adequate furnishings.

4. The chairperson introduces the parents to all committee members present and sees that everyone is seated comfortably before the staffing begins. Seating should be arranged in a nonthreatening manner and should allow everyone present to see and hear what is happening.

5. The chairperson reads the annual goals that were established for the child at the beginning of the school year by the CST.

6. The chairperson calls on the teacher and asks for a progress report on each annual goal as stated in the IEP. The teacher gives the following information to the committee:
    a. The progress made on each goal
    b. Whether the services were adequate to meet the goal, and whether additional services are needed

    c. Data, charts, graphs, etc., to back all statements regarding the child's program

    d. Recommendation for placement for the coming school year, based on the above information

7. The chairperson will call on the specialists who have been involved with the child's program. If they are unable to be in attendance, the teacher will read the progress notes they have written. These progress notes should:

    a. Review the programs they have worked on with the child

    b. Report progress made on the programs

    c. Make suggestions based on the child's particular needs concerning what services and other programs will be needed in the future, and how much time should be allotted to these programs

8. The chairperson calls on the school district representative. He or she:

    a. Asks any questions of the other committee members regarding the student's program and progress

    b. States what placement options are currently available in the district

    c. Relates what services the school district will provide for the child based on the child's needs as stated by the teacher and specialists

9. The chairperson calls on the parents. The parents:

    a. Add any information to what has already been given

    b. Ask any questions about their child's progress or programs

    c. State what they feel the child's needs are in relation to the school placement and services needed

10. The chairperson opens the staffing to discuss the topic of what the least restrictive environment for this child is for the coming year.

11. The teacher writes a summary of the content of the IEP staffing and attaches it to the student's permanent IEP. He or she also makes sure all necessary signatures and dates are obtained on the IEP.

12. The chairperson verbally summarizes the decisions made at the staffing.

13. If everyone is in agreement, the chairperson closes the staffing. If there is disagreement, the chairperson records what additional information is needed and sets a date for another staffing.

SUMMARY

This chapter has provided an overview of the procedures for developing, implementing, evaluating, and monitoring IEPs. Specific emphasis was given to the functions and responsibilities of the CST, and to the selection and use of IEP forms designed to meet the letter and intent of PL 94-142. In addition, a quality check form for evaluating the technical adequacy, functionality, and generality of annual goals and short term objectives was provided, along with examples of its use.

DETERMINING PRESENT LEVELS OF PERFORMANCE

Jeff is a student in a classroom serving moderately and severely handicapped children. He is 10 years old and has been in this program for the past 2 years. In addition to his placement in this classroom, he also attends a regular classroom for 1 hour a day and participates in physical education and social activities with other children. It is the desire of Jeff's parents and the CST to focus his program on the attainment of skills necessary to enable him to function more appropriately in the regular classroom.

Strengths and weaknesses (a)

Strengths / Sources

—age-appropriate fine motor coordination / teacher and physical therapist
—follows simple directions / teacher
—performs verbal and motor imitations / teacher and speech therapist
—identifies basic needs with single and multiple word utterances / teacher and speech therapist

Weaknesses / Sources

—physical aggression / teacher and psychologist
—easily distracted / psychologist
—not toilet-trained / teacher
—unable to work in groups of 3–5 children without disruptions / teacher
—complies with instructions 20% of time / teacher and parent
—does not talk in phrases and sentences / speech therapist

Categorizing strengths and weaknesses (b)

Pre-instructional skills / Sources

—follows simple directions / teacher
—performs verbal and motor imitations / teacher and speech therapist
—unable to work in groups of 3–5 children without disruptions / teacher
—complies with instructions 20% of time / teacher and parent

Summary: Jeff follows simple directions and has verbal and motor imitation skills. He is easily distracted and is unable to work in groups of 3–5 children without being disruptive. Though he follows directions, he complies with instructions appropriately only 20% of the time.

Communication skills / Sources

—identifies basic needs with single and multiple word utterances / teacher and speech therapist
—does not talk in phrases and sentences / speech therapist

Summary: Jeff can communicate his basic needs by making verbal requests consisting of single and multiple word utterances. However, he does not speak in phrases and sentences.

Motor skills / Sources

—age-appropriate fine motor coordination / teacher and physical therapist

Summary: Jeff has age-appropriate fine motor coordination.

Self-help skills / Sources

—not toilet-trained / teacher

Summary: Jeff is not able to toilet himself.

Social skills / Sources

—physical aggression / teacher and psychologist

Summary: Jeff is physically aggressive toward others.

DETERMINING PRESENT LEVELS OF PERFORMANCE
(continued)

Statement of present levels of educational performance (c)

Jeff follows simple directions and has verbal and motor imitation skills. He is easily distracted and is unable to work in groups of 3–5 children without becoming disruptive. Though he follows directions, he complies with instructions only 20% of the time. He can communicate his basic needs by making verbal requests consisting of single and multiple word utterances. Jeff has age-appropriate fine motor coordination but is unable to toilet himself. He demonstrates physical aggression toward others in school settings.

6

Methods for Influencing Behavior Change in the Classroom

After reading this chapter, you should have an understanding of:

1. How to recognize inappropriate behaviors, and how behaviors are acquired
2. How to change behavior using the behavior modification approach, techniques for increasing appropriate behaviors, and techniques for decreasing inappropriate behaviors
3. How to define behaviors in observable and measurable terms
4. Procedures for measuring behavior and behavior change, including how to graph and analyze information
5. The use of single subject behavior modification intervention designs
6. Management techniques to use when working with groups of children
7. How to program for generalization and maintenance of behavior

INFORMATION NEEDED TO IMPLEMENT behavior techniques in the classroom is presented in this chapter with the express purpose of simplifying staff duties while enhancing child progress. The reader requiring additional information is referred to the extant literature on the topic of classroom behavior modification (e.g., Epstein, Cullinan, & Rose, 1980; Jones & Kazdin, 1981; Sprick, 1981).

Anyone who has worked in a classroom can recall one or more situations where the students appeared to have more control of the classroom than did the teacher. Johnny may have been busy putting a "kick me" sign on Susan's back. Susan, meanwhile, was trying to see how long she could balance her chair on two legs. Bill was trying to rescue Barry the goldfish from a certain death by drowning by putting Barry in with the hamster. This description may even describe what some teachers consider to be a "good day," but most observers would agree that there is a need for change in the behavior of some students or, in other words, a need for "behavior modification."

Changing behavior is not new to teachers. When a teacher succeeds in getting a student to answer the question, "Who was the first president?" with "George Washington" rather than "I don't know," then the teacher has engaged in a form of behavior modification. The same thing is true when a teacher succeeds in getting Bill to leave the goldfish in the goldfish bowl. The intent of this chapter is to deal with behaviors that align more closely with the latter type of behavior.

Behavior can be managed on at least four levels. The first level of behavior management is prevention of problems by planning and structuring the classroom program. The second is establishment of a high level of appropriate behavior by maintaining a high frequency of reinforcement for such behavior. The third level is teaching children how to cope with their frustrations and thereby giving them acceptable alternatives to disruptive behavior. The final level is direct intervention, dealing with problems after they occur. The focus of this chapter will be on prevention of problems, reinforcement, and on direct intervention strategies.

INAPPROPRIATE BEHAVIOR:
RECOGNITION, DEFINITION, AND ACQUISITION

How does one go about recognizing an inappropriate behavior? Someone might say, "It's easy. Just watch William for 5 minutes. Now, that's inappropriate!" And it may very well be inappropriate for William, in that class, at that time. But what is inappropriate for one person, in one place, at one time may be perfectly appropriate under different conditions. For example, it may be inappropriate if William is sitting at his desk tapping his pencil rather loudly while the class is engaged in taking a test. But, on the other hand, if the class was listening to a John Phillip Sousa march, the same tapping might be very appropriate.

Because what is and is not appropriate is relative to the situation in which the behavior occurs, there are several aspects that should be considered before calling a behavior inappropriate. It is important to remember that behavior change should result in the student learning to do more for him- or herself, or make the student more acceptable to others in his or her environment. Perhaps the first consideration is whether the behavior interferes with the student's (or other students') right to accomplish the objectives that school staff are trying to have students achieve. These general objectives will vary from class to class and school to school but will almost always include things such as getting a quality education, learning to get along socially with others, and providing a learning environment without disruptions. Each teacher will have to establish the objectives of her class. Once these have been established, they can be used as criteria to help decide which behaviors are inappropriate, e.g., those that, if changed, will result in benefits of some type for the individual. A note of caution might be wise here. A class objective should never be established solely for the convenience or preference of the teacher. If the only reason a teacher describes a student's behavior as inappropriate is because he or she does not want students to do it then the teacher has *not* been fair to the student. For example, if a teacher has imposed a "no one will talk" rule so that he or she may spend time writing a novel, then the teacher has done a great disservice to her class because students could benefit greatly from discussing and helping each other with a topic during that time.

Other considerations in deciding what is and isn't appropriate in a classroom deal with the strength of the behavior. The strength of the behavior can be described in terms of the frequency (how often), the duration (how long), the rate (how quickly), the magnitude (how vigorous), or the latency (how long between the occurrence of a stimulus event and the beginning of a response) of a behavior.

The strength of a behavior becomes important when one considers that a behavior at one level of strength may not be inappropriate while at a higher or lower level it might be inappropriate. For example, one would probably not consider it inappropriate for a student to be out of his seat without permission once or twice a month. But what if it were once or twice a day, or once or twice an hour or even once or twice a minute? At what point does it become inappropriate? The answer depends on determining the point at which the behavior interferes with the learning of the student or others. Another example of determining an inappropriate behavior might be how long it takes a student to complete an assignment. At some point the teacher might decide that Sally is progressing at less than an acceptable rate because it takes her too long to complete the assignment.

In order to be successful at changing inappropriate behaviors, it is necessary to be familiar with how behaviors are acquired. Behavior is established and/or maintained by the events that precede (antecedents) and follow (consequences) the behavior. Individuals perform those behaviors that produce desirable changes in the environment. Tommy disrupts a class by making funny noises because when he does, people laugh and Tommy likes to hear people laugh. When Judy has been working at a lesson for more than a few minutes and is tired, she is likely to throw a tantrum because the teacher will then sit her in the corner, and she will not have to work on her lesson. Most teachers are able to indicate with accuracy what the antecedents and/or consequences are that are maintaining certain behaviors. But there are many more instances where it may be difficult to determine what consequences are maintaining a behavior.

As a general rule, teachers should assume that inappropriate behaviors displayed by students have been learned. The teacher may not always be able to pinpoint exactly what consequences helped establish or maintain a particular behavior, but there are several areas that should be considered. As previously stated, most behavior can be traced to the natural consequences that follow the behavior. These can include consequences produced by the teacher or other class members, or can include those that naturally occur, such as getting out of doing work when one disrupts the class. Another important area to consider in trying to determine how inappropriate behaviors are established is *shaping*. Shaping refers to the process of gradually establishing a new behavior, in this case an inappropriate behavior, by repeatedly reinforcing minor improvements toward that behavior (Panyan, 1980). This shaping, or what Patterson (1971) called accidental training, can often occur unintentionally by one of several processes.

A student might be ignored until he or she acts inappropriately. At that point the teacher may attend to the child and thus, if the child is seeking attention, the teacher may be reinforcing inappropriate behavior. This happens more often than educators would like to admit. If a child is quietly sitting at his or her desk, it is less likely that the teacher will attend to that child than one who is being a little disruptive. Consequently, the student sitting quietly at his desk may behave inappropriately in order to obtain some of the teacher's attention.

A second way that inappropriate behavior is often shaped is by receiving attention after inappropriate behavior. This method is not too different from the one just discussed except that the teacher may not have to ignore a child to cause inappropriate behavior. The child may already have in his repertoire a set of inappropriate behaviors. If the teacher gives a great deal of attention to those behaviors when they are exhibited, then those behaviors may be maintained by that attention. At this point, it may be good to re-emphasize the fact that attention in and of itself is neither a reinforcer (a stimulus that increases the future probability of a behavior it is contingent upon) nor a punisher (a stimulus that decreases the future probability of a behavior it is contingent upon). What one student considers to be a very unpleasant form of attention, a different student, or that student at a different time, may consider to be a very desirable consequence to his or her behavior.

A third process that often establishes inappropriate behavior is to require too much behavior of a student before providing positive consequence for appropriate responses. Very often in educational settings, students are asked to do tasks that they have never before accomplished. When these tasks are too difficult or the criteria are set too high, one can expect the student to exhibit inappropriate behavior. For example, when Calvin is promoted from the 1st to the 2nd grade and the 2nd grade teacher asks Calvin to sit at his desk and work on a workbook for an hour in the morning and an hour in the afternoon, it may be too difficult for Calvin if his 1st grade teacher never required Calvin to sit for more than 15 minutes at a time. When the criteria are too difficult for the student, one can be assured that other inappropriate behaviors will be exhibited by the student, even if these inappropriate behaviors are merely incorrect responses. Often the inappropriate behaviors will be more disruptive in nature than merely making incorrect responses.

CHANGING BEHAVIOR

One solution for inappropriate behavior that is promulgated by this chapter is to influence behavior, that is, to change or to modify it. Behavior modification as a solution has not been universally embraced. There are those who oppose behavior modification for several reasons. Perhaps the most frequently given argument is that it takes too much time. Behavior modification techniques can, in some instances, be extremely time consuming. However, the amount of time taken to gain control of an inappropriate behavior must be weighed against the amount of time that is needed to deal unsuccessfully with the inappropriate behavior. Another argument given for opposing behavior modification is that it doesn't work. This argument can be refuted simply on the grounds of the vast amount of literature available reporting successful use of behavior modification techniques (Epstein et al., 1980; Jones & Kazdin, 1981; Sprick, 1981). Many oppose behavior modification on the grounds that it is "just bribery." The term bribery implies the use of reinforcement to get an individual to commit an immoral or illegal act. Teachers do not try to teach their students immoral or illegal acts. Furthermore, children are no different than adults in that most of what they do occurs because they anticipate some future consequence (a payoff). Most teachers would not continue teaching if they did not receive a paycheck, nor would most other adults continue in their job if they did not receive compensation. Even within the area of social behavior, most adults would not continue to speak or be friendly to those people around them who never returned the courtesy by speaking back. Why should children or students be treated differently than these adults are in terms of consequences? Another reason given by many as to why they do not use behavior modification is that they do not know how. The remainder of this chapter is directed toward remedying this last situation.

Responsive Teaching

In order for behavior modification to be useful to teachers, the approach must be: a) responsive to the objectives of the teacher who is charged with the responsibility of changing student behavior in appropriate ways, b) responsive to conditions and limitations of the particular classroom setting, and c) responsive to the needs and abilities of the students. It is for these three reasons that Hall (1971a) coined the term *responsive teaching*. Because behavior modification has become extremely sophisticated and has been used in a variety of situations with a variety of behaviors, responsive teaching is necessary to make the procedures feasible and worthwhile. If behavior modification cannot be applied by the typical teacher in the classroom, then behavior modification has become too sophisticated and it has become a useless procedure for practical situations. The following information about procedures, approaches and techniques has been described as *The Responsive Teaching Model* and has been used by many teachers.

The responsive teaching model has several essential elements: a) It requires precise observation and measurement of behavior while focusing on procedures that assure the reliability of these measurements and other recording techniques. These techniques are ones that can be used by the teachers while they carry out their other responsibilities. b) The model requires the use of graphs for charting the behaviors recorded. c) It requires application of systematic antecedent (stimuli that precede a response) and consequent (events or stimuli that follow a response) procedures in the classroom setting in order to bring about behavior change. d) It requires the use of single subject reversal and multiple baseline designs (Hersen & Barlow, 1978; Kazdin, 1982) that allow each person or teacher to analyze experimentally what he or she does and then to verify teaching procedures scientifically. e) Its goal is to bring about mutually reinforcing interactions between parents, teachers and the students.

It is extremely important that the teacher be mentally, physically, and technically able to carry out the procedures required to modify the behavior of individual students in the classroom. An outside consultant could easily be asked to come into the classroom and modify a child's behavior. If this is done, it is very likely that when this individual leaves the classroom, the child's behavior will return to its old pattern.

DEFINING BEHAVIOR

First, teachers must determine exactly what aspect of behavior they wish to change. This means defining the behavior accurately. In order to define behavior accurately and appropriately, the definition must be stated in such a way that it has the following characteristics:

1. It is observable and measurable (Hall, 1971a). There are many things that happen in a classroom that cannot be observed. For example, a teacher may say that a child "knows" his math problems. It is just not possible to observe directly that a child "knows" anything. It is possible to observe when a child responds correctly in a given situation. However, knowing is not an observable behavior. It is an inference made by the teacher. Another example might be trying to record when a child is "not trying." If "not

trying'' refers to a child who is not motivated to attempt a behavior, then the behavior becomes one that is not observable. A teacher may not be able to determine when the child is ''not motivated'' and when he or she is ''unable'' to perform a particular behavior.

2. The definition must enable the teacher to differentiate the particular behavior in question from other behaviors. If a behavior concerns a student being out of a seat *without permission,* then it is important that the behavioral definition clarifies that being out of seat is not, in and of itself, the important aspect of the behavior. Rather, the critical component is being out of seat without permission. Another example might be defining talking as an inappropriate behavior. It is important to note that one does not want to turn a student into a mute. One may however, want to shape when and where a student talks.

3. The behavior should be defined specifically enough to allow independent observers to agree on when the behavior does or does not occur (Hall, 1971a). It is important to define behaviors so that they may be measured reliably and consistently. Without such specificity, there may be confusion as to whether or not the behavior did occur.

4. The definition of behavior must be held constant across time so that the changes in behavior can be accurately measured. If one changes the definition of the behavior, then the measurement of the strength of that behavior is going to change accordingly. This makes it extremely difficult to determine whether or not procedures in effect at that time were having any impact on the strength of the behavior.

A few examples of some well-defined behaviors that might be of concern in an academic classroom follow:

In-seat behavior—buttocks in contact with seat of chair and feet flat on the floor with body and head oriented toward the front of the room

Hitting—striking another student with either hand with the result that the student struck cries or complains to the teacher about being hit

Not completing assignments—not turning in written assignments within 15 minutes of the assigned deadline.

Each of these definitions meets the four guidelines previously specified. While the language used to define them may seem stilted, it is necessary for precise measurement.

MEASUREMENT OF BEHAVIOR

Once the behavior has been defined, it is important to determine how often the behavior is currently occurring or how long it lasts when it does occur. That means it is necessary to measure the behavior. As mentioned before, reliability of measurements is one of the essential aspects of behavior modification. It is important to distinguish actual changes in behavior from changes that appear to be there but in actuality are the reflection of inaccurate measurement. Chapter 7 on data collection provides extensive coverage of techniques and examples of behavior measurement; thus, they are mentioned only briefly here. There are several techniques for measuring behavior:

1. *Measure the end products of behavior.* Behavior sometimes results in permanent products that are tangible and that can be observed and counted. For example, students' written answers to math problems can be observed. Direct products are some of the most useful items for a teacher in terms of measurement because they provide permanent records, they are precise, are often a result of important academic behavior and can be saved for later comparisons and analysis.

2. *Event recording.* This technique is used when a behavior does not result in a permanent product. The teacher counts the number of times a particular behavior occurs. For example, the teacher might want to record how many times a child is out of his or her seat without permission. This could be accomplished by making marks on a piece of paper or by using a wrist counter such as a golf counter.

3. *Duration recording.* This technique is used to discover how long a particular behavior lasts. One simply records the amount of time that elapses between the beginning and the end of the behavior. A stopwatch is the most efficient tool for duration recording although clocks and conventional watches can be used if extreme precision is not required.

4. *Latency recording.* There will be instances when one is not interested in knowing how long a behavior lasts but is concerned with how much time elapses between when a behavior should start and when it actually does. For example, if the teacher asks a child to be seated and 15 minutes elapses between the time of the request and the time the child actually is seated, then the teacher may want to record latency of that behavior.

5. *Interval recording.* Interval recording is a technique for observing one or more behaviors concurrently. The observation time is divided into a number of intervals. For example, a 10-minute observation period may be divided into 20 30-second intervals. After having defined the behavior or behaviors in question, the teacher will observe during each of the intervals and record whether or not the behavior occurred during the interval. Note that how many times the behavior occurred during each interval is not in question. The important aspect is whether or not it occurred at all. Obviously, this does not provide an exact measurement of the behavior. It does give an estimate of the behavior, however. The advantage of interval recording is that more than one behavior of a particular child or the behavior of several children can be observed concurrently.

6. *Time sampling.* This procedure is similar to interval recording in that the observation session is divided into intervals of time. But with time sampling, rather than observing whether or not behavior occurred during the interval, the behavior is recorded as either occurring or not occurring at the end of the time interval. For example, a school day may be divided into 30-minute intervals. Every 30 minutes the teacher would record whether or not a particular behavior was or was not occurring at that particular moment. This procedure is also an estimate of the strength of the behavior. It is generally a less accurate estimate than interval recording and obviously less accurate than event recording, but again, the advantage is that more than one behavior can be recorded simultaneously, and, with time sampling, the teacher does not have to give undivided attention during the total observation period.

7. *Placheck.* This procedure is useful for obtaining data on a group of children. To use it, one picks random or preset time periods for recording data, e.g., every half hour. One may even set a timer to ring at the selected time. The observer looks up and rapidly counts the number of students engaged in the target behavior and then rapidly counts the number of children present. A proportion or percent is then calculated. The advantages of this technique is that data can be collected for groups of children even though the number present may vary from time to time.

Graphing

Graphing raw data is a useful procedure for summarizing information and allows the teacher to analyze quickly the progress a student is making. In graphing behavior, the vertical axis is used to indicate the strength of the behavior. The horizontal axis is used to indicate the time dimension. (Refer to Chapter 7 for an extensive explanation of graphing.) Figures 6.1, 6.2, and 6.3 show three graphs that are examples of the strength of behaviors that may be of interest to teachers.[1]

Figure 6.1 shows a graph of the rate at which John is able to do math problems on several consecutive days.

Figure 6.2 shows the frequency Jane cried during a 40-minute observation session across several days.

Figure 6.3 shows the duration of Frank's playing behavior during several recess periods.

BEHAVIOR MODIFICATION INTERVENTION DESIGNS

The literature in the field of behavior modification includes numerous intervention designs (Hersen & Barlow, 1978; Kazdin, 1982) to demonstrate the

---

[1]The figures in this chapter are included with the permission of the first author.

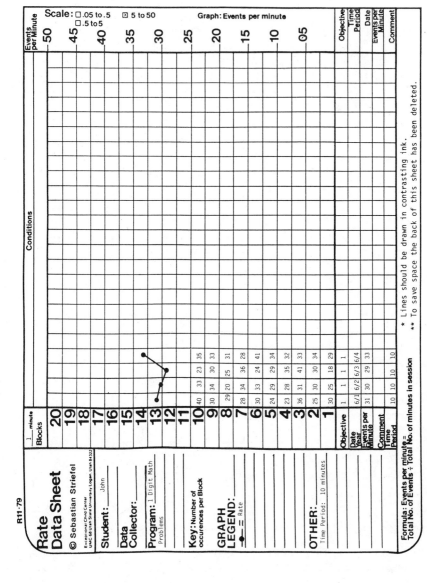

Figure 6.1. Rate of doing math problems.

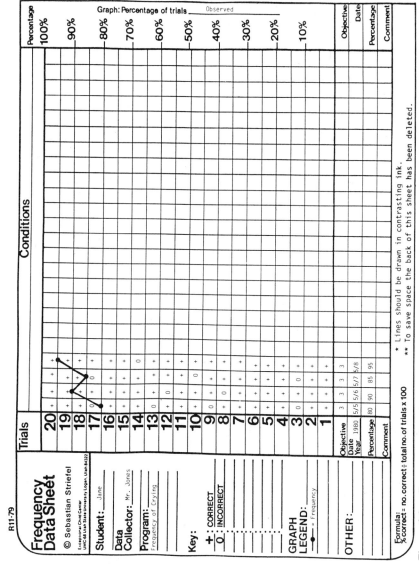

Figure 6.2. Frequency of crying.

123

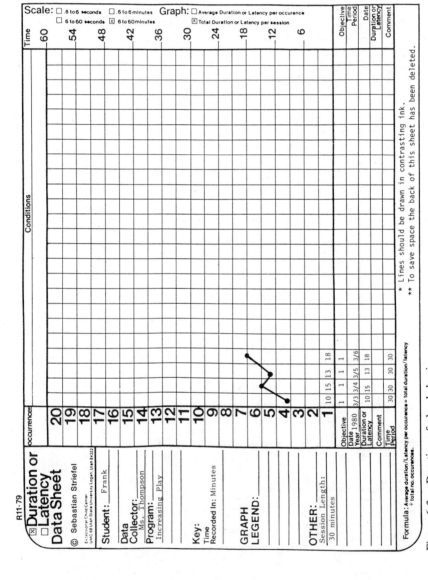

Figure 6.3. Duration of play behavior.

124

effectiveness of procedures used. Many of these designs are extremely complicated and require a great deal of time and personnel. Two of the designs that are not extremely complicated and are useful in the typical classroom situation are discussed here.

The Reversal Design

This design is capable of demonstrating that a procedure implemented by the teacher is in fact having an effect on the behavior. Figure 6.4 is a record of the rate of arguments of a student during a tutoring session. It can be seen that during the first baseline (sessions during which the strength of the behavior is measured but no intervention made), the rate of arguments is about 3 per minute (i.e., $93 \div 30$) and varied from 2 to about 4 per minute. Beginning with the seventh session, the teacher began to ignore the subject when he disagreed with her directives. This resulted in the behavior decreasing to zero and remaining there for three sessions. On the fourteenth session there was a reversal (baseline 2), or return to the original condition, during which the teacher attended to arguments. This resulted in the behavior returning to approximately the same levels as before intervention (baseline 1). On the eighteenth session the teacher again began to ignore the behavior (intervention 2) that resulted in a decrease in the behavior to almost a zero.

The purpose of a reversal design is to demonstrate that the intervention made by the teacher does in fact have an effect on the behavior. If an intervention does have an effect on the behavior, then each time the intervention is implemented, the behavior will change in the desired direction. When the intervention is removed (a return to baseline), then the behavior should return to its previous level. There will be exceptions to this type of reversal for some behaviors. An example of this might be teaching a child to interact appropriately with other students. The baseline may show that the child has almost no appropriate interactions with other students. When an intervention is implemented to increase interactions, the behavior may increase to an appropriate level, but when there is a reversal to baseline conditions, the behavior may not return to its original levels because the child has found that it is fun to interact with others. He or she has learned how to do it, has no desire to stop interacting, and so continues to interact. For most teachers this is of little concern given the fact that the main objective was to teach appropriate interactions. There may be some concern by teachers if they wish to demonstrate that the procedures that they implemented did in fact have an effect on the behavior. If a behavior can be reversed by a mere return to baseline conditions, the teacher's job is unfinished. It means that the teacher needs to carry out additional activities to program for generalization of the skill so the skill is maintained by the natural environment and does not return to the inappropriate level when intervention is removed.

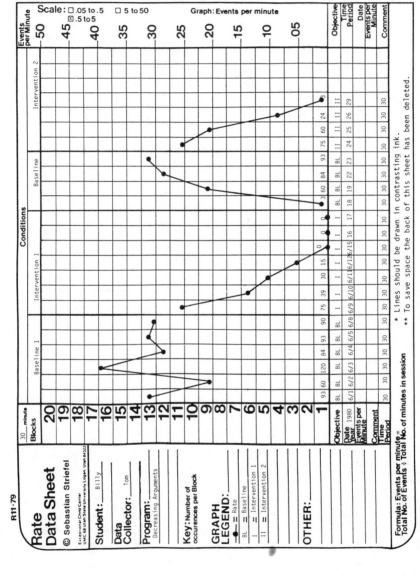

Figure 6.4.   Rate of arguments using a reversal design.

The Multiple Baseline Design

A design that can be used to demonstrate control even when the behavior does not return to baseline after the intervention is withdrawn is the multiple baseline design. The multiple baseline design is used with several behaviors, several students, or the behavior of one student in several situations or settings. In the example given in Figure 6.5, the duration of tantruming for a student is recorded in two different settings. Baseline data are collected on the duration of tantruming in reading and math sessions daily. On day 5, an intervention strategy, in this case a response cost procedure (each time the response occurs, the consequence costs the student something, e.g., points), is implemented for tantruming in the reading session only. Tantruming decreased during reading but not during math. Baseline data are continued in the math session until day 10. At that point, the same intervention procedure is implemented in the math session and tantruming also decreased in math sessions. This procedure demonstrated that the intervention was effective in both settings because there was no change in tantrum behavior until the response cost procedure was implemented in reading and math respectively. Multiple baselines can be used to demonstrate that the intervention strategy was the variable that caused the behavior to decrease if the behavior changes after the intervention strategy is implemented (and only after) sequentially in each setting (e.g., reading and math), for each behavior or for different students.

TECHNIQUES FOR INCREASING BEHAVIORS

In a normal classroom situation the teacher is usually interested in either increasing the strength of an appropriate behavior or decreasing the strength of inappropriate behavior. There are several techniques or procedures that are used to increase the strength of behaviors.

Reinforcement

Reinforcement is technically defined as the procedure for increasing the strength of a behavior by presenting a reinforcer immediately after (contingent upon) that behavior. This, of course, begs the question "What then is a reinforcer?" First of all, a reinforcer is not a static thing. What is a reinforcer today may not be a reinforcer tomorrow and vice versa. Technically, re- inforcers are stimuli, which, when applied contingent upon behavior, will increase the probability that the behavior will occur again. More simply, a reinforcer is a payoff that is sufficient enough to get a student to produce the behavior desired by the teacher/therapist. For example, assume that Bobby, who seldom follows instructions, is given an instruction and he complies. Being allowed to play with one of his favorite toys will result in an increase in following instructions if the toy is a reinforcer. The toy is a reinforcer if instruction following in the future increases in compliance with requests by the

R11:79

☒ Duration or ☐ Latency Data Sheet

© Sebastian Striefel

Exceptional Child Center
UMC-68 Utah State University Logan, Utah 84322

Student: Dorothy M.

Data Collector: Sally Weber

Program: Decreasing Tantruming

Key:
Time Recorded In: Minutes

GRAPH LEGEND:
● = Duration of tantrums during reading
▲ = Duration of tantrums during math.

OTHER:
Session Length: 30 Minutes

Formula: Average duration/Latency per occurrence = total duration/latency ÷ total no. occurrences.

Scale: ☐ .6 to 6 seconds ☐ .6 to 6 minutes ☐ 6 to 60 seconds ☒ 6 to 60 minutes

Graph: ☐ Average Duration or Latency per occurence ☒ Total Duration or Latency per session

Time: 60 54 48 42 36 30 24 18 12 6

Conditions

occurrence	BASELINE	RESPONSE COST READING	RESPONSE COST MATH

20
19
18
17
16
15
14
13
12
11
10
9
8
7
6
5
4
3

| | Reading 2 | | | | | | | | | | | | | | | | | | |
| | Math 1 | | | | | | | | | | | | | | | | | | |

Objective																			
Date 1980	BL	BL	BL	BL	BL	6/4	6/5	6/6	6/7	6/8	6/9	6/10							
Year	6/1	6/2	6/3																
Duration or Latency	15	14	16	15	14	11	11	8	13	14	2	0	1	0	0	0	0		
	13	16	14	15	16	11	13	15	11	11	14	13	12	10	5	0	0		
				See Back of Page		12	13	14	15	12	12	12	12	12				
Comment	*	*	*	*	*	*	*	*	*	*	*	*	*	*	*	*	*		
Time Period	30	30	30	30	30	30	30	30	30	30	30	30	30	30	30	30	30		

Objective
Time Period
Date
Duration or Latency
Comment

* Lines should be drawn in contrasting ink.

128

Date	Comments
6/1	Reading period duration = 15 minutes; Math period duration = 13 minutes
6/2	" = 14 " " = 16 "
6/3	" = 16 " " = 14 "
6/4	" = 15 " " = 15 "
6/5	" = 14 " " = 16 "
6/8	" = 13 " " = 14 "
6/9	" = 8 " " = 13 "
6/10	" = 2 " " = 15 "
6/11	" = 0 " " = 14 "
6/12	" = 1 " " = 13 "
6/15	" = 0 " " = 10 "
6/16	" = 0 " " = 5 "
6/17	" = 0 " " = 1 "
6/18	" = 0 " " = 0 "
6/19	" = 0 " " = 0 "

Figure 6.5. Duration of tantruming using a multiple baseline design.

B-79

129

teacher. The easiest way to decide what to use as a reinforcer often consists of observing what the child chooses to do when given the opportunity to decide on any of a number of activities, e.g., during free play. The activity chosen will usually serve as a reinforcer for the child. Since a behavior is strengthened or weakened depending on its consequences, it is necessary to rely as heavily as possible on the use of reinforcement and to avoid the use of punishment whenever possible. Reinforcers for students include anything that can increase future behavior such as teacher praise, peer recognition, toys, edibles, liquid, activities such as being the first to line up for some activity, stars on the chart, and so on. Hall and Hall (1980a) and Sulzer-Azaroff and Mayer (1977) provide extensive lists of potential reinforcers. In addition, Cautela (1981) provides a variety of reinforcement survey schedules for use with children of different ages in different settings such as school or home. Shevin (1982) provides a set of guidelines for appropriate selection and use of food and drink as reinforcers in the classroom. Striefel (1974) has also outlined several procedures for selecting potential reinforcers:

1. Ask the learner.
2. Question others who have been associated with the learner and have had ample opportunity to observe his or her likes and dislikes, e.g., parents, teacher, ward personnel.
3. Observe the learner in his or her natural environment where a number of potential reinforcers are available to see what the child does with free time in such a situation.
4. Provide the child with several choices by placing four or five potential rewards (piece of candy, a little cake, chips, a drink, a toy) on a table. Allow the child to sample each, replace missing items, and ask the learner to take one. Repeat this procedure until a clear preference is established, e.g., 10 trials, and then remove and use the most preferred item.

It is important to keep in mind that for any given student a particular item may or may not be a reinforcer (Striefel, 1974). The only way to determine accurately whether or not an item is a reinforcer is to try that item and see whether or not changes in the behavior of the student occur.

After determining which reinforcers work well and which do not, the teacher might then prioritize each reinforcer according to the following specific characteristics:

1. *Strength*:   Rank from strongest to weakest. It is also necessary to consider the satiation curve of the reward, i.e., how long does it maintain its initial strength? For example, with a walk, the learner may become tired; thus, the walk may temporarily lose its reinforcing capabilities. Edibles are very subject to satiation.
2. *Disruption*:   How difficult is it to dispense the reward, i.e., how upsetting is it to the training situation? A piece of hard candy may be easy to

dispense, but if the learner requires 3 or 4 minutes to eat it (thus does not concentrate on the task), it can be extremely disrupting. It is also essential to consider the disruptive characteristics of a reward if it is to be used in group instruction.

3. *Satiation*: What is the potential for satiation? Will the reinforcer have any long-lasting effect?

4. *Measurability*: Can it be measured in quantifiable amounts for duplication by others? Items such as candy and cereal are relatively easy to measure (one piece of candy, 2 teaspoons of cereal), while social rewards (e.g., praise or a smile) are more difficult to measure, due to individual tutor difference.

5. *Social Acceptability*: Certain reinforcing activities may upset those who have to work with the learner. Preferred learner rewards, such as twirling or ripping pages out of a book, may be labeled "bizarre" and "socially unacceptable" by staff or parents. It is necessary that the tutor be as willing to give the reward as it is for the learner to want the reward (McCormack, 1977).

6. *Natural*: Certain potential reinforcers are readily available on a daily basis in the normal environment (e.g., natural reinforcers such as social praise and physical contact). Others (artificial) are available only in certain settings or in programmed environments (e.g., M & Ms, marshmallows, pretzels). Artificial reinforcers may be more effective in establishing new behaviors in some cases where natural reinforcers have failed; however, Baer (1981b) has pointed out that whenever one uses artificial reinforcers, one should be aware of it and be prepared to do all that is necessary to maintain the behavior in environments where artificial reinforcers are not available. In essence, be prepared to program for generalization to natural reinforcers in the environment.

In using reinforcement procedures, there are several rules or guidelines (Striefel, 1981) to keep in mind about their use: a) The reinforcer should be delivered contingent upon the desired response. The conditions under which the reinforcer will be delivered should be clearly specified. b) Reinforcers should be delivered immediately after the desired behavior occurs. If a reinforcer is delivered more than a couple of seconds after the desired behavior, one of several things might occur. First, an inappropriate behavior may have occurred between the time the desired behavior occurred and the reinforcer was delivered. If an inappropriate behavior has occurred, then the reinforcer was supplied contingently, not upon the desired behavior, but upon the inappropriate behavior. Thus, inadvertently, the inappropriate behavior, not the appropriate behavior, was reinforced. Second, if more than a few seconds elapse between the time an appropriate behavior occurs and the time that reinforcement is delivered, the behavior being reinforced may not be clear to the student. In other words, the student may be confused about exactly what behavior is being reinforced. c) Whenever a student is being reinforced with a tangible reinforcer such as food, a toy, or a token, that tangible reinforcer should always be preceded by social praise that can be delivered in-stantaneously, providing immediate reinforcement (Striefel, 1974). The social stimulus becomes a secondary reinforcer (a reinforcer that acquires reinforcing power by being paired with a primary reinforcer like food) by associating it with the tangible reinforcer. This becomes important later when a teacher tries to gradually eliminate the tangible reinforcers being given to the student to have the behavior respond to reinforcers that occur naturally in the environment (Baer, 1981b). d) Caution should be used to avoid satiating a child on the reinforcer, whether it be tangible or social. Satiation can be avoided by using small amounts of the reinforcer (edible) or allowing short exposures to the tangible reinforcers. e) When choosing a reinforcer for a particular child, it is important to keep in mind that what works well with one child may not work at all with another child. Additionally, what works well with an individual at one particular time may not work at a different time. Consequently, it cannot be assumed that a particular reinforcer will work for a child every time. f) In most normal situations, people do not receive reinforcement after each occurrence of a behavior. People receive reinforcement on an intermittent basis. Most people are paid every 2 weeks or once a month rather than after each minute, hour, or day's work. Similarly, every time an individual smiles and says something pleasant to a passerby, the individual does not receive in return a similar smile. But on an intermittent (periodic) basis, the stranger smiles back thus reinforcing smiling behavior. It is important for teachers to plan for generalization of responses (Baer, 1981b) and for the delay and intermittency of reinforcement that commonly occur in normal society. Teachers must move from a continuous reinforcement situation to an intermittent reinforcement situation. When teach-ing a new behavior, it is important that each correct response be followed by reinforcement. This will allow maximum learning and provide for the efficient use of time. When the behavior is learned, it is important to move to an intermittent reinforcement schedule or one in which on the average every other response is reinforced. This continues to perhaps an average of every third response, then an average of every fourth response, and so on, until the student is functioning at a level in which he or she maintains a high rate of behavior and yet receives the reinforcement only occasionally. A teacher will need to practice using intermittent reinforcement schedules in order for the process to work efficiently.

Shaping and Chaining

Through the proper use of positive reinforcement and nonreinforcement, one can establish behaviors in a person's repertoire that have not been exhibited by the person previously. These might be entirely new responses and/or behavior sequences. One process that can be used to do this is called "shaping"

(Panyan, 1980). It is used to change existing simple responses into new more complex responses by reinforcing minor improvements or steps (successive approximations) toward a terminal or target behavior.

Just as reinforcement affects the frequency of a response or how often it occurs, it can also affect the topography of the response. Topography refers to the physical aspects of the responses that compose the learned behavior (the form of the behavior, the force, its duration). Using the example of pushing a doorbell button to ring the doorbell, the topography of the behavior includes how hard the button is pushed, whether it is pushed with a finger or fist, and how long it is pushed. If reinforcement is delivered in shaping this response, the behavior and its topography are reinforced.

A decision must be made as to what the terminal or final behavior is going to be before attempting to shape a behavior. After this decision has been made, a typical shaping procedure is to observe the subject to identify an initial response that is related to the terminal response along some meaningful dimension (e.g., a sound from a word that is to be shaped). The terminal response is typically a behavior that the subject does not currently exhibit. The intitial response, on the other hand, must be a behavior that the subject does perform frequently. For example, a teacher may wish to teach Johnny, a nonverbal child, to say the word ''ball.'' Saying the word ''ball'' is the terminal behavior. This terminal behavior is not currently in Johnny's behavior repertoire. Consequently, it would be impossible to reinforce the actual behavior of saying the word ''ball.'' One can, however, reinforce approximations of that behavior that the student frequently exhibits. For example, one might begin by reinforcing any sound whatsoever that Johnny makes when asked to say ''ball.'' When Johnny is consistently making some sound when asked to say ''ball,'' one may reinforce only sounds that begin with the letter ''b.'' Next, one might reinforce the sound ''ba'' and not reinforce other sounds that do not begin with the letter ''b.'' Subsequently, one reinforces only sounds that are more and more like the sound ''ball'' until finally Johnny is saying the word ''ball'' when given a directive to say that word.

Occasionally, it may be important to set the occasion for either an initial response or one of the intermediate responses to occur. For example, at a specified time each day, the trainer may sit down at a table with a child and have available a paper and pencil and instruct the subject to watch what the trainer is doing. As the trainer draws a straight line (modeling), he or she might ask the subject to do the same and provide verbal instructions. In the beginning, the trainer reinforces any attempt on the part of the subject to pick up the pencil and draw a line. Gradually, the trainer will require the line to be straighter in order for the subject to get reinforcement. A similar tactic could be used to teach writing letters of the alphabet. In shaping it may be useful to undertake a task analysis in which a behavior is broken down into small steps (Striefel, 1974, 1981). Doing so may be useful in determining potential components of the behavior that a child already possesses that can be shaped via reinforcement into the final desired behavior.

The process of connecting all the steps of a complex behavior into one smooth sequence is called chaining (Ashcroft, 1982). This chaining process of connecting the steps of a behavior can involve a forward or backward process. It's like viewing one frame at a time of a filmstrip of a complex behavior when the film is run forward or backward. For example, the behavior of putting on a coat can be divided into steps, i.e., touching the coat, picking it up, slipping the left arm into the left sleeve, and slipping the right arm into the right sleeve. In forward chaining, the child is reinforced first for touching the coat. Next, reinforcement is delivered only after the child has touched the coat and picked it up. The child is then reinforced only for touching, picking up, and slipping the left arm in the left sleeve. The process continues until the child performs the entire behavior in the correct sequence. In backward chaining, the process is similar except that the first step reinforced is the last step in the sequence. For example, reinforcement is delivered after the child slips his or her right arm in the right sleeve when the left arm is already in the left sleeve. The next step to be reinforced is putting the left arm in the left sleeve and the right arm in the right sleeve when already holding the coat, and so on.

In chaining, as each step is mastered, it is linked to the next step until the entire behavior is performed in a smooth sequence. Shaping can be considered a process of chaining small steps of a behavior into a smooth, complete behavior.

The Instructional Control

If the behavior in question is in the individual's repertoire and the child can understand the instructions given, then telling the child how to do the behavior can be a useful technique for increasing the accuracy of the behavior. For example, with some students it may be sufficient to merely explain individual steps in the process for completing long division. This explanation may give them sufficient information to complete the terminal behavior accurately.

Visual Control or Modeling

For individuals who do not yet function at a level where instructional control is adequate to assist them in gaining new behavior or in learning complex behaviors, visual control by modeling may be a technique that is extremely useful (Striefel, 1981). Modeling merely consists of showing the individual how to do the behavior that is being taught. For example, rather than tell the student how to do math problems, it may be necessary to solve a math problem on the blackboard. In using this technique to teach new behavior, a few things can be done to facilitate the procedures. Select behaviors that are within the developmental level of the child, break the behavior into small steps as appropriate for the child, be sure the child is attending before modeling, and be sure each approximation or correct imitation by the student is followed by reinforcement. Additionally, it is often very helpful to start with simple responses when modeling to give the student a degree of success before moving to more complex behaviors.

Role Playing

This technique is useful in refining a behavior that is in the repertoire of the student or for establishing a new behavior for which the student has already mastered the individual components. Model and give instructions to the individual concerning how to perform the behavior, and then allow the student to practice this behavior while giving feedback on the student's performance. This provides an opportunity for the student to acquire or increase his or her accuracy on the particular behavior (McKay, Davis & Fanning, 1981). Role playing provides the student with auditory (instructions), visual (modeling), and kinesthetic cues (practice) while getting feedback on performance. As such, the student is provided with multiple cues allowing him or her to focus on the elements needed to acquire the behavior. It has been known for some time that individuals differ in terms of how they typically process information (Bandler & Grinder, 1979). Some do better with visual information, others with auditory information, and still others with kinesthetic information. Role playing can include all three.

Prompts and Fading

If the individual does not have a particular skill in his or her repertoire, and that skill or behavior is desired, one method of teaching that behavior is to give the individual either verbal or physical prompts (assistance). As the assistance is gradually removed (fading), have the individual do more and more of the task him- or herself until he or she can perform the behavior independently (Striefel, 1974). For example, in teaching Jerry to write letters of the alphabet, one may initially hold Jerry's hand with the pencil in his hand and help him make the movements necessary to draw the letters. Slowly over time, the trainer would exert less pressure on the student's hand until such time as the student is performing the task on his own. A different way of teaching the same skill would be to have pages of completely written letters of the alphabet and ask the child to trace the letters. As the child is able to trace the letters, one begins to fade or remove parts of the letters so that the child is required to trace parts of the letters and then draw from memory the parts that are missing. Eventually the child must draw the complete letters by memory. Commercial materials for such tasks are available in any school supply store.

Establish Stimulus Control

Students often have behaviors in their repertoire that are displayed in inappropriate situations. It is important to teach students when behaviors are appropriate and when they are not appropriate. Stimulus control refers to behavior that is under the control of certain stimuli or events. If a behavior is reinforced when one stimulus is present and is not reinforced in the absence of that stimulus, the subject learns that he or she is to respond in the presence of that stimulus and not in its absence. An example of this might be when a student learns to talk loudly during recess but does not talk loudly during math class. Establishing stimulus control of a behavior is a matter of consistently reinforcing the desired behavior in the presence of some stimulus and withholding reinforcement from that behavior in the absence of that stimulus. Under some conditions it may be desirable not to merely withhold reinforcement in the absence of a stimulus but to discourage the behavior by withdrawing privileges or in some other way mildly punishing the behavior when it occurs in the absence of the stimulus. See Chapter 3 for more information on the use of stimulus control in the educational setting.

Contingency Contracting

Another procedure for increasing the frequency or the strength of behavior is called contingency contracting (Sulzer-Azaroff & Mayer, 1977). In contingency contracting the teacher arranges the conditions of the teaching environment so that the student is able to obtain something that he or she wants, or that he or she wants to do, if and when the student completes a task or behavior that the teacher wants the learner to complete. This procedure can be formal or informal. In either case, what is expected of the student and what will be given to the student if he or she completes the task must be clearly understood by both the teacher and the student. The conditions are often written out to make remembering them easier. Contingency contracting is sometimes call "Grandma's Law," which says that "if you do 'x,' then you can do 'y'." For example, "if you eat all your spinach, then you can have some cake."

An example of a simple kind of contract is the use of a token system. In a token system, there are specific written rules, which, when followed, earn the student tokens. If rules are broken, then the student may lose tokens. The numbers of tokens to be earned or lost for various behaviors are specified along with what can be purchased with the tokens and how many tokens each item or activity will cost (Drabman, 1976).

To be a viable contract, the terms of the behavioral contract must offer as a reinforcer something that is a) desirable and b) not easily obtainable outside the conditions of the contract. In addition to this, there are several rules or suggestions concerning contingency contracting that should be followed: a) A contingency contract should be fair. In essence, the size of the reinforcement provided should be equal to the work required, that is, the payoff should be related to the size of the job. For example, it is unfair to have a contract specifying that if a child does 2 minutes of work he can see one movie. It is probably fair to say that if he does 80% of his math problems correctly for a week, he will be allowed to go to one movie. b) The contract should be clear and unambiguous. It should specify in clear terms the requirements that are expected of the child and the rewards that would be delivered. c) The contract should be honest. The content of the contract should be carried out immediately in accordance with the terms of the contract. d) The contract should be positive. As much as possible, the contract should contribute positive experiences, not take away experiences. Although it is not always possible to limit a contract strictly to rewarding students for positive behavior, it should be done as much as possible. It is useful to avoid including too many instances that specify that if a student performs a certain behavior the privileges are taken away. e) The contract should be carried out systematically. This results in advantages for both the student and teacher. Children are eager to perform, not timid or aggressive, as often occurs with coercive techniques, and they are less likely to become unmanageable.

In a contingency contract it is necessary to specify the task and to identify the appropriate reinforcers. The wording of the contract should resemble the form "If you do x, then you may do y." The "you" can refer to an individual or a group. It is harder to use contingency contracting with a group because there may be individual differences in rates of responding, or differences in what the individuals find reinforcing.

Reinforcing events can be entertaining (for example, talking with the teacher, playing games, going to a movie), or academic (reading 10 minutes of a favorite book or completing math problems). It is critical that in a contingency contract, the amount of work required and the criteria required for completion of that work be specified clearly. It is often very helpful if the actual physical areas in which the tasks are performed can be separated from the areas in which the reinforcing events are carried out. This clearly delineates for the student that he or she has ceased working for the reinforcement and is now consuming the reinforcer.

In using contingency contracting, it is necessary to be able to specify the behaviors that the trainer wants the student to perform. Often, an appropriate type of behavior is one that corresponds to a student's deficiencies in skill or to one he or she engages in too often. If the teacher is not currently aware of what the students' academic deficits and/or excesses are, an achievement test can often provide the information. Once the deficits/excesses have been identified, whether they are academic or consist of inappropriate behavior of some sort, one can list each of these tasks and break them down into small steps, usually in task analysis sequence. One procedure that has proven to be helpful is to use a series of task cards. Before each class period the teacher can make a list of task cards for each student. The task cards should specify: a) the beginning and end of the task, b) the criterion to measure successful completion of that task, c) the kind of reinforcing events that are available, d) the amount of time the student has to complete the task, and e) the amount of time that is available for consuming the reinforcer. The student at this point would come to the teacher, get a task card, and choose a reinforcer from the menu. This constitutes a semi-formal contract. The student is then allowed to work on the task that was chosen and when it is successfully completed the student is allowed to take part in the activity chosen from the menu.

There are five levels of contracts that are delineated by how much control the two parties of the contract have in establishing the content of the contract. The levels of control begin with the teacher controlling all the major aspects of the contract. The final level is where the student controls the content of the contract. Obviously it is desirable to move a student as quickly as possible from level 1 to level 5.

Level 1 Level 1 is a teacher controlled contract in which:

1. The teacher determines the amount of reinforcer to be given.
2. The teacher determines the amount of task to be required.
3. The teacher presents the contract to the student.
4. The student accepts the contract and performs the task.
5. The teacher delivers the reinforcing event.

Level 2 Level 2 is a contract partly controlled by the student. The student assumes joint control with the teacher over either the amount of reinforcement earned or the amount of the task required.

Level 3 Level 3 is a contract controlled equally by the teacher and student. There are three possible forms that might be practiced by each student: a) The student and teacher share joint determination of both the amount of reinforcement and the amount of the task. b) The student is responsible for determining the amount of reinforcement while the teacher retains control of the amount of the task. c) The student is responsible for the amount of the task while the teacher retains control of the amount of reinforcement.

Level 4 Level 4 is a contract in which the teacher has partial control. There are two forms of a contract that might be practiced by the student here: a) the student has full control over the amount of reinforcement and shares with the teacher joint control over the amount of the task, and b) the student has full control over the amount of the task and shares with the teacher joint control over the amount of reinforcement.

Level 5 Level 5 is a student controlled contract in which:

1. The student determines the amount of reinforcement.
2. The student determines the amount of the task.
3. The student agrees to his own contract.
4. The student performs the task.
5. The student delivers the reinforcer to himself.

TECHNIQUES FOR DECREASING BEHAVIOR

As stated earlier, it is advisable to use positive techniques for increasing appropriate behavior rather than to use negative techniques for decreasing inappropriate behavior. However, there are situations in which inappropriate behavior must be dealt with directly. In each of these cases, reinforcement should be given for behavior that is incompatible with the inappropriate behavior. Several techniques for decreasing behavior are explained below.

Differential Reinforcement of Competing Behaviors

One of the most productive techniques for decreasing inappropriate behavior is to reinforce the child for engaging in appropriate behaviors that are incompatible with the inappropriate behavior. For example, if the behavior the teacher is trying to limit is being noisy or talking out, the teacher might be successful by providing frequent reinforcement to the child when he or she is quiet. The student cannot be quiet and talk out at the same time. As the frequency of being quiet increases, the frequency of being noisy will automatically decrease. This technique can be used in conjunction with other techniques for decreasing behaviors.

Extinction

Extinction can be defined as withholding or removing the reinforcers that are maintaining a behavior. It is often thought that ignoring inappropriate behavior is the equivalent of using an extinction procedure. This may often be the case, but is not necessarily so. If attention is, in fact, reinforcing or maintaining an inappropriate behavior, then by ignoring the student, one will, in fact, extinguish that behavior. But as is often the case, the teacher's attention is often only a small part of what is reinforcing an inappropriate behavior. For example, if Judy makes faces and funny noises during class, the teacher may ignore that behavior and the behavior might continue at the same strength. This may occur because what is reinforcing making faces and funny noises is not the teacher's attention but the laughing and the attention of the other students. A teacher may or may not be able to remove the attention of the other children in the class. It is the inability to control all the potential reinforcers that produces the biggest disadvantage in using extinction and is the major reason why extinction is not always effective in decreasing behavior.

When using the extinction procedure, keep in mind that the behavior will increase in strength immediately following the initiation of extinction and then will decrease very slowly thereafter. The initial increase may last for two or three sessions. Extinction works best on new behaviors. If one can identify what is reinforcing a new inappropriate behavior as it starts to develop, extinction is probably an excellent choice for dealing with that inappropriate behavior.

Structural Rearrangement

Often, decreasing inappropriate behavior is simply a matter of rearranging or eliminating factors that encourage disruptions, for example, moving a disruptive student to the opposite side of the room from an individual with whom he or she typically interacts, or removing distracting materials. Obviously, this technique is neither always possible nor always desirable. It is not always possible in that the environment may not play a major role in a particular disruptive behavior. It is not always advisable in that there will not always be someone around in the future who is willing to rearrange the environment to encourage the student to behave appropriately. But, in some situations a simple solution for an inappropriate behavior is rearranging the environment by removing either the child or the distracting stimuli within the environment.

Response Cost

Another procedure that is used to decrease an inappropriate behavior is termed *response cost* (Striefel, 1972). In this procedure, a response that is inappropriate costs the student something. This loss could be less recess time, missing out on group activities, or losing special privileges. The loss or response cost is made contingent on the occurrence of the behavior to be decreased. As with other negative procedures for decreasing inappropriate behaviors, it is always important to reinforce behaviors incompatible with the behavior to be decreased.

Timeout

This procedure, referred to technically as "timeout from reinforcement" (Hall & Hall, 1980b), is a procedure to decrease the frequency of a behavior. It is accomplished by removing the student from the reinforcing environment contingent upon inappropriate behavior. Removal can be accomplished by removing the student from the environment or by removing the reinforcing events, people, or stimuli from the immediate area of the student. There are several considerations when using timeout:

1. Immediately after an inappropriate behavior occurs, apply timeout by one of the following methods.
    a. Take the individual to a timeout room. The timeout room should be a small room that is free from interesting and potentially reinforcing articles and free from danger. Ethically, and in many cases legally, the room will have an observation window so a teacher can monitor the activities of the student while in the timeout room.
    b. Look away from the child for 10 to 20 seconds.
    c. Turn the child's chair away from the group for a period of 10 to 20 seconds.
    d. Seat the child in the corner away from interesting activities and stimuli.
2. As the child is placed in a timeout area, either say nothing at all, or at most, one simple statement such as: "You cannot stay here if you _____ " (fight, scream, throw things).

3. In using a timeout room, swiftly move the child there without conversation, place the student in the room, and close the door.
4. Leave the child in the timeout room for no more than approximately 2 minutes if he or she is quiet. If the student tantrums, cries, or screams, start timing the 2 minutes when he or she has terminated crying or screaming.
5. When the timeout time is up, take the individual out of the timeout room and back to his or her regular activities without any further comment.
6. Do not discuss the reasons for the timeout with the student at this time.
7. Ignore undesirable behavior that does not merit going to timeout. This means, do not comment on the behavior, do not attend to it, do not suddenly look at the child when it occurs.
8. Reinforce desirable, cooperative play without interrupting it, as well as behaviors that are incompatible with the behavior you wish to eliminate.
9. Always reinforce the child for appropriate behavior.
10. When using a timeout program with a particular student, be sure that the program is used consistently. If you are using a timeout room, be sure to record for each and every instance of using the room, why the child was placed in timeout, when the child went in, and when the child came out. This record is often required by law.

Because timeout is one of the more effective procedures for decreasing inappropriate behaviors, it is one that is used quite often in a variety of situations. Because of its frequent use, it is also subject to frequent misuse. There are certain rules and suggestions that should accompany using a timeout procedure, especially when using a timeout room. These will ensure that the timeout is used effectively and efficiently as well as prevent misuse of the procedure and safeguard against adverse public reactions. These safeguards include:

1. Use the term "quiet place" rather than timeout room.
2. Be sure that there is adequate lighting and carpeting on the floors. Placing a child in a room without furniture and nothing but cold floors is considered unkind and unethical by many individuals.
3. Remove all dangerous objects that the child could use to hurt him- or herself such as objects with sharp corners or anything that could be thrown or swallowed.
4. Be sure that the child can be observed by someone present to monitor him or her without it being known by the child (in case an emergency should occur), and that there is a timer available to measure the length of time the child is in the timeout room.
5. Use a timeout room only after more positive procedures like reinforcing alternative responses, modeling, extinction, response cost, and milder forms of timeout have been attempted and have proven ineffective. It is

also important that these alternative procedures be documented as to their ineffectiveness for this particular behavior of this child.

6. Obtain the consent of the child, the child's parents, and of appropriate supervisors before using the timeout room procedure. Be sure that you are operating in accordance with state and federal laws and policies concerning the use of timeout.

7. Explain the procedures to visitors before they enter the timeout area so they are aware of all of the safeguards that have been used.

Overcorrection

Overcorrection (Sulzer-Azaroff & Mayer, 1977) is a mild punishment procedure designed to minimize negative reactions such as screaming and crying, which often occur when intense punishment is used. Overcorrection is most appropriate when the problem is frequent, deliberate, severe, or very annoying (Azrin & Besalel, 1980). The following procedures are necessary for overcorrection to be effective:

1. Restitutional overcorrection, or overcorrecting the environmental effect of an inappropriate act, requires the student to restore the environment to a much better state than before the inappropriate act took place. For example, the student who has overturned his desk may not only be required to put it back in its correct, upright position, but also to clean, dust, and polish the desk.

2. Positive practice overcorrection includes requiring the disrupter to intensively practice exaggerated correct forms of relevant behavior. It involves repeated practice of a positive behavior. For example, the student who has overturned the desk would be required to straighten, dust, polish, and clean other desks in the room in addition to his own. An additional example of overcorrection is seen in the case of a child hitting another individual. The student might be required to apologize to that individual as well as to any other individuals present. In addition, he may be required to write 25 times, "It is all right for me to be angry, but it is not all right for me to hit other people. I will not hit other people" (or some similar statement).

Overcorrection has advantages and disadvantages. The advantages of overcorrection are:

1. It minimizes the disadvantages of punishment in that it is less likely to produce excessive withdrawal, aggression, or negative self-comment. It is not a painful procedure. It involves having an individual engage in positive behavior. Thus, the student might well learn appropriate behavior from this procedure.

2. Overcorrection often brings rapid and long lasting reduction of inappropriate behavior.

3. The procedure is educative. It teaches the student appropriate behaviors.

The length of time required for restitution in an overcorrection procedure should be longer than the amount of time it takes to restore the environment, but should not be excessively long—2 to 15 minutes beyond the time needed to restore the disrupting environment is usually sufficient. It is important that the overcorrection activity be performed without allowing the student to pause and that it involves the aversive features of additional work and effort. The difficulties or disadvantages in using overcorrection are:

1. Research on its use to date has been conflicting. Thus, the conclusions are based on differing results.
2. It is often difficult to select the restitutional activity. This activity *must* be relevant to the misbehavior if it is going to result in the elimination of a behavior and replacement with a more appropriate behavior.
3. In order to ensure consistent implementation of the consequences, it requires a one-to-one ratio between the teacher and the student. Caution must be exercised so that extreme force is not used when the student refuses to engage in the overcorrection procedure. There is no justification for injuring the individual. It is better to remind the child that a more severe disciplinary action will be used, establish self-correction for any disruption, and discuss the need for self-correction before an incident occurs (Azrin & Besalel, 1980).

Other Forms of Punishment

The presentation of aversive stimuli (spanking, shock, etc.) contingent on inappropriate behaviors is not a recommended procedure and should be reserved as a last resort. There are ethical and legal concerns involved. If aversive stimuli are to be used, several precautions are in order.

1. Be sure all other avenues for changing the behavior have been explored and are documented.
2. Be sure that a meeting has been held with administrative personnel and parents to discuss the need for aversive stimuli, obtain agreement for their use; and specify precautions or guidelines to be used.
3. Be sure that the offense warrants the punishment and that the behavior is clearly defined so the trainer knows when to use the aversive stimuli.

GROUP MANAGEMENT TECHNIQUES

There are a number of techniques that can be used successfully to teach appropriate behavior and decrease inappropriate behavior in a group of individuals. These techniques use many of the procedures that have already been outlined. A list of such techniques and a brief explanation of each follows.

Classroom Rules

Once a set of rules has been established for the classroom (including items such as: a) requiring that permission to do things can be obtained only by raising one's hand and being called on by the teacher, b) requiring that no student is to be out of his or her seat without permission, and c) requiring that no student talk without permission), then members of the class can be reinforced for following the rules. This can be done effectively by using a timer that is set for various time intervals during the day. When the timer goes off, all children who are engaged in appropriate behavior gain points, get to go to recess early, or are allowed to participate in special activities at the end of the day. Those not engaged in appropriate behavior lose points, do not get to go to recess at all, are not allowed to participate in special projects at the end of the day, or have to do extra work.

The Good Behavior Game

The good behavior game can be used with a group of students to encourage appropriate behavior (Sulzer-Azaroff & Mayer, 1977). To accomplish this game, the class is divided into teams (2 or more). At that point, rules of appropriate and inappropriate behavior are established. Violation of these rules result in marks being placed on the board by the teacher. The criterion for winning is variable and is established by the teacher and perhaps the students. For example, less than five marks on the board may mean that both teams win, or the team with the fewest marks at the end of the day may be declared the winner. Winners receive special privileges such as being first in line for lunch, wearing victory tags, receiving extra recess time, or participating in special projects. The losers can be required to continue to work or, in some instances, may even get extra work to do. The advantages of the good behavior game are that children enjoy it, it is easy to implement, teachers respond to teams and not to each individual, and it makes good use of peer pressure. There are some disadvantages of the game, one of which is that some individuals may decide not to play so that they need to be placed on a team by themselves.

Contingency Bank

Another procedure that is often very successful is called the contingency bank (Sulzer-Azaroff & Mayer, 1977). A special area is set up that contains a variety of activities in which most or many of the students enjoy participating. Laminated bank checks are imprinted with the name of the teacher and each check can be cashed for varying amounts of time within the special activity area. A student who receives a check for engaging in appropriate behavior may go to the contingency bank to redeem the time printed on the check. When a student arrives at the bank, he or she deposits the check, sets a kitchen timer for the amount of time on the deposited check, and is allowed to freely engage in the activities located at the bank. A student who overstays the earned time may be denied the use of the bank for the rest of that day or some other time period. Generally, a well-stocked contingency bank can handle 7 to 10 students at a time without direct adult supervision.

Grab Bag

The grab bag procedure is used to increase desirable behavior by reinforcing individuals within the group for engaging in appropriate behavior (Sulzer-Azaroff & Mayer, 1977). This procedure is designed to allow the teacher and the students to designate the desirable behaviors. Students who exhibit these desirable behaviors are allowed to reach into a grab bag and pick something out for themselves. The items within the bag can include notes that indicate a certain amount of free time, extra recess time, bubble gum or opportunities to engage in activities such as jumping rope.

Home Reports

The home reports procedure is used to reinforce children's school activity. A daily note is sent home to the parents indicating that the student was in compliance with the rules and was exhibiting appropriate behavior (Bailey, Wolf & Phillips, 1970). The parents then would allow the student to engage in special activities such as extra television time, special desserts, or family games.

"Warm Fuzzies" and "Compliment Meters"

This procedure is designed to encourage as much class participation in identifying and reinforcing positive behavior in each other as possible (Sulzer-Azaroff & Mayer, 1977). Note cards are made available for students to write compliments to each other that would make the other person feel warm and fuzzy. These note cards then may be collected throughout the day or might be given to individuals directly. After the class as a whole has delivered a certain number of notes, they may earn a class picnic, a popcorn party, extra time for recess, or a story read by the teacher. Only positive comments should be written on the cards. For example: "I like the way you helped John," "The picture you drew is pretty," or "You have a very pretty smile."

Slot Machine

The slot machine procedure is a game in which a target behavior or behaviors for the class period or day is selected (Sulzer-Azaroff & Mayer, 1977). A kitchen timer is set to go off at a random interval. When the timer sounds, one or more participants who have been engaging in the desired behavior throughout the interval are selected to take chances at the slot machine. The slot machine can be as simple as three to five paper cups turned upside down. Under each cup is a slip of paper that describes some reinforcing activity or event: 10 minutes of free time with a buddy or one ice cream bar at lunch. The participant receives the reinforcer under the cup that he or she selects. Initially, the time interval should be very short when introducing this game, but as children get used to the game, the length of the time between the ringing of the buzzer can be extended.

GENERALIZATION AND MAINTENANCE

All educational and behavioral programs must plan for generalization (Baer, Wolf, & Risley, 1968) and maintenance so that the behavior occurs in different settings, with different people, with different cues, with different reinforcement schedules; and with natural reinforcers replacing artificial reinforcers. Techniques to help accomplish this goal include:

1. Training should include a variety of settings, people, and stimuli, each of which can be faded in slowly over time or can be present throughout training (Striefel & Owens, 1980). Some of these settings and people should be from within the community and outside the school (Wehman & Hill, 1982). Development of a generalization matrix with people on one axis and settings on the other can be extremely useful to a teacher for identifying several settings and people to program for generalization of skills (Striefel & Owens, 1980; Whitney & Striefel, 1981).
2. Reinforcement schedules should be thinned out so that behavior can be maintained on an intermittent schedule.
3. Consequences should gradually be delayed so the student learns to react for longer and longer periods of time before reinforcement is forthcoming.
4. Artificial reinforcers not normally available in that environment should gradually be replaced by reinforcers that occur naturally in the environment in which specific behaviors are appropriate.
5. Procedures for transferring control from one stimulus to another should be developed and implemented. Sanok and Striefel (1979) reported a procedure in which control of behavior was transferred from one trainer to another in a 20-minute period by gradually having the second trainer take over the functions of the first trainer while the first trainer was present. Teachers should also master strategies such as fading, matrix training, and time delay to transfer control of behavior from one stimulus that already controls the desired behavior to another stimulus that does not (Striefel & Owens, 1980). Fading was discussed earlier in the chapter, so it will not be rediscussed. Matrix training has been used successfully with severely retarded students to obtain generalization of verb-noun instruction-following skills (Striefel, Wetherby, & Karlan, 1978). Twelve nouns occupied one axis and twelve verbs occupied the other. The training sequence consisted of combining the first verb with each of the first two nouns (e.g., push car, push plane) until mastery was obtained, then combining the second verb with the second and third nouns (e.g., lift plane, lift glass) until mastery was obtained, and so on for each additional verb and noun. Eventually, subjects were able to combine a new noun or new verb with any previously trained verbs or nouns after training with only one example. Similar matrices can be used for other skill areas. Time delay has been used successfully to shift control of motor behavior from

visual models to verbal instructions (Striefel, Wetherby, & Karlan, 1976, 1978). To do so, subjects were trained to imitate motor behaviors. A verbal instruction was then paired with the behavior being modeled. Next, a time delay of 1/2 second was inserted between the presentation of the verbal instruction and the modeling of the behavior. After each correct response, the length of the time delay was increased by 1 second. The subjects quickly learned to respond to the verbal instruction before the visual model was provided. The use of time delays is useful for obtaining generalization of skills across stimuli.

A program that does not plan for generalization and maintenance is very likely to fail because any change in the situation, people present, or stimuli used will result in a loss of appropriate behavior and a return of inappropriate behavior.

7

A Classroom
Data Collection
and Analysis
System

After reading this chapter, you should have an understanding of:

1. Data collection from an educational perspective, including a definition of data and how it is related to child progress and the rationale for implementing a data collection system
2. The preliminary procedures that must be implemented before data collection can begin, such as defining behavior
3. Behavior measurement, including the different aspects of behavior about which data can be collected
4. The different types of measurement systems and the importance of reliable data
5. The various forms that can be used in implementing data collection systems, and the steps involved in implementing a data collection system
6. The process for selecting the appropriate data collection system
7. Data analysis and decision making

THE PROCESS OF EDUCATING children with handicapping conditions relies heavily on the collection of timely and appropriate data so decisions affecting child progress can be made on the basis of that progress or lack thereof. This chapter takes a detailed look at the various aspects of data collection and analysis.

Instructional data collection and analysis is, perhaps, the most important aspect of teaching exceptional children, for, without collecting and analyzing data, it may neither be possible to determine the effectiveness of the instruction nor to know what modifications in the instruction are appropriate (Fredericks, Anderson, & Baldwin, 1977). According to McCormack (1976), "systematic instruction refers to the modification of instruction based on the analysis of information collected regarding previous performance" (p. 1). Such a systematic approach to instruction implies a need for constantly interfacing the acts of teaching with those of monitoring and evaluating what is being taught, or in other words, collecting and analyzing data. In order to provide efficient, individual programming, a teacher must be able to measure accurately the skills and capabilities that a student possesses. He or she must further be able to track the student's progress or lack thereof. "Implied in this tracking procedure is the necessity to respond to the data collected. This ability to respond to the data and to modify programs accordingly is the essence of individual programming" (Fredericks et al., 1977, p. 101).

Data collection and analysis provide the specific information that will allow the teacher to make intelligent and informed decisions regarding both the individual learner and instructional materials. They are, therefore, viewed as necessary skills for every teacher. This is neither a recent nor a novel concept in the field of education. Teachers have been "tracking" (in a gross sense) their students' performance by routinely employing such items as grades, report cards, and anecdotal entries in students' files. As the need for more refined reporting of classroom performance has become necessary, so have procedures for collecting and analyzing data.

The data collection process allows the teacher and/or therapists to respond to the data collected, analyze them, and employ them as a tool for decision-making procedures in the classroom. Recording information about students' performances may or may not cause the teacher to change a child's program or the way it is being presented. If the student is doing well, making few errors, and exhibiting satisfactory progress, the data collected are used only to monitor the student's progress. When little or no progress is being made, however, the data are used in a different fashion. They should serve as an impetus for the teacher and/or therapist to revise or modify the student's instructional program.

INSTRUCTIONAL DATA COLLECTION
FROM AN EDUCATIONAL PERSPECTIVE

Definition and Rationale

Data consist of information, facts, or figures from which conclusions can be made (Guralnik, 1976). Teachers have routinely collected certain data on normal children in the classroom. Those data generally consisted of the number of items performed correctly and have often been labeled "measurement of permanent records." Permanent records were used to make routine classroom decisions such as course grades, class advancement, and in which group (fast or slow) to place a child. Such data collection has been useful but has not carried over to programs for those with handicaps, and when it has, it has often been found to be insufficient. When it has carried over to programs for handicapped persons, this may, in part, be due to the Education for All Handicapped Children Act (PL 94-142), which requires programs to be individualized for each handicapped student. Also, the diversity of these programs often requires more complex and specific data collection systems.

The process of modifying instructional programs based on the collection and analysis of previous performance data is called systematic instruction. Systematic instruction is the essence of individual programming. Instructional data collection and analysis can provide a teacher/trainer with the information necessary to determine the effectiveness of specific instructional programs and to determine what modifications in the program are necessary and/or appropriate. Appropriate and timely modifications in instructional programs contribute to effectiveness and efficiency in the education and training of students with handicaps. In order to use data effectively, the teacher/trainer must know how to: a) collect, b) communicate, c) analyze, and d) use data appropriately. These skills are a necessary part of systematic instruction and, thus, a necessary skill for each teacher/trainer.

Data are collected: a) to determine a child's individual skills and deficits, b) to determine entry levels on specific curricula, c) to determine annual goals and short term instructional objectives, d) to determine progress or lack of progress in achieving established goals and objectives, e) to determine if program modifications result in the desired change in child progress, and f) to determine if the intervention has been executed as it was designed. In addition, data are important because: a) subjective human judgments are often inaccurate, b) without accurate data, the process of determining what to change when progress is not occurring, and choosing appropriate intervention strategies may be less efficient, c) baseline data are needed for comparison purposes, d) communication with parents and other professionals is facilitated, and, e) conditions that influence the occurrence of a behavior may be identified. Appropriate data collection and analysis provide an accountability system for parents, supervisors, and state and federal agencies, and to the public in general. Accountability is something that educators and agency personnel have learned is a necessary part of survival and a requirement by many funding agencies.

DEFINING BEHAVIOR

The first step in developing a data collection system is to be sure that all behaviors that one is interested in increasing or decreasing are defined in *observable* and *measurable* terms (Hall, 1971a). The reasons for defining behaviors in observable terms include: 1) general terms are too ambiguous, 2) general terms are hard to quantify, 3) objective terms ensure that all observers observe the same behavior, 4) objective terms decrease the likelihood that observers will begin to observe something else over time (observer drift), and 5) objective terms increase communication (Ascione, 1977). In general, for a behavior to be observable in an educational setting, the behavior must be *seen, heard,* or *felt.* If a behavior can be seen, heard, or felt, it can be defined in measurable terms. Furthermore, a behavior has been adequately defined when two or more individuals can independently agree on when the behavior has or has not occurred (Bijou, Peterson, & Ault, 1968; Hall, 1971a; Striefel, 1981). The degree to which they agree on what they observed is called *reliability.* Generally, the higher the reliability, the better the definition of the behavior, although there are exceptions (Hawkins & Dotson, 1975).

BEHAVIOR MEASUREMENT

Be aware of behaviors that have been defined in an unobservable or ambiguous manner. Such behaviors cannot be accurately or reliably measured. The opinion of an observer falls into this category. An individual's thought is not observable, and therefore, not measurable until the thought is written down or verbalized. Once the thought has been written down or verbalized, what has been written or said becomes observable and thus potentially measurable.

Since behavior is not static, what is being measured in most educational situations are changes in some aspect of the behavior. The four most common aspects of a behavior change are: a) frequency, or how often a behavior occurs, b) rate, or how often a behavior occurs in a given time period, c) latency, or how much time elapses after a cue is given before the behavior occurs, and, d) duration, or how long the behavior lasts.

The two most commonly used methods for measuring behavior in educational settings are direct measurement of permanent products (Coopers, 1981; Hall, 1971a) and direct observation. Automatic recording (measurement) of behavior by machines and narrative recording is not discussed in detail in this book. Individuals interested in more information about such concepts are referred to the *Managing Behavior Series* published by H & H Enterprises (Hall 1971a, 1971b, 1971c). In the direct measurement of permanent products, one relies on permanent, tangible products of a behavior that can be observed or counted. Permanent products have more often been associated with academic tasks and have been overlooked as a useful measure for other types of tasks. Common examples would include written assignments such as math and spelling, and art products such as drawings and paintings. The end results are fairly permanent and can be reviewed repeatedly for grading purposes. Stokes and Baer (1977) provide a list of examples of potential tasks more appropriate to students with handicaps that can be measured by permanent product measures, e.g., number of steps taken as indicated by footprints on carpet, and amount of paint removed. Automatic machine records are also permanent products, e.g., records from instruments that measure muscle tension and skin temperature.

Direct observation typically refers to observation of ongoing behavior. Thus, the end product, the behavior, is often present for very short periods of time, unless, of course, one videotapes or films the behavior so that it becomes a permanent product. The direct observation method consists of an observer looking at, listening to, or touching to feel a behavior and then making a record of that experience. In a classroom situation, there are two types of behavior that are observed. The first consists of observing discrete behaviors that should occur only when a cue or signal is given. The time period from when the cue is presented to termination is known as a trial. Since the onset of the trial and its termination are controlled by the trainer, collecting data on the occurrence or nonoccurrence of the behavior is relatively simple once the behavior has been adequately defined. The second type of behavior consists of what is known as a free operant, which means that the behavior is due to occur whenever and as often as the individual exhibits the behavior. Accurate observation of such behavior can be more difficult, since a behavior may occur so seldom that it is difficult to observe.

In measuring behavior, perhaps the most difficult and complex decision a teacher, therapist, or other professional has to make is what kind of data are most appropriate for a certain behavior or program. The first point to be made in addressing this question is that the data collection system should not determine what kind of program is to be conducted. In other words, one should not decide to collect a certain type of data, such as frequency or duration, and then write or modify a program to fit that kind of data. Among other things, the data should be informative about the effectiveness of the program. Therefore, the data system should be selected after the program is intact or after the behavior to be changed is defined. There is an exception. Occasionally, a program is written or a behavior is defined that does not state the terms in an observable and measurable manner. If this is the case, *no* type of data can accurately be collected; consequently, the program or behavior definition is in need of revision.

DATA COLLECTION SYSTEMS

Assuming that the program is written or behavior is defined in observable and measurable terms, how does one decide what type of data to collect? The type of data system that should be used depends on what change is expected in the behavior and on factors such as availability of observers. These factors are addressed in more detail below. But first, definitions of the different types of data collection methods are discussed.

In most situations, behavior may change in one of four aspects: a) frequency, or how often a behavior occurs, b) rate, or how often the behavior occurs in a given time period, c) duration, or how long the behavior lasts, or d) latency, or how much time elapses after a cue is given before the behavior occurs. Other facets of behavior can also be changed such as the intensity (loudness of a person's voice), but these are not addressed here.

There are four types of data collection systems that give exact measurements of behavior: frequency, rate, duration, and latency. In addition, there are two data collection systems that give estimates of behavior: interval and time sampling.

Exact Measurement Systems

Each of the four measurement systems that follow gives an exact measure of behavior when properly applied. To be properly applied, the behavior must be *adequately defined* and the observer must be trained in the use of the definition and in the specific technique to be used. Any data collection system can fail if observers are not properly trained and if behaviors are not defined so that two or more individuals can agree on when the behavior has or has not occurred.

Frequency   Measurement of the frequency of behavior occurrence is sometimes called "event" or "tally" recording because frequency data collection refers to the number of times or how often a behavior occurs. It can be used with both discrete behaviors and free operants. In a classroom situation, frequency data are often used with discrete behavior that should only occur when a cue or signal is given, such as a question being asked or request being made by the teacher, i.e., "Point to the red one." In such cases, the information is collected on how often the behavior correctly occurred given some number of opportunities for it to occur. In essence, the data consist of a proportion composed of two frequencies: the total number correct and the total number of trials. Examples of discrete behaviors are: How many times out of ten trials is the student able to identify the letter A? How many times out of five trials is the student able to imitate such behaviors as drinking from a glass or setting a table?

Frequency data are also appropriate in cases where a specific cue is not given for the behavior to occur (free operants). In such cases, one is interested in how often a behavior is occurring because its frequency seems unusually high or low. Examples might include determining how often a child leaves his or her seat without permission, how often a child teases classmates, or how often a child asks for help. In frequency recording, one can make a mark on any piece of paper each time the behavior occurs, use a golf counter, or a data sheet. Data sheets are often the best for classroom use, as pointed out later in this chapter.

Rate Discovering how often within a given time period a behavior occurs is referred to as rate measurement. Sometimes it is not sufficient to merely know how many behaviors, such as math problems, a child completed, but rather to know as well how long it took. For certain skills such as math problems, a teacher may use rate to determine whether or not a child's performance is up to grade level or whether it is sufficient for moving on to the next task. The teacher may also use it to evaluate changes in performance across days or weeks. Rate can be used with both discrete behaviors and free operants. Examples of discrete behaviors in which rate might be useful include the number of words read per minute, the number of items sorted into categories per minute, and the number of letters a child can recognize per minute. Examples of free operants in which rate might be useful include the number of spontaneous utterances per minute and the number of times a child hits him- or herself per minute. To record rate, one needs a watch and a data sheet or permanent product.

Duration Measurement of how long a behavior lasts is known as duration measurement. Sometimes it is more important to know how long a behavior lasts than to know how often it occurs. For example, if two children each throw one tantrum per hour, but for one child it lasts 1 minute and for the other it lasts 45 minutes, the duration of tantrums is more useful than knowing only frequency. Duration measurement can be used with both discrete behaviors and free operants. Examples of discrete behaviors in which duration measurement might be useful include how long a child makes eye contact with the teacher when he or she calls the student's name, how long a physically involved child can remain in an upright sitting position when placed there, and how long a child can work independently after being given an assignment. Examples of free operants in which duration might be useful include how long a child sucks his or her thumb, and how long a child is out of his or her seat. To record duration, one needs a watch, preferably a stopwatch, and a data sheet.

Latency Measurement of latency refers to how much time elapses between the presentation of a cue, such as a request for a child to sit down, and the occurrence of the behavior. For example, a child may sit down every time you ask him or her to but it may take 1–3 minutes to do so. In such situations, latency measurement would be useful for increasing the child's responsiveness in terms of responding sooner and would allow the teacher to monitor changes in performance objectively. Since latency measurement requires the presentation of a cue, it *is not* used with free operants, but rather, only with discrete behaviors. However, a teacher/therapist can manipulate the environment so that as many opportunities of the discrete behavior as possible are available. Examples of discrete behaviors in which latency might be useful include how long it takes a student to begin working after an assignment has been given, how long it takes a child to start to clear the table after being instructed to do so, and how long it takes a child to sit down after the school bell rings. For latency recording, one needs a stopwatch and a data sheet.

Estimate Measurement Systems

The two data collection systems that follow, interval recording and time sampling, do not give exact measures of behavior, but rather give estimates of the occurrence of behavior. If they are properly applied, the estimates they provide can be sufficient for dealing with particular classroom situations in which it might be difficult or impossible to use one of the exact measurement systems, e.g., behaviors that occur too often to be counted, last for a long time, or involve observation of more than one student or behavior.

Interval Interval measurement provides an estimate of how often a behavior occurs. It is best to use frequency or duration techniques (which give exact measures) when possible, but sometimes practical considerations prevent using these preferred techniques. For example, suppose one needed to record three or four different behaviors simultaneously. It becomes nearly impossible to accurately record each occurrence of each behavior. Interval recording helps solve this problem. Interval data are collected by recording the occurrence or nonoccurrence of one or more behaviors during each of a series of equal time intervals. To use interval recording, the total session time is divided into equal time intervals of some length, say 10 seconds, and the observer records whether or not the behavior(s) occurred during each of these intervals. Each interval is represented by a box on a data sheet. How many times each behavior occurred (frequency) is *not* noted. If the behavior occurred at all during the interval, then it is recorded as having occurred. Short recording periods of 5 seconds are usually interspersed between each of the observation intervals. This provides time to record the occurrence or nonoccurrence of the behaviors during the previous time period. Thus, a session may have a 10-second observation period, a 5-second record period, a 10-second observation period, etc. The major advantage of this system is that it can be used to collect simultaneous data on two or three behaviors or children. It provides a simultaneous *estimate* of both the frequency and the duration of each behavior. Interval recording is the most complex of the data collection systems and requires the undivided attention of the observer as well as an audiotape or timer that indicates to the observer when each interval begins or ends. Regardless of how many times the target behavior occurs during an interval, the observer only records whether or not the behavior occurred and makes no attempt to count numbers of occurrences, thus, the term "estimate measurement system." Interval recording can be used with both discrete behaviors and free operants and would typically be used to record the same type of behaviors as for frequency or duration. The difference is that interval recording would be used to record behaviors that occur so rapidly that they cannot be counted and to record several behaviors or the same behavior of several children simultaneously. Interval recording would generally not be used to record responses on a program in which a specific number of trials are conducted since other data collection systems are more useful and accurate.

Time Sampling   Time sampling also provides an estimate of how often a behavior occurs, but it is generally a less accurate estimate than interval recording. Time sampling does not require constant observation of the child, but it does use intervals of equal length. The difference is that the intervals are usually of longer duration (e.g., 5 minutes) and the observations are made only at the end of each interval. At the end of the interval, usually signaled by a timer, audiotape, or clock, the observer looks up and records whether or not the behavior is or is not occurring at that exact moment.

In time sampling, an observer can observe and record data on several behaviors or children *consecutively* by arranging for the time sampling intervals to end at different times. It also allows a teacher to take advantage of natural time intervals that occur in the classroom, e.g., the end of each half hour of instruction. As with interval recording, time sampling provides an estimate of behavior and can be used with the same discrete behaviors and free operants for which one might record frequency data. It should be noted that a low rate discrete behavior can be missed using this method.

A "Levels of Assistance" Measurement System

An additional data collection system, the levels of assistance system, is in reality a frequency data collection system. It is often thought of as a separate data method because of the feature of recording the frequency of how much assistance is given the student by the trainer or teacher. Such a system is extremely sensitive in situations in which the learners make small gains, or the teacher desires to manipulate the type or amount of assistance being given to the child.

This system requires the development of a "hierarchy of help." This task is arbitrary and will vary. One such hierarchy is:

0 = Refuses the step/no response
1 = Requires total manipulation to complete step
2 = Requires manipulation to begin step then completes step independently
3 = Begins step independently but requires a physical prompt to complete step
4 = Requires that the step be modeled
5 = Requires verbal assistance
6 = No assistance required

Generally, a code is assigned to each level of help. Often, the code is merely a number or letter representing each level of help. The data are collected by recording, for each occurrence of the behavior, the level of help that was needed for the student to complete the behavior. The frequency of the various levels of help can then be determined.

A Group Multi-Behavior or Multi-Step Measurement System

When a group of students is taught, or more than one behavior or step in a program are conducted during a session, special considerations need to be made. The type of data that are collected will be frequency (most common), duration, or latency, but the mechanics of recording these data will be different in that data for different students' behaviors or steps will need to be recorded separately without the hassle of numerous papers to handle. Details for recording these types of data are given below.

Data Collection Guidelines

Before discussing in detail various data sheets and how they are used, a few general comments about data collection should be made. The efficiency of any classroom data-keeping system is a function of the definitions of behavior, training of observers, type of data collected, the frequency of data collection, the analysis procedures that are used, and the reliability of the observations. Several general rules for data collection are:

1. Care should be exercised in deciding what type of data to collect. Careful planning will preclude spending a lot of time collecting data and then finding out that the necessary decisions cannot be made because the wrong data were collected.
2. Only enough data to meet the needs of the situation should be collected. Data collection and analysis is time consuming. If one is not going to use the data, it shouldn't be collected.
3. Raw data (the individual response data that are collected during a session) need to be summarized so that they may be analyzed. The most efficient way to do this is to graph the information right on the data sheet (see sections below concerning data sheets). Graphing this information is a very useful means of visually displaying the data to facilitate program decision-making and communicating program progress to parents and other professionals.
4. Data should (with rare exceptions) be recorded and reviewed daily. The intent of monitoring data on a daily basis is to discover problems as quickly as possible and to intervene to correct the problem. Doing so prevents minor problems from becoming major problems, ensures that a child does not become discouraged because he or she cannot perform the prescribed behavior, and avoids boredom caused by continuing a program once a skill has been mastered.

The necessity of recording and reviewing data daily is important to the educational progress of each and every student. If a student progresses very slowly, then each day the child spends on a task but makes no progress becomes a major concern. The best method for a teacher to accurately determine if a student is making progress is to record and analyze objective data.

Data Recording   To ensure that a child learns as efficiently as possible, certain practices should be followed (Fredericks et al., 1977). First, let the child know what he or she is expected to do by giving the student a cue, signal, request or condition that does or can be made to influence the occurrence of a behavior. A verbal cue might be, "Look at me" or "Sit down." A nonverbal cue might be ringing a bell or clapping your hands.

Rules for Delivering Cues   It is important to be consistent in delivering cues in order to ensure that the child learns as quickly as possible and does not become confused. Thus, the verbal and nonverbal cues should be repeated exactly as stated in the program on each and every trial. A cue should *only* be presented *once*, and then a correct response or assisted response from the child should be required. Speaking clearly and loudly enough to be heard is important.

After the cue is delivered, the child will respond either correctly or incorrectly (note that if a child gives no response, it is an incorrect response). Each response must be followed by a consequence. A consequence is feedback immediately following a response that increases, decreases, *or* does not affect the future occurrence of a response. A consequence that increases the strength of a behavior is a positive reinforcer (e.g., praise such as "Good talking" or "Neat job," candy, juice). These are examples and may or may not work with a particular child. A consequence that decreases the strength of a behavior is a punisher, (e.g., saying "No, that is not right," or physically leading a resistant child through the task). A consequence, even one that has increased or decreased a behavior in the past, may, under some circumstances, have no effect on the behavior it follows.

Rules for Delivering Consequences   Every response must be immediately followed by a consequence that will let the child know if his or her response is correct or incorrect. Every *correct response* should be followed by an immediate reinforcer (within 1 second of behavior occurrence), a functional reinforcer (something that will increase the same response the next time the cue is presented), or a reinforcer that occurs naturally in the environment whenever possible instead of an artificial reinforcer (one that does not ordinarily occur in the training environment). Verbal praise should always precede or be delivered simultaneously with a backup reinforcer (food, juice, etc.) after a correct response. If a child does not respond or responds *incorrectly,* go through the correction procedure *exactly* as listed on the program cover sheet.

Probes   A probe is used to determine if a child will perform a specific behavior when presented with a specific situation or cue. A probe may be used to determine whether a child will still perform a previously trained behavior or if he or she will perform a behavior that is being considered as a possible goal or objective. A probe consists of one or more trials (presentation of cue and opportunity to respond) on the behavior of interest. Correct responses should be followed by reinforcement to maintain the highest level of child motivation (Striefel, Wetherby, & Karlan, 1978).

Cautions in Data Recording

The system designer should be aware of certain precaution areas in data recording and be prepared to deal with them effectively. These cautions refer to those in which an observer other than the classroom's teacher or therapist goes into another person's classroom or home. Handling problem areas is easier if observers are conscious of the following principles. First, teachers and students may be reactive to classroom observation (Mash & Terdal, 1981). The degree of reactivity can be minimized by making sure that those being observed are aware of the reason for the observers' presence (more applicable to teachers than to children with handicaps), and that observers do not disrupt the classroom routine by interacting with individuals being observed or by making noise. Over time, most individuals habituate and ignore the observers; thus, their behavior returns to its natural level. Second, observation must occur at times when the behavior of concern is likely to occur. In classroom training programs where data are collected during specific training sessions, this is almost automatic. In other cases, one must match the time for observation to the behavior of concern. Third, observers must be trained to use the specific observation system, and behaviors must be defined in observable terms, or agreement between different observers will be low. In addition, one must be aware that over time, if the behavior is not defined clearly and the definition followed closely, observers change what they observe and record, a phenomenon called "observer drift." This can be controlled by use of a training tape of predetermined criterion for the behaviors of interest on which observers must regularly reach agreement. An additional concern is one in which observer expectancy can influence what is observed. Individuals tend to see what they want to see. The use of naive or unbiased reliability checkers can help to control for this factor.

Reliability

It is critical that two or more observers simultaneously observing a behavior agree to a high degree on when a specific behavior has occurred or not occurred. The percentage of agreement between observers is called reliability. If interobserver reliability is low, great care must be taken in making decisions based on those data since their accuracy is questionable. A rule of thumb is that the percentage of agreement between two observers should be 80% or better (Sulzer-Azaroff & Mayer, 1977). Reliability problems can be minimized by using clear behavioral definitions, training observers to a predetermined criterion on the behavior(s) of interest (videotapes are useful for this purpose), periodically having observers again meet criterion on a training tape, and being sure that observers are motivated to make accurate observations. The easiest way to determine the coefficients of agreement is to divide the number of agreements by the number of agreements plus the number of disagreements:

$$\text{coefficient of agreement} = \frac{\text{number of agreements}}{\text{number of agreements} + \text{number of disagreements}}$$

A whole variety of other methods for computing reliability exists. Interested readers are referred to Ciminero, Calhoun, and Adams (1977), and Cone and Hawkins (1977).

FORMS FOR DATA COLLECTION

General Information

The following sections discuss a set of five data collection forms that have been used to collect data in a variety of educational settings. The forms were designed for flexibility and have been used for almost every conceivable type of data in the educational setting by teachers, aides, volunteers, physical and occupational therapists, speech pathologists, and psychologists. The forms consist of: a) a Frequency Data Sheet, b) a Rate Data Sheet, c) a Duration or Latency Data Sheet, d) a Time Sampling or Interval Data Sheet, and e) a Multi-Behavior/Step/Student Data Sheet. (A completed sample of each of these forms is included at the end of this chapter (pages 175–179) as Figures 7.1–7.5[1].) Each of the different data sheets (each can be printed on a different color paper) has space for collecting raw data and has a built-in graph that can be used to summarize the data.

All five forms use the same general format; thus, each form has certain common characteristics, and each has some unique characteristics. For ease of explanation, each area of the data sheet has been numbered, both within the text and on the forms themselves. Unless otherwise stated, the information for each area of the data sheet is the same for all five forms. The reader will find it useful to refer back and forth between the five forms while reading the instructions that follow. Each area discussed has a circled number on the data sheet that corresponds with the area number (e.g., area 1 = ①on the data sheet).

Instructions for Use of Forms

Area 1—Title The name of each data collection sheet is printed in the upper left hand corner of the form (e.g., Frequency Data Sheet—Figure 7.1, Rate Data Sheet—Figure 7.2). Two of the data sheets (Duration or Latency—Figure 7.3 and Time Sampling or Interval—Figure 7.4) can be used for

---

[1]The data forms in this chapter are included with the permission of the first author and are available from him.

collecting either of two types of data; thus, they have a pair of boxes for checking off the type of data that will be collected. For example, if duration is the type of data to be collected, a check mark would be placed in the blank square located to the left of the word "Duration" in the upper left hand corner of the Duration or Latency Data Sheet.

Area 2—Student The full name or code number of the student about whom data will be collected is entered here (see area 2 on Figure 7.1).

Area 3—Data Collector The name(s) of the person(s) who will collect the data is entered here (see area 3 on Figure 7.1).

Area 4—Program The name of the program for which data are being collected is entered here (see area 4 on Figure 7.1).

Area 5—Key This area includes prerecorded codes and/or space for additional codes that will be used to record responses when collecting data (see area 5 on Figure 7.1). For example, the code + is equal to a correct response, 0 is equal to an incorrect response, and S is equal to a self-corrected response. For the Duration or Latency Data Sheet (Figure 7.3), the key is used to record the time units (seconds or minutes) in which responses will be recorded (see area 5 on Figure 7.3). For the Time Sampling or Interval Data Sheet (see area 5 on Figure 7.4), the space is used to code behaviors (e.g., H = hitting, A = attending), or students (e.g., JJ = John Jones, HH = Harriet Happy).

Area 6—Graph Legend Included in this section will be the symbols to be used to plot the different data points on the graph (see area 6 on Figure 7.1) along with an explanation of what is being graphed. For example, if a solid circle (●) is going to indicate percent correct and an open circle (○) is going to represent percent approximations, the legend would read: ● = % correct and ○ = % approximations.

Area 7—Interval Length or Other Only the Time Sampling or Interval Data Sheet includes a space for interval length (see area 7 on Figure 7.4). Since behavior is recorded at the end of or during a specified time interval for time sampling and interval recording, respectively, the length of the interval needs to be specified and entered in the space entitled "Interval Length." The remaining four forms (Figures 7.1, 7.2, 7.3, and 7.5) have a section entitled "Other" for recording any other relevant information.

Area 8—Formula Included in this section for each graph is a mathematical computation formula for changing raw data into one meaningful number or percentage that can be plotted (see area 8 on Figure 7.1). For example, the formula for percentage correct on the Frequency Data Sheet is: % correct = number correct ÷ total number of trials × 100.

Area 9—Referent The referent area is located just to the right of the title on each data sheet and differs for the five types of data sheets. This area indicates whether data are being recorded in trials, blocks, intervals, occurrences, behaviors, students, or steps (see area 9 on Figures 7.1–7.5).

Area 10—Numbering   The section directly below the referent section is prenumbered from 1 to 20 for four of the data sheets (see area 10 on Figures 7.1–7.4). The fifth form (the Multi-Behavior/Step/Student Sheet—Figure 7.5) has blanks. Numbers (and a brief description) should be entered on this sheet as appropriate, beginning at the bottom and moving upward. These numbers serve to indicate the step for which the observer should record data.

Area 11—Objective   This row is used to identify the short term objective (from the child's IEP) for which data are being recorded in the trial column above (see area 11 on Figures 7.1–7.5). Data for only one objective are recorded in any one column.

Area 12—Date/Year   This row is used to identify the date on which the data in the column were collected (see area 12 on Figure 7.1). Do not put data for more than one date in a single column. Note that several columns may be used to collect data for the same day.

Area 13—Percentage   This row is to be used to record, numerically, the percentage that will be graphed (see area 13 on Figure 7.1). *Note:* if *exactly* 20 trials are conducted during a session, the percentage can be found by adding up the number of correct (or incorrect, etc.) trials, finding that number under "Trials" on the data sheet, and then looking directly across the sheet to the column labeled "Percentage" to locate the corresponding correct percentage. Percentage correct can also be computed by dividing the number of trials correct by the total number of trials in that session, and multiplying by 100 [i.e., % correct = (no. correct ÷ total no.) × 100]. Compute the percentage and record it in the percentage row below the data to which the percentage refers. If more than one column is used in a session, enter the percentage beneath the last column used. The Rate and Duration or Latency Data Sheets do not include percentages.

Area 14—Comment   This row is to be used to draw attention to any written comment you make on the back of the data sheet (see area 14 on Figure 7.1). If you make a comment, place an asterisk (*) in this row below the data about which you are commenting. Then turn the page over, record the date, and make your comment. This row can also be used to give special instructions from the teacher to some other person who is conducting the program. A circle (O) can be entered to draw the person's attention to the special instruction on the back of the data sheet.

Area 15—Time Period   On programs where the total amount of session time is variable, this row is used. This area is present only in the Rate and Duration or Latency Data Sheets (see area 15 on Figures 7.2 and 7.3). Indicate for each session the length of the session in minutes. This should equal the length of the time block (1 minute, 5 minutes, etc.) multiplied by the number of time blocks used.

Area 16—Conditions   This space can be used to record different teaching conditions such as "baseline," "intervention," and "return to baseline" (see area 16 on Figure 7.4). It can also be used to note teaching variables such as different teachers or different locations. Simply draw a heavy line through the column at the end of a condition and label the condition in the space provided.

Area 17—Data Boxes There are 20 blank boxes in each column for the recording of data (see area 17 on Figures 7.1–7.5). Beginning at the bottom of a column, enter for each successive trial/block/interval, a symbol that represents the student's performance. No symbol should be used that has not been printed or listed in the key. Mark each trial with the appropriate symbol. If more than 20 trials are given, merely continue in the next column (begin at the bottom).

Area 18—Graphing For ease of reading, graphing should be done using a brightly colored pen or pencil. Be sure to use a color different from what has been used to complete the rest of the data sheet (see area 18 on Figures 7.1–7.5). Graph the number or percentage that has been entered in the percentage row (area 13). If only one column has been used for the session, graph the data by placing a solid circle (data point) in the middle of the column at the point corresponding to the correct percentage as listed at the right. If more than one column has been used for one session, a data point should be placed in the middle of the last column used for that session. Connect the data points for all sessions with a straight edge, using a brightly colored pen or pencil.

Area 19—Scale This only applies to the Rate and Duration or Latency Data Sheets (see area 19 on Figures 7.2 and 7.3). Choose and mark (x) the appropriate scale that will best suit the data you will be graphing. The scales are .05 to .5, .5 to 5, and 5 to 50 for rate, and .6 to 6 seconds, 6 to 60 seconds, .6 to 6 minutes, and 6 to 60 minutes for duration/latency. Depending on which scale is chosen, adjustments need to be made on the graph scale. These are quickly accomplished by moving the decimal position as appropriate. For example, if the first scale is chosen, one may place a decimal two places to the left of each number of the graph scale. Thus, on the Rate Data Sheet, 50 becomes .50, 45 becomes .45, and so on (each square then represents .025 events per minute). Likewise, the decimal can be moved one place to the left for latency or duration so that 60 becomes 6, etc.

Area 20—Graph In this section, enter and/or underline the information that will be represented by a graph (see area 20 on Figure 7.1). Generally, the percentage of trials correct will be graphed.

Vignette Examples for Each Data Sheet

To clarify the use of each data form, examples are presented below for reader convenience. A vignette is presented for completion of each form as shown in Figures 7.1–7.5. The reader is referred to the section on data collection systems (pages 153–161) for descriptions of each data collection method.

Example Using Frequency Data Sheet—Vignette 1 Read the vignette and instructions that follow, and look at the completed data sheet (Figure 7.1) as necessary.

Sam B. is a 6-year-old child in Ms. Thompson's room. Sam is severely retarded but has no other physical handicaps. Sam is working on a program called "Word Identification: Men and Women." Sam is currently working on objective 2 of the program, which states: "Sam will point to the word "men" when asked, after being given printed cards including one with the word "men" in large print and two with the word "women" in small print, on 9 out of 10 trials." The data for Sam are:

February 1: Sam pointed to 12 out of 20 correctly.
February 2: Sam pointed to 15 out of 20 correctly.
February 3: Sam pointed to 22 out of 25 correctly.

Area 1—Title Because the title was preprinted, no action was needed.

Area 2—Student "Sam B." was entered in area 2 on Figure 7.1.

Area 3—Data Collector "Ms. Thompson" was entered.

Area 4—Program The name of the program, "Word Identification: Men and Women," was entered.

Area 5—Key No additions were needed.

Area 6—Graph Legend The legend "—•— = % correct" was entered.

Area 7—Other Nothing was needed for this example so it was left blank.

Area 8—Formula Because the formula was preprinted, no action was needed.

Area 9—Referent Because the referent was preprinted, no action was needed.

Area 10—Numbering The numbers were preprinted, so no action was needed.

Area 11—Objective The number 2 was entered.

Area 12—Date/Year The year 1982 was entered in the year blank and 2/1 in the first column. The completed data sheet for Vignette 1 includes 2/2 in the second column and 2/3 in the third and fourth columns. The 2/3 is entered in two different columns because on that date more than 20 trials were conducted and, thus, more than one column was used.

Area 13—Percentage There were exactly 20 trials conducted on February 1; thus, the percentage correct can be found by counting the number of correct trials (12), locating row 12 in the trials column and moving across the page to the right ot the percentage column, which indicates that 12 out of 20 is 60%. The number 60 was entered in the percentage row under the first column. Similarly, for February 2, the percentage correct was 75% (15 out of 20). The number 75 was entered in the percentage row under the second column. On February 3, there were not exactly 20 trials conducted. Therefore, the correct percentages cannot be found by using the data sheet. The percentages correct must be figured using the formula: % correct = (number correct ÷ total number of trials) × 100. In this case 22 out of 25 is 88% correct. The number 88 was entered in the percentage row under the *fourth* column, not the third column.

Area 14—Comment Nothing was needed for this example.

Area 15—Time Period The time period was not relevant to this data sheet.

Area 16—Conditions It was not necessary for conditions to be specified for this example.

Area 17—Data Boxes In the first column, 12 pluses (+) and 8 circles (○) were entered. The second column has 15 pluses (+) and 5 circles (○) and the third and fourth columns combined include a total of 22 pluses (+) and 3 circles (○). Note that only the first five spaces from the bottom of the fourth column are marked. They represent trials 21–25.

Area 18—Graphing For the first column, a data point was placed at the 60% level. For the second column, a data point was placed at the 75% level. For the *fourth*, not the third column, a data point was placed at the 88% level. Note that no data point is placed in the third column. The data points are all connected, using a straight edge.

Area 19—Scale A scale was not relevant to this data sheet.

Area 20—Graph The word "Correct" was entered in the blank space to represent information marked in the area labelled "graph."

The Frequency Data Sheet is now completed for the vignette provided. If everything is not clear, reread the section entitled "Forms for Data Collection" (pages 161–164), as well as the example.

Example Using Rate Data Sheet—Vignette 2 The Rate Data Sheet (Figure 7.2) was completed for the vignette that follows.

> Billy T. is a 10-year-old child with cerebral palsy who attends Mr. Jones's resource room. Billy is nonverbal, but has developed a functional communication system by turning his eyes to the right to respond "yes" and to the left for "no." Billy has some gross control of his upper extremities but almost no use of his legs. Billy is currently working on a program entitled "Fine Motor: Sorting Tableware." Billy is working on objective 1 of the program, which states: "Billy will sort tableware at the rate of at least 3 pieces per minute during a 30-minute period on 2 consecutive days." Each session is broken into 5-minute segments. For example, a 30-minute session would contain six 5-minute blocks of time. The session is broken into small blocks so that Mr. Jones will be able to determine whether or not Billy's rate varies during different parts of the session. Variability, if it is evident, might be due to factors such as fatigue or boredom. The data for Billy are:
>
> May 6: Session length was 30 minutes. Billy sorted the following numbers of tableware correctly during the 5-minute blocks: 5, 6, 4, 8, 5, and 7.
>
> May 7: Session length was 30 minutes. Billy sorted the following numbers of tableware correctly during the 5-minute blocks: 7, 8, 7, 10, 8, and 9.
>
> May 8: The session length was only 20 minutes due to a field trip. Billy sorted the following numbers of tableware correctly during the 5-minute blocks: 8, 9, 11, and 8.

Compare the information provided above with the completed Rate Data Sheet (Figure 7.2). If questions exist, the reader should reread the instructions and the vignette.

Example Using Duration Data Sheet—Vignette 3 The following vignette was used to complete the Duration Data Sheet (Figure 7.3).

> Terry B. is an 8-year-old severely retarded child who is in the Special Education program of the Woodrow Wilson Elementary School. Beverly T. is currently working on a program to decrease the amount of time that Terry has her hand in her mouth. The program has been titled "Decreasing Mouthing of Hand." Terry is working on objective 2 of the program, which states: "Terry will have her hand in her mouth less than an average of 30 seconds per occurrence on 2 consecutive days." The amount of time Terry has her hand in her mouth is recorded in seconds for each occurrence. The data for Terry are:
>
> | January 5: | Session length was 30 minutes. The lengths of time, in seconds, Terry kept her hand in her mouth for each of 11 occasions were: 30, 35, 40, 30, 43, 17, 103, 21, 4, 15, and 38. |
> | January 6: | Session length was 35 minutes. The lengths of time were: 15, 12, 40, 43, 18, 12, 7, 35, 60, and 15. |
> | January 7: | Session length was 30 minutes. The lengths of time were: 103, 115, 48, 48, 17, 13, 22, 17, 32, and 40. |

Check the information provided against the completed Duration Data Sheet (Figure 7.3). Reread the instructions and vignette as necessary.

Example Using Interval Data Sheet—Vignette 4 The Interval Data Sheet shown in Figure 7.4 was completed by using vignette 4.

> Ms. Step is the teacher of the special education classroom at the Robert F. Tucker Elementary School. Zachary B. is a severely retarded 8-year-old child. Zachary is physically normal. Due to some fine motor coordination problems, Zachary has had some difficulty eating as neatly as his parents and the teacher would like. Ms. Step and the parents determine that there are two main behaviors that contribute to Zachary's sloppy eating. The first is pushing food off of his plate while trying to scoop food, and the second is dropping food from his spoon as he carries it to his mouth. Ms. Step develops a program of positive reinforcement and timeout (from the spoon for 10 seconds) for the two behaviors listed above. Ms. Step decides to observe these behaviors for 5 minutes during each day's lunch period. She decides to use the interval data sheet (Figure 7.4) because counting individual pieces of food pushed or dropped would be far too difficult. She decides to use 10-second observation intervals, followed by 5-second record periods. An audiotape and earphones are used to cue the observer on when to mark the intervals. Three days of baseline and 2 days of treatment are included in Table 7.1.

Check the information provided against the completed Interval Data Sheet (Figure 7.4). Reread the instructions and vignette as necessary.

Example Using Multi-Behavior Data Sheet—Vignette 5 The Multi-Behavior Data Sheet shown in Figure 7.5 was completed using Vignette 5.

> David B. is a moderately retarded adult who lives at a group home for retarded adults. Mr. Wilson, the houseparent, is currently teaching David a cooking skill,

Table 7.1. Intervals during which behaviors occurred

	Baseline			Treatment	
	3/1	3/2	3/3	3/4	3/4
Pushing food off tray = P	1, 2, 13 14, 15, 18, 19	11, 14, 15, 19	3, 4, 5, 6, 8, 11, 16	5, 10, 13, 16, 18	3, 7, 10, 12, 14
Dropping food from spoon = X	12, 13, 19, 20	1, 3, 7, 8, 10 11, 13, 16, 18	1, 3, 4, 7, 9, 12, 13, 14, 16	1, 4, 5, 7, 9, 11, 15, 20	2, 4, 7, 8, 9, 12, 19

toasting bread in a pop-up toaster, each morning. This task has been broken into eight small steps, each of which is taught once each morning. The steps are: 1) locate bread, 2) untwist bread tie, 3) remove two slices, 4) twist bread tie, 5) place bread in toaster, 6) push button down, 7) wait until bread pops up, and 8) remove bread. Mr. Wilson is interested in three aspects of David's performance: a) the steps David performs correctly (without assistance), b) the steps David performs correctly after being given a verbal prompt, and c) steps that David does not perform correctly. David has completed 3 days of training. The data for David are:

May 4: David completed all of the steps after being given a verbal prompt.

May 5: David failed to remove the tie from the bread bag, was able to remove the bread from the toaster without any assistance, and required verbal assistance on all of the other steps.

May 6: David's performance was identical to that on May 5, with the exception that he was able to remove the bread from the bread bag without any assistance.

Mr. Wilson decided to graph the percentage of steps that were correct (without assistance).

Compare the information in the vignette with the completed Multi-Behavior Data Sheet (Figure 7.5).

The process for completion of a Multi-Step or Multi-Student Data Sheet is the same as for a multi-behavior example except that steps or student names are entered on the data sheet in place of behaviors in area 10.

DECIDING WHICH DATA SHEET TO USE

The decision-making process that follows is used for deciding which data collection sheet to use in any given situation. The flowchart on pages 170–171 provides a visual picture of the complete decision-making process. To use the flowchart, one begins with the "Start" circle and proceeds by following the arrows. Each question in the decision triangles is answered with either a "yes" or a "no" and the appropriate branch arrow is followed to the next step to be completed. It would be helpful for the reader to read through the complete flowchart before proceeding further.

Previously, it was mentioned that there are four basic changes that can be made in the strength of a behavior. The frequency (how often it occurs) can be increased or decreased. The rate (how quickly it occurs) can be increased or decreased. The duration (how long it lasts) can be increased or decreased. The latency (how long between a cue and when the behavior begins) can be increased or decreased.

In deciding which aspect of a behavior to modify, it is important to remember that with some behaviors one may be able to modify more than one aspect of the behavior. For example, a teacher could desire to increase the frequency and decrease the latency of some behavior such as following instructions. In such a case, the teacher should decide what is the most important aspect of the behavior to modify first and answer the questions in the flowchart concerning the less important aspect. Later, the teacher can modify the second aspect of the behavior.

Vignette 6 that follows describes a child and a behavior. Read the vignette and then use the flowchart (pages 170–171) to determine how the decision was made and which type of data to collect.

> Calvin is a 6-year-old, mildly retarded child. Mr. Ferguson is teaching Calvin how to tie his shoes. This has been defined as "tying his shoes in a standard bow that stays tied for at least 20 minutes during normal activity." Mr. Ferguson works individually with Calvin on three specific occasions during each day. This task has been broken down into a series of individual behavior, none of which can occur simultaneously. The whole series of behaviors begins when Mr. Ferguson asks Calvin to "tie his shoes."

What data collection sheet should be used?

The correct decision arrived at is to use the multi-behavior/step data sheet. The information that follows should clarify how the question in each decision triangle of the flowchart was answered to arrive at the final decision. The following questions should have been asked and answered as indicated in Table 7.2.

DATA ANALYSIS

Data analysis is the process of reviewing the collected information in order to make needed modifications in the instructional program. Through data analysis, questions about the individual learner's progress can be answered. Information collected from instructional sessions, logically recorded and analyzed, makes it possible to assess the effectiveness of changes in instructional conditions in order to effectively assist the individual learner.

Data Patterns

The information recorded on the data sheet provides the teacher with a record of performance. The teacher will monitor the learner's performance daily to determine whether or not the student's performance is adequate. If performance

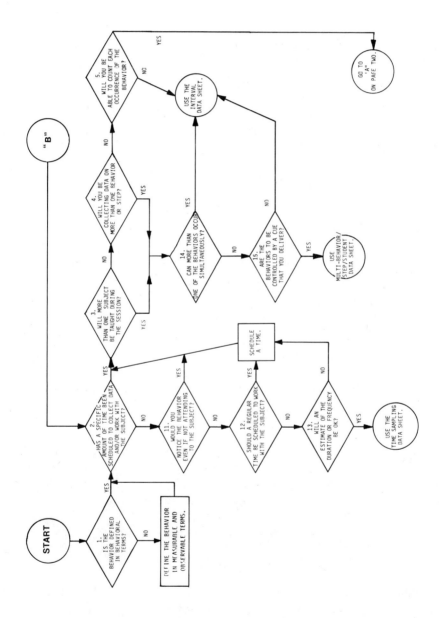

START

1. IS THE BEHAVIOR DEFINED IN BEHAVIORAL TERMS?

NO → DEFINE THE BEHAVIOR IN MEASURABLE AND OBSERVABLE TERMS.

YES →

2. HAS A SPECIFIC AMOUNT OF TIME BEEN SCHEDULED TO COLLECT DATA AND/OR WORK WITH THE SUBJECT?

YES →

NO →

11. WOULD YOU NOTICE THE BEHAVIOR EVEN IF NOT ATTENDING TO THE SUBJECT?

YES → SCHEDULE A TIME.

NO →

12. SHOULD A REGULAR TIME BE SCHEDULED TO WORK WITH THE SUBJECT?

YES → SCHEDULE A TIME.

NO →

13. WILL AN ESTIMATE OF THE DURATION OR FREQUENCY BE OK?

YES → USE THE TIME SAMPLING DATA SHEET.

NO →

"B"

3. WILL MORE THAN ONE SUBJECT BE TAUGHT DURING THE SESSION?

YES →

NO →

4. WILL YOU BE COLLECTING DATA ON MORE THAN ONE BEHAVIOR OR STEP?

YES →

NO →

14. CAN MORE THAN ONE OF THE BEHAVIORS OCCUR SIMULTANEOUSLY?

YES → USE THE INTERVAL DATA SHEET.

NO →

15. ARE THE BEHAVIORS TO BE CONTROLLED BY A CUE THAT YOU DELIVER?

NO → USE THE INTERVAL DATA SHEET.

YES → USE MULTI-BEHAVIOR/STEP/STUDENT DATA SHEET.

5. WILL YOU BE ABLE TO COUNT EACH OCCURRENCE OF THE BEHAVIOR?

NO → USE THE INTERVAL DATA SHEET.

YES → GO TO "A" ON PAGE TWO.

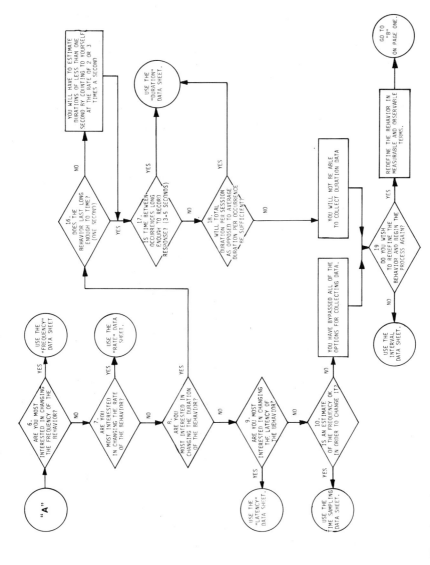

Flowchart of procedures for selecting the correct data sheet.

Table 7.2. Process of deciding which data sheet to use

Question	Answer	Instructions	Comments
1.	Yes	Go to 2.	
2.	Yes	Go to 3.	Mr. Ferguson will work with Calvin on 3 occasions each day.
3.	No	Go to 4.	This is an individual program.
4.	Yes	Go to 14.	Behavior broken into several steps.
14.	No	Go to 15.	Steps cannot occur simultaneously.
15.	Yes	Use Multi-Behavior/Step.	Mr. Ferguson will control the cue.

is adequate, the program should be continued as it is. Adequate performance is defined as those cases in which the data show that the child is continuing to make progress toward the program goals or objectives on a day-to-day basis as indicated by *increasing percentages* of correct behavior over days. If performance is not adequate, the data will help the teacher determine facts or factors that are affecting the student's performance. If a child is not making progress, it is assumed that the trainer will first check to be sure the program is being conducted correctly; thereafter, the trainer should consider several alternatives (Fredericks, Baldwin, Grove, Hanson, McDonnell, Riggs, Furey, Jordan, Gage, Lebac, Alrich, & Wadlow, 1975) based on the data pattern available. Some sample data patterns and suggested actions to take when encountering them follow:

Data Pattern	Alternatives
1. $----+-+$ $--+-+++$	If the child is making consistent gains but has not yet reached criterion, *the current program should be maintained.*
2. $+++++++$ $+++++++$	If the child is consistently making correct responses, without errors, on each step of the program, *probe ahead to determine if the child can perform at a more advanced step of the program.*
3. $+-+++++$ $+++++++$	If the child is making consistent gains and has met the individual criterion set for the program (e.g., rate frequency, percentage), *move to the next step on program.* This pattern is different from #2 above in that the child may have made errors on previous trials or steps of the program.
4. $++++---$ $+++--+-$	If the child is having intermittent success, particularly if progress drops off toward the end of the sessions, *change the reinforcer(s) being used with the program or alter the program slightly.*

5. $---+---$ If the child is making no progress from one day to the
    $----+--$ next, consider several options. First, *consider modifying the program by adding additional steps via task analysis procedures*. Smaller steps should make the task easier by providing additional support to the child performing the task. It may, on the other hand, also increase the number of program sessions needed for the child to reach the terminal objective. Second, *consider modifying the program itself by changing the cues or materials*. Third, *pinpoint specific variables, such as materials presented, the way in which they were presented, the type of learner responses expected, the sex of the tutor and the location in which the program is being conducted*. Any one of these may limit improvements in a child's performance. Last, *probe backward to determine if the child has mastered previous steps*.

Identifying Variables   The preceding data patterns will often call for the specified changes. However, there are other possible factors that might result in inadequate student performance. These factors should be isolated and then modified so that they no longer prevent skill acquisition. The factor(s) may be variables relating to the situation such as the trainer or training environment, or to personal factors (such as fatigue or the task being too difficult). The teacher, therefore, must look through all the data for variables that are consistently present when the student exhibits poor performance.

It is generally easier to examine situation variables first because there are few of them, and they are often easy to change. Examples of situation variables include:

1. Poor performance with a specific trainer
2. Poor performance with a trainer of a specific sex
3. Poor performance at a specific time of day
4. Poor performance in a specific environment

If this analysis results in identifying factors that appear to vary consistently with performance, the teacher should systematically reverse the factor to determine if it is actually the causal factor. For example, if the data appear to indicate that the learner performs poorly in the afternoon, the teacher might schedule the instruction and instructor in the morning for a week. After the week ends, the teacher should assess whether the performance has improved. If it has, the teacher may then schedule the instruction and instructor for the afternoon. If performance is poor, the teacher may have identified a causal factor.

If none of the situation variables seem to be present consistently when the student performs poorly, the teacher will have to initiate an analysis of the personal variables. To do this, the teacher must know exactly what transpired in each instructional session. The instructional sequence and the data sheet should provide the teacher with the necessary information. Items that initially might be checked include questions such as those listed below.

1. Was the student's performance consistently poor at the beginning or end of the session? This might indicate that session length or attentional factors are of concern.
2. Did the order of stimulus presentation appear to affect performance?
3. Are there any specific tasks in which the learner consistently erred?

Again, as with situation variables, the objective of the analysis is to identify potential factors, to manipulate them to determine if they are the causal factors, and, if they are, to modify them to eliminate their negative effect.

SUMMARY

This chapter has provided the different data collection systems that have proved useful in classrooms for handicapped children and youth. Timely collection of the appropriate data is essential to effective decision making concerning child progress. Examples were provided on the application of the different systems, along with a method for determining what type of data to collect in any given situation. Analysis and graphing of data were also stressed.

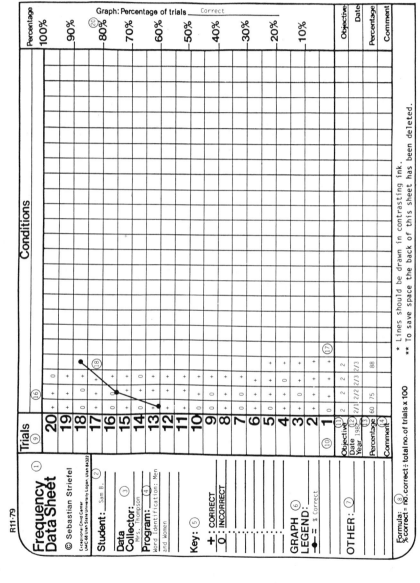

Figure 7.1. Vignette 1, using the Frequency Data Sheet.

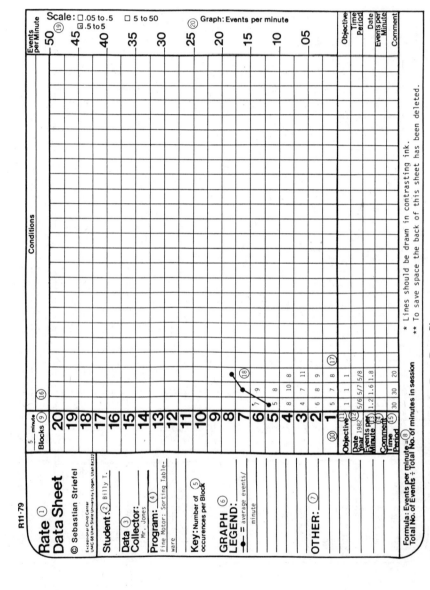

Figure 7.2. Vignette 2, using the Rate Data Sheet.

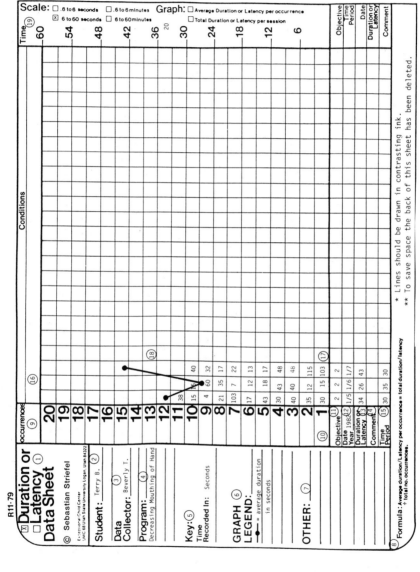

Figure 7.3. Vignette 3, using the Duration or Latency Data Sheet.

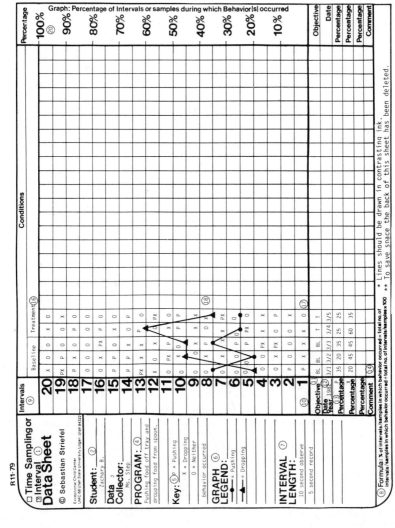

Figure 7.4. Vignette 4, using the Time Sampling or Interval Data Sheet.

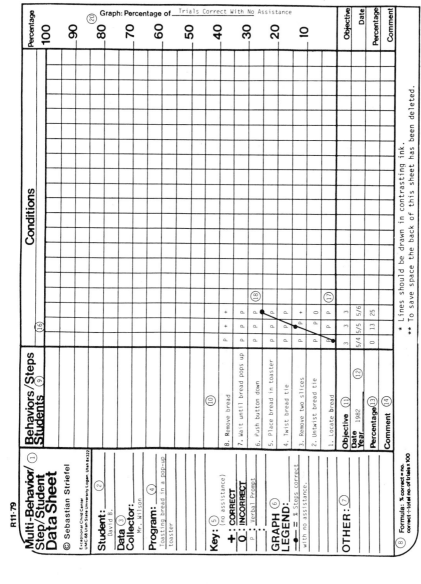

Figure 7.5. Vignette 5, using the Multi-Behavior/Step/Student Data Sheet.

179

8

Curriculum:
Its Selection,
Development,
and Use

After reading this chapter, you should have an understanding of:

1. The rationale for selecting a behavioral philosophy for curriculum development and use, including the components of a curriculum system
2. The role of instructional methodology in implementing an effective curriculum system
3. Learner analysis, the relationship between assessment and curriculum selection, and the criteria useful in the selection of curricula
4. The role of commercial programs and materials
5. The role of classroom or in-house developed curricula, including steps to follow in in-house curriculum development
6. The process of instructional task analysis
7. Writing the instructional sequence
8. Conducting an individual teaching session
9. The role of group programming, including incidental teaching

SO THAT STUDENT PROGRESS is maximized, a curriculum should be developed or selected for children on the basis of their individual needs. A curriculum system must be combined with the other components of a special education program (see previous chapters) if it is to be effective. An eclectic approach to the selection and use of curriculum materials is suggested. That is, commercial and "in-house," or teacher-developed, materials should be used to supplement and complement each other. Activities from several programs can be used to teach the same skill. No material meets *all* the individual needs of the child with handicaps. The spirit of exploring, defining, and responding to individual needs inherent in an eclectic approach will help to ensure that a curriculum system never becomes stagnant, but rather reflects changes based on the individual makeup and needs of the student.

In keeping with this philosophy of flexible, individualized curriculum selection and development, the authors have developed the Program Assessment and Planning Guide for Developmentally Disabled Children (PAPG) (Striefel & Cadez, 1983), discussed later in this chapter. The expansion of the PAPG system and/or development of similar systems is entirely possible and is encouraged. Teachers can add their own programs to available commercial systems and create an individualized curriculum system tailored to their own situation. A school district might even choose to put all the programs developed by their staff on a word processor so they are readily available for future use.

THE BEHAVIORAL PHILOSOPHY FOR CURRICULUM DEVELOPMENT

Both teacher-generated or "in-house" programs and commercial materials can be incorporated into any educational setting. What is basic to any curriculum philosophy and system is an organized approach to selecting, developing, and utilizing instructional programs, and a method of determining their effectiveness. The organized approach that has been set forth in this text is a behavioral intervention approach where behaviors are defined and data are collected on a daily basis (see Chapter 7) to determine child progress and program effectiveness.

The behavioral approach can incorporate the best characteristics of both the developmental and functional models. The developmental model assumes that if the sequence and average age for achievement of specific skills within a normal population of children has been determined, one can determine the appropriate annual goals and short term objectives for a child with a handicapping condition (Adams, 1982). The developmental model further assumes that 1) the sequence of development is simple to complex, 2) complex behavior consists of a combination of more simple behaviors, and 3) certain behaviors are acquired before others because of a developmental hierarchy (Adams, 1982; Haring & Bricker, 1976). Thus, it is assumed that all children, whether normal or with handicapping conditions, acquire skills in the same sequence at the same developmental rather than chronological age.

When the functional model is utilized (Brown, Nietupski, & Hamre-Nietupski, 1976; Whitney & Striefel, 1981), goals and objectives are selected because of their relationship to the student's current or future functioning in the community. Thus, in order to be functional, the skills must generalize to other people and situations, and be maintained over time. It may be difficult to determine what behaviors are required for a specific child or youth for his or her present or future environment. A developmental sequence can be used to estimate what is or might be appropriate. It is false to assume that the two models are or need to be mutually exclusive. The behavioral approach can encompass both developmental age-appropriate skills and functional skills as guidelines in the selection of annual goals and short term objectives. When combined with observable, measurable definitions of behavior, task-analysis procedures, and ongoing data collection, the approach offers a viable means for curriculum development and use. Once the philosophy of development and intervention has been established, methodology and material selection and/or design is the next hurdle for the teacher or therapist implementing programs for children with handicaps.

THE ROLE OF INSTRUCTIONAL METHODOLOGY

The *methodology* by which program content is taught should "reflect the systematic conceptualization and implementation of an empirically validated psychology of instruction" (Fink, Kuombs, Sandall, & Taylor, 1977, p. 8). To be empirically validated, a *written* data-based communication system in the classroom is necessary. This system should enable the teacher to coordinate the effort of various professionals and paraprofessionals and monitor the specifics of learner performance more easily. Such a system requires (McCormack, 1976; Whitney & Striefel, 1981):

1. Measurable and functional behaviors
2. Descriptions of training procedures in clear, operational terms
3. Procedures for assigning who does what with whom, where, when, and how
4. Systematic methods of recording learner behavior on each task regularly
5. A systematic method of comparing learner behavior on each task across time so that pupil progress is established
6. A systematic method of analyzing all data on common ordinates for all learners and tasks
7. A systematic method for ensuring that skills acquired generalize to other times, people, and locations

These procedures are, to a great extent, based on Glaser's (1974) and Fink's et al. (1977) conceptualization of the four major concerns of the psychology of instruction: a) an analysis of the content of competent performance, b) a description of the initial state of the learner, c) a description of the conditions that foster the acquisition of competence, and d) an assessment of the effects of instructional implementation. To the teacher, this implies learner analysis, review of existing materials or development of new materials, goal setting, instructional analysis, reinforcement, instructional presentation, program monitoring, generalization of skills, and incidental teaching.

LEARNER ANALYSIS

Effective teaching and curriculum management stem from knowing the student who is being taught. When one considers the student, a learner analysis is an excellent method of summarizing and putting into a usable format information about the learner. The teacher or therapist puts together information collected during initial and later assessments of the learner and is thus able to develop a statement of the student's learning style, including any performance constraints (e.g., physical handicaps that may exist and limit individual performance on a given task).

A thorough learner analysis should include:

> ...information about the student, which would enhance the student's attainment of objectives, information such as instructional strategies, e.g., fading, shaping, modeling, backward chaining, etc., interest areas for reinforcement purposes, language level, and behavior management techniques that have been used with this student and found to be successful. Any physical/medical constraints (including effects of medication) should also be indicated when they have instructional ramifications (McCormack, 1977, p. 8).

Once information regarding the learner has been synthesized and summarized, proposed goals can be established. The approval and finalization of the goals for each individual client signals the beginning of the curriculum selection process by the teacher or therapist. Essentially the teacher or therapist has two options: available commercially marketed materials or "in-house" staff-designed materials. It is essential that the teacher or therapist review existing curriculum materials that are currently available in their setting so time is not wasted with inaccurate programming decisions.

Material Decisions

Materials serve as the vehicles of instruction, bringing the learner in direct contact with the chosen task. They must always be selected to suit learner characteristics, planned objectives, and strategies (Laycock, 1982). Several facets need to be considered prior to selection of materials:

1. Real objects or materials should be used rather than contrived ones. It may be easier to teach a child with handicaps to button or snap using a dressing frame, but time must be taken after the skill is learned on the frame to generalize the skill to the child's own clothing.
2. Objects should be used initially that differ only in regard to the critical dimension of the instruction. For example, when teaching colors, examples should vary only in color, not size and shape. This prevents misconceptions on the part of the learner.
3. Selected objects or materials should be functionally useful, e.g., sorting utensils has greater functional usefulness than sorting colored straws.
4. Safety is another facet that should be given considerable attention. Sharp corners and edges, small, loose, easily swallowed parts, and objects with

cords or plastic coverings that can suffocate and strangle a person should be avoided.

5. Cost effectiveness includes selection of objects or materials that are sturdy, easily cleaned and maintained, and easily obtained for replacement. Many a good program has been jeopardized because the materials have been lost or damaged and cannot be replaced.

6. Materials and objects should be attractive, colorful, and inviting enough to hold the learner's attention.

Close attention should also be paid to the physical arrangement and storage of materials for ease in handling by the teacher or therapist during instructional sessions. Other factors that affect material use are directly related to various handicapping conditions, such as easily manipulated materials for the physically handicapped and various textured materials for the visually impaired.

COMMERCIAL PROGRAMS AND MATERIALS

Commercial resource materials and programs should be examined carefully for their applicability and appropriateness for the target population. A specific procedure for analyzing commercial programs and materials will provide the reviewer with objective information from which an informed programming decision can be made. A questionnaire such as the one in Figure 8.1 is suggested for evaluating commercial materials.

Additional criteria to determine the appropriateness and applicability of instructional aids are listed below (McCormack, 1977):

1. Are instructional objectives stated?
2. Are prerequisite skills required of the learner to effectively use the material stated?
3. Are prerequisite skills required of the teacher to effectively use the material stated?
4. Is the presentation mode appropriate for the learner?
5. Does the instruction follow a logical sequence?
6. Are the directions complete and accurate?
7. Is the teaching strategy clearly and completely indicated?
8. Are storage and/or retrieval requirements difficult?
9. Will preparation time prevent regular use?
10. Is the answer key (if provided) useful, or can one be easily constructed?
11. What student/teacher ratio is necessary to use the material?
12. Is the material capable of maintaining instructor interest?
13. Is the procedure for detecting errors and making corrections sufficient?
14. Is the stated mastery level (criteria for success) indicated?
15. Are there alternative approaches to using the material to attain the same objective?

Title/Program: _____

Publisher: _____

Author(s): _____ Copyright Date: _____

Cost: _____

Sex or Cultural Bias   Designed for Ages:_____
Yes ☐   No ☐

Designed for specific handicapping conditions of:_____

1. High or low structure? (Circle one)
2. Who is primary interventionist?
3. Staffing pattern required for effective use?
4. Age equivalent referenced in program?
5. a. Are there behavioral objectives?
    b. Are they properly stated?
    c. Is there a criteria for performance?
6. a. Are these consumable materials?
    b. If so - do they constitute a high portion of total cost?
    c. Is the program reusable?
7. a. Is there a recordkeeping system?
    b. Does it provide sufficient information to evaluate child's progress
        and program effectiveness?
    c. Does it provide daily, weekly, quarterly, semi-annual, or annual
        records? (Circle one(s) that apply)
    d. Is it time consuming or easy to use?
8. a. Is there a procedure included in the program for periodic evaluation?
    b. Does this procedure appear to be cumbersome or easy to administer?
    c. Does it appear to provide adequate and relevant information?
9. Could a parent or paraprofessional easily understand and use this
    program?
10. Is this program based on test sample items, developmental levels, or both?
    (Circle one)
11. Are objective activities:
    clearly stated   Yes ☐   No☐
    lengthy or short (circle one)
    appropriate for intended population   Yes ☐   No ☐
    easily modified and adapted for use   Yes ☐   No ☐
    or
    are adaptations or modification already stated   Yes ☐   No ☐
12. Are there additional support materials available?   Yes ☐   No ☐
13. Is specific staff training required for use of program?   Yes ☐   No ☐
14. What is your overall rating of this program?

        ☐   ☐   ☐   ☐   ☐
     excellent   good   fair   poor   unable to rate

Figure 8.1. Curriculum evaluation sheet.

16. Is the material capable of maintaining interest?
17. Is the material durable?
18. Is the teacher's guide (if one is provided) complete?
19. How often will it be necessary and how difficult will it be to replace
    consumable parts of the material?
20. What are the strengths and weaknesses of the validation information
    provided?

21. What is the cost/price/value estimate?
22. Are the material's technical aspects (e.g., size of print, quality of pictures) acceptable?

Overall, each program and curriculum system should be modifiable so as to be appropriate for:

1. Individual (one-to-one) instruction
2. Small group instruction
3. Meeting the specific needs of the student population
4. Use by paraprofessionals, practicum students, student teachers, tutors, and aides, without difficult instructions or sophisticated training being necessary
5. Use with the data recording and monitoring system employed by the teacher

The scope and sequence of the commercial materials being used should cover the skill areas that are being taught. For example, commercial materials and programs can be categorized according to the major program areas outlined in the Program Assessment and Planning Guide (PAPG) (Striefel & Cadez, 1983): language, math, reading, writing, music, social skills, motor, home-living, and self-help. Although its uses have changed with recent revisions, the PAPG is basically a curriculum guide, an assessment, monitoring and training tool, and was originally designed for use in demonstration classrooms. It is now being commercially disseminated for use in other educational settings and is primarily a planning instrument; i.e., the PAPG cross-references materials that can be used to plan instructional programs for the child or youth with developmental disabilities.

The PAPG includes objectives designed to cover 26 categories of behavior, with the intent being to increase the rate of acquisition and improve the performance of the behavior to more closely approximate that of a normal child. The 26 skill areas are: 1) gross motor, 2) fine motor, 3) receptive language, 4) expressive language, 5) social, 6) social language, 7) eating, 8) dressing, 9) toileting, 10) personal hygiene, 11) safety, 12) music, 13) writing, 14) reading, 15) math—numerations and operations, 16) seasons and time, 17) money, 18) calendar skills, 19) volume measurement, 20) linear measurement, 21) housecleaning, 22) clothing care, 23) kitchen and cooking, 24) survival and security, 25) appliance operation, and 26) travel. The 26 skill areas are divided into three areas on the basis of age of onset of the skills in normal children. The three areas are *basic skills, preacademic/academic skills,* and *prevocational/homeliving skills.*

As a curriculum guide, the objective statements in the PAPG are arranged in a developmental sequence, and the user is referred to a marketed program or programs that can be used to teach each objective. By stating the objective in behavioral terms, programs can be written to meet a child's exact needs if existing programs referred to in the PAPG are not adequate or if no program is listed (note Figure 8.2 for an example of the PAPG format). The PAPG provides over 1,400 items in the 26 skill areas that can be used as a resource for planning individualized programs.

As an assessment and monitoring system, the PAPG can be used to assess a child's performance level in determining skills and deficits. Results can be used to make placement decisions and to design the child's IEP. The student profile, a component of the PAPG, is a written record that may be used in the regularly scheduled staffings or IEP meetings when the child study team meets. It can also be used for keeping a specific record of daily and quarterly progress for each individual child. Narrative reports and parent/teacher interviews are also facilitated by this record. Although the PAPG should not be used as the only assessment tool, it can help to determine placement in instructional programs. The PAPG is a record that can be transferred with the child when he or she leaves one educational setting for placement in another.

As a training tool, the PAPG provides the trainee with an overall educational planning guide for the child, an appropriate developmental sequence for most subject areas, and a resource file that contains appropriate instructional programs and suggestions for teaching each objective. Various resources have been utilized both in writing the items in each skill and in selecting the materials and activities used to teach them.

The PAPG provides the teacher and trainee with a potential educational plan for the child. This plan is analyzed into a sequenced series of behavioral objectives that are used as a "standard of reference" in the development of the student's IEP. Annual goals may be developed from the instructional objectives drawn from each of the curriculum areas of the PAPG. These are then utilized in preparing the IEP, which is then written and approved by the child study team, and implemented both in the home and in the educational setting by home trainers, teachers, therapists, and parents.

CLASSROOM DEVELOPED MATERIALS

Planning appropriate individualized instruction for clients is an important part of the program planning process. "In-house" or staff-developed programs should be written in areas or on tasks where commercial materials are unavailable or not functional. As in the case of commercial materials, educational materials produced by staff should be appropriate for:

1. One-to-one instruction
2. Small group instruction
3. Specific needs
4. Use by paraprofessionals, parents, or tutors without the need for use of sophisticated training methods

PROGRAM ASSESSMENT & PLANNING GUIDE

Striefel and Cadez © 1983

Objective Number	Objective Statement	Developmental Age	Resources
	Safety		
1.	When told "no" the student will cease what she or he is doing at least momentarily 75% of the time.	9 – 12 months	POPC 0-092
2.	When presented with a hot object where heat is felt without touching the object and the verbal cue, "No, Hot!" the student will move immediately away from the hot object.	12 – 14 months	TMSH V2 (1) – I Safety
3.	When told "no" the student will cease what she or he is doing 90% of the time.	14 – 18 months	POPC 0-092 Portage S #39
4.	When given an edible and inedible substance and the verbal cue, "Point to the one you can eat," the student will point to the edible substance 100% of the time.	24 – 30 months	TMSH V2 (5) – A Safety POPC 2-252
5.	When shown a toy on a stair step or some other inappropriate place and a toy on a shelf or in an appropriate place and the verbal command "Put the toy where it belongs," the student picks up the toy in the inappropriate place and puts it in a safe location.	30 – 36 months	POPC 2-295

* POPC – Performance Objectives for Preschool Children
  TMSH – Teaching Moderately and Severely Handicapped
  Portage – Portage Guide to Early Education

Figure 8.2. PAPG format sheet.

The ever present need for materials and programs that do not currently exist prompts professionals to develop their own. Staff-developed materials are often needed to supplement or fill in gaps in commercially prepared courses of study (Kohfeldt, 1976). Activities such as design, production, evaluation, and revision of programs and materials should be an ongoing process in special education programs. The end product of this development process should include a series of instructional sequences written in an easy-to-use format and filed by the program area and the objective. Eventually, these program sequences can be compiled into programmed curriculum manuals categorized into specific units. Units would be conceptually organized by content. For example, a calendar skill unit would consist of days, weeks, months, and years.

Time spent in designing and developing programs is conserved when an organized program development procedure is followed throughout the process. In 1975, Hofmeister described a "mini" educational research and development (R & D) model based on a more extensive model described by Borg and Gall (1971) for designing and field testing parent training packages. This model has direct application for classroom staff in developing "in-house" curricula. The seven major stages in the "mini" R & D model are described as follows:

1. Definition of curriculum content. During this first stage, instructional needs of the student are analyzed (learner analysis), and a search for existing materials is conducted. If materials are found that require certain adaptation before they meet the instructional needs of the learner, as identified by the learner analysis, then such adaptations are made, and the program goes through a "mini" field test prior to its initial use with the intended student. Such adaptations might include visual pictured steps in a procedure for a student who does not read, enlarged printed materials for a visually impaired student, or use of an electronic response mechanism or switch by a motorically involved individual. If the search for existing curriculum materials fails to produce any possibilities, even ones that can be used with modifications, then the complete procedure as outlined in the model needs to be followed to develop quality instructional programs for students.

2. Development of a prototype. The second stage of the R & D model as described by Hofmeister (1975) involves the development of a prototype instructional program. The instructional programmer first completes a concept analysis and/or a task analysis of the concept or procedure to be taught, then the programmer constructs a rough draft of the program format complete with materials, a process description, student outcomes, and an established criteria that must be met on each step before proceeding to the next step.

3. Critique by experts. After a prototype or a completed draft of the program is finished, the instructional programmer should ask his or her colleagues and/or a district curriculum specialist to quickly review the program for

any suggestions or changes that might be made prior to its initial use. Once revisions and changes are made, then the programmer tries out the program.

4. Programmer as parent* or paraprofessional. In this stage, the instructional program developer takes the role of a parent or paraprofessional and uses the program with several children with developmental disabilities to see if it works and to make modifications as needed.

5. Volunteer as parent. After further revisions have been made based upon data gathered in stage 4, paraprofessionals, parents, or clinicians are asked to use the program with children to make further revisions and modifications before the individual formative evaluation is initiated.

6. Formative evaluation. In this stage of the R & D model, field test versions of the program are used by the staff or volunteers with various children, and data are gathered to identify any phase or step of the program needing revision prior to the final summative evaluation stage.

7. Summative evaluation. In this final stage, a second group of staff or volunteers use the revised programs, and controlled data are collected over a period of time to determine program effectiveness.

*Note: The term "parent" is used throughout the R & D model described by Hofmeister (1975) due to the fact that he was designing programs for use by parents. "Paraprofessional" or "staff member" can easily and appropriately be substituted for "parent" in this model.

INSTRUCTIONAL TASK ANALYSIS

Task analysis is the breaking down of a task or objective into subtasks or subobjectives usually defined as a step, phase, or frame (Bateman, 1967; Engelmann, 1970; Fredericks, Riggs, Furey, Grove, Moore, McDonnell, Jordan, Hanson, Baldwin, & Wadlow, 1976; McCormack, 1977; Semmel & Thiagarajan, 1973). Task analysis aids the teacher or therapist both in determining what to teach and in what sequence it should be taught (McCormack, 1976).

Like any other learned behavior, accurate task analysis depends mainly on the ability to logically sequence the learning experience so that each subtask acts as a building block or foundation for the next subtask to be learned. The four major steps in development of task analysis are: a) deciding on a method, b) breaking the *content* of the task into teachable components, c) determining the methodology or *process* of teaching the task, and d) teaching the task (Gold, 1976, 1977).

Deciding on a method is an important first step; it entails considering both the learner and how the task should be performed (i.e., what the most appropriate, efficient, and effective way is of teaching *this* child *this* task) Watching competent performers of the task, or finding out how others routinely perform the task, should broaden the teacher's base of options on how a task should be performed. (For example, there are at least six variations of how to tie a shoe—experimentation would most likely prove there are even more.)

Analyzing the *content* of the task is an important second step. Essentially, this entails breaking the task down into teachable components. Conducting a complete task rehearsal (completing the task oneself) several times will help to isolate the essential steps and the minor variations so that the task can be written down in a step-by-step sequence (Adams, 1982). Table 8.1 gives a step-by-step sequence of brushing teeth.

Of course, not everyone will brush their teeth in the exact manner nor require the same number of steps as described in Table 8.1. A content task analysis is somewhat arbitrary in that there is no absolute number of steps for any given task. The steps should be logically sequenced and/or proceed from simple to complex. The adequacy of a given subtask sequence of tasks is determined by whether the learner demonstrates the desired behavior or not.

Process analysis is the third step and involves three decisions by the teacher or therapist. First, a decision as to what "format" should be used needs to be made, including answering such questions as how the task will be

Table 8.1. Task analysis on brushing teeth

1. Choose own toothbrush.
2. Put toothbrush on counter.
3. Turn cold water on.
4. Pick up and wet toothbrush.
5. Turn off cold water.
6. Pick up toothpaste.
7. Unscrew cap with dominant hand while still holding toothbrush in dominant hand.
8. Put cap on counter.
9. Hold toothbrush correctly in dominant hand.
10. Squeeze toothpaste onto brush.
11. Pick up cap with dominant hand (while still holding toothbrush).
12. Screw cap on toothpaste tube.
13. Put toothpaste on counter.
14. Wet toothbrush under cold water.
15. Brush upper back teeth on the one side.
16. Brush upper teeth on other side.
17. Brush lower back teeth on one side.
18. Brush lower back teeth on other side.
19. Brush front teeth—down on upper, up on lower.
20. Turn cold water on.
21. Rinse brush.
22. Put brush down in correct place (holder).
23. Rinse mouth (hand method).
24. Reach for (paper) towel.
25. Put (paper) towel in hand.
26. Wipe mouth.
27. Dry hands.
28. Inspect mouth corners for paste.
29. Throw paper towel away or hang up cloth towel.

presented to the learner and in what way the teaching material will be organized. One kind of format is used for learning one-step behaviors, such as naming colors or learning which public restroom to use. Another kind of format is used for learning multiple-step behaviors, such as putting on a shirt or toileting. Formats for one-step behaviors include, among others:

1. Simple discrimination (e.g., which is correct?)
2. Match to sample (e.g., which is like this one?)
3. Paired associate format (e.g., flash cards)
4. Odd or different (e.g., which one does not belong?)

Formats for multiple-step behaviors may include:

1. Forward chaining
2. Backward chaining
3. Total task (present the whole task on each trial with assistance, as needed)
4. Organized exposure with feedback (used for nonsequenced tasks such as social behavior at parties)

The second decision in process analysis concerns "feedback," i.e., how to ensure that the learner knows what is wanted and if he or she is achieving it. The trainer provides the learner with information before, during, and after the learner's behavior. Feedback may be verbal, nonverbal, or a combination of both. For children with handicaps, feedback almost always includes a reinforcement component, e.g., in addition to being told "you pointed to the right one," the child might be given a raisin to eat if it has been determined that this child will work to earn raisins.

The third decision involves "procedure"—a description of the proposed training plan. This usually involves a description of the actions of the trainer, outlining how feedback procedures will be used so that the trainer will know how to implement the task analysis.

The fourth step in task analysis is to *teach the task*. Implement the first three steps and then teach. However, even when a task is carefully planned, someone will inevitably not learn or at least not learn part of what is being presented. In that case, the process task analysis should be redone. It may also be necessary to determine if there is some type of reinforcer that can be used that hasn't been, or whether or not the reinforcement being used is actually increasing the probability of the behavior's occurrence. For some children with developmental disabilities, it is very difficult to find a functional reinforcer that will increase the probability of the desired response. In such cases, one must continue to search for viable alternatives. One might examine the method to see if the information can be given more quickly or if there is a format that may be more effective than the one being used, (e.g., would the task better fit a backward chaining or total task approach, or are presentation or environmental factors inhibiting progress?).

What if the student still doesn't learn the task after redoing the process task analysis? This may mean that the trainer was not familiar enough with the task at the onset. In this case, he or she should redo the content task analysis by breaking the unlearned steps into even smaller components so that the subtasks will be even simpler.

If the learner still doesn't respond correctly, redo the method. There may be an entirely different way of doing the task or the part of the task the person is having trouble with that has not been tried. As a general rule, if it does not work, try another method (Gold, 1977). However, use this decision as a last resort since it involves start-up time and thus, slows the program down.

After the task has been sufficiently analyzed and the skills of the learner have been determined via assessment and observation, several alternatives for teaching each objective can be selected from commercial or "in-house" curricula. Continual review of current materials and programs will produce an extensive resource file of appropriate activities that can be "rounded out" with additional staff-generated activities. When several alternatives are available for teaching each objective, program planning time is greatly decreased for the teacher or the therapist.

WRITING THE INSTRUCTIONAL SEQUENCE

What specifically is an instructional sequence? McCormack (1974) says that it is "a series of systematically controlled situations conducted in order to bring about a specific change in the student's behavior." To write an instructional sequence, the following tasks are necessary (McCormack, 1974):

1. Identify and write a terminal objective by focusing on an objective that will teach the child a *functional* skill.
2. Task analyze the terminal objective.
3. Determine what materials will be needed to conduct the sequence.
4. Determine how the teacher should arrange and/or use the materials.
5. Determine what the teacher's actions should be.
6. Determine what the student's response should be.
7. Determine what the teacher should do if the student responds correctly.
8. Determine what the teacher should do if the student does not respond correctly.

In addition, the instructional sequence must include the mastery criteria used and a method for collecting information on student performance (the data collection procedure).

Identifying and Writing the Terminal Objective

Once the learner has been pretested and the data analyzed to determine which skills he or she can and cannot perform, the teacher must translate an observable skill into a clearly written behavioral objective. When developing the objective, certain instructional considerations should be kept in mind:

1. Is the skill being taught functional? Will the child use the skill to maintain or improve his or her daily living conditions?
2. Has the wording of the objective included consideration for generalization of the skill? Many times a child will display the response for the teacher but the skill may not occur (transfer) in the presence of the parent. When writing the terminal objective, the teacher should try to incorporate as many conditions as possible that will validate whether or not the behavior has been learned (e.g., if the skill being taught is color discrimination, then several different types of objects should be used rather than similar sized and shaped objects; in this way the teacher will ensure that it is indeed the color rather than similarity in objects to which the child is responding).
3. Has the wording of the objective included a specific observable action verb? In a behavioral objective, the teacher should avoid such words as "recognize," "understand," or "indicate" because each person working with the student would have too much latitude in determining just *how* a student shows recognition and understanding, thus increasing the chance of unreliable data collection. The action element of the objective should be stated in observable and measurable terms, e.g., the student will point to, verbally name, or touch.
4. Under what conditions will the behavior take place? This, of course, will vary from objective to objective, but the conditions should reflect concern with generalization. Instead of stating that the child will emit the behavior in only one location or at one time of day, the objective should be stated so that the behavior occurs under several different conditions.
5. What kind and how much assistance will the teacher or the instructional material give? Is the student to perform the objective independently? If the assistance is "minimal," then the kind of minimal assistance to be provided should be specified.
6. How well and how quickly must the skill be performed in order for the behavior to be considered mastered? Mastery criteria must be determined and included in the written objective or stated somewhere on the program format sheet. Often, resources will provide information about mastery criteria on certain skills and thus aid the programmer in making a reasonable decision, e.g., Baer (1981b) has pointed out the relationship of fluency (high rate, accuracy or short latency) to obtaining generalization of skills.
7. What materials, if any, will be needed for the student to perform the objective? In an objective concerned with eye-hand coordination, a spoon might be used, whereas in an objective dealing with a receptive language skill, the only stimulus may be a verbal cue from the teacher. If part of the

stimulus is to be an object, then the objective should include what the object will be and if relevant, what its characteristics are (e.g., a 10″ rubber ball).

By specifying information from each concern in the following manner, a "skeleton" of a behavioral objective is developed.

Functional skill: eating with spoon
Specific Action: hold spoon in fist
Assistance: shown how by the teacher
Criteria: four out of five trials
Materials: spoon, dish with soft food, (e.g., mashed potatoes)
Generalization: different spoons, dishes, food, locations and people

By combining all the necessary ingredients, the objective can be written in several, equally correct ways. For example: "The student will hold a spoon in his fist and feed himself in imitation of the teacher or any other adult in any location, when given a spoon and dish containing soft food on four out of five trials." Or: "When given a spoon and a dish containing soft food and shown how to use the spoon to scoop and eat, the student will imitate correctly four out of five trials for any adult in any setting."

Task Analyzing the Terminal Objective

Initially, this planning should begin on scratch paper since the analysis will be modified and revised several times. Isolating and writing down all the component subtasks regardless of order is a complex job, but an excellent starting point. Rearranging the steps into a logical pattern according to complexity or operation is much easier and begins to give the program a prioritized order (Howell et al., 1979). An example of a single step task is: "The learner will point to a specified colored card from a set of nine different colored cards on verbal request, without assistance, nine out of ten trials" (Gold, 1976). Because there are nine different colored cards, the programmer may want to break the sequence into nine different steps, one step per color. However, the behavior (pointing) remains constant. Only the color of the stimulus (card) changes as the sequence of steps progresses.

In a multiple-step task such as a task analysis for toothbrushing, the sequence is a combination of chained multiple behaviors. In forward chaining, the first behavior is taught, then the second behavior is added, then the third behavior, etc., until the student is able to demonstrate the whole task. The sequence of objective components may vary. Actually, the teacher should teach (and program for) many small behaviors before the total behavior is attained, e.g., in teaching eating as a functional behavior, many small behaviors such as grasping the spoon need to be taught prior to the accomplishment of the total behavior, functional eating.

Backward chaining follows the same sequence except that the steps are taught in reverse order so that step 20 is taught first, step 19 next, then step 18, and so on, until all the steps are achieved. Tasks such as dressing and learning one's phone number or address are often taught more quickly using the backward or reverse chaining technique in programming. Tasks that involve delivery of natural reinforcers when completion of the task is achieved, such as going outside when completely dressed or hearing another person's voice after dialing a phone number, are often taught easily by the backward or reverse chaining technique because the completion step (the last step) or natural reinforcer is in every instructional session. Thus, reinforcement occurs more often. No matter what technique is used, it is important to write down the sequence of steps in the program, to perform the behaviors to be taught, to arrange the steps either in order of operation or complexity, and to modify, if necessary, the sequence, size, or number of steps in the program.

Program Format

Instructional sequences can be written in various formats designed to help the teacher and paraprofessional determine the procedure in which the terminal objective will be taught. One such format, the curriculum program format,[1] is the result of several evaluations and subsequent revisions. The format sheet has been used to write instructional programs for all types of children with handicaps.

The curriculum format has several uses besides being a good method for determining if all components of an instructional sequence have been covered. These uses include:

1. A written program is available for staff who might need to teach the same skill at some future time.
2. Use of a common format should increase communications between staff and allow integration of skills from one session to another session.
3. The format allows an easy method for training classroom volunteers to conduct programs because once they learn the format, their questions on future programs should be limited to content.
4. The format can easily be used by parents in conducting programs in the home.

There are two major components in the curriculum format: a) the header, and b) the sequenced content of each program. When writing programs, both components should be completed by the author. The student information in the header should not be filled in on the master copy of the program. This information is added after the program is photocopied and assigned to the

---

[1]The curriculum program format was adapted from material by McCormack (1976) and is reproduced here with the permission of the first author.

student. Figure 8.3 depicts the curriculum program sheet and includes the instructions for using it.

Determining the Instructional Procedure

After deciding what suitable materials are needed for the instructional program, a general procedure or instructional format should outline what the teacher or trainer will do or say to the student. The more carefully this portion of the program is written initially, the easier it is to identify steps that may be causing difficulties or contain gaps via the data collection system. Using as few words and actions as possible without sacrificing clarity increases the probability of child success. Utilizing a program format sheet such as the one in Figure 8.3 helps the programmer be succinct and accurate in outlining the program and prevents program components from being forgotten. Verbal and physical cues should also be noted in this segment of the program so these cues remain as consistent as possible from step to step of the program.

Determining What the Student's Response Should Be

It is equally as important to define what the student's response should be as it is to clearly outline the procedure for the trainer. If the student response is not clearly defined, it is extremely difficult to determine when or even if it has occurred. What, specifically, is a correct response? It should reflect the "verbing" component of your behavioral objective, i.e., the child should exhibit an observable, measurable, and quantifiable type of behavior. For example, the student should: a) *verbally name* a presented color, or b) *point to* the letter named, or c) *orally read* the days of the week from the blackboard. An important factor to consider before continuing further is the relationship between the physical and verbal cues entered in the "what you do and say" column and the specified response stipulated in the "what the student does" column of the curriculum program format sheet. If the child is told to *point to* a color card, that is exactly what he or she is to do—not touch, not pick up, but point to. A direct correlation must exist or learner confusion will result. If trainer direction and anticipated learner response are not consistent, then one or the other must be rewritten so they match.

Reinforcing the Correct Response

Deciding the type and frequency of reinforcement that will maximize student performance is essential. Children will perform instructional activity only if it "pays off" frequently and sufficiently enough. (Note Chapter 7 for an overview of reinforcement procedures.) Giving a token and praise after each correct response, or tickling the child and praising verbally after each correct response helps motivate children to respond. Often, because reinforcement preferences vary to a great degree from child to child, the particular reinforcement that works should be selected by the teacher specifically for each child and changed as needed. Reinforcement preferences should be determined prior to instruc-

INSTRUCTIONS FOR USING THE
CURRICULUM PROGRAM FORMAT SHEET

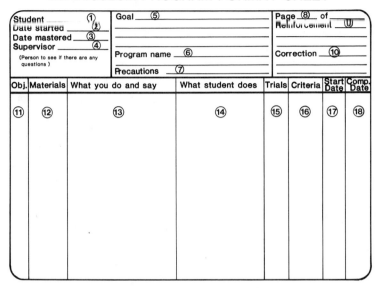

1. STUDENT: The Client/Child's Name.

2. DATE STARTED: The first day the program is used with the student.

3. DATE MASTERED: The date that the learner met the criterion for the program as set in the GOAL.

4. SUPERVISOR: The person who is in charge of monitoring the program to insure that it is being used correctly.

5. GOAL: What you want the student to be able to do when s/he completes the program. The goal should be stated behaviorally and include a) conditions, b) behavior, and c) criterion.

6. PROGRAM NAME: This is a short title to be used to refer to this program. It should be the type of activity you are teaching, i.e., color recognition, counting objects, self feeding, etc.

7. PRECAUTIONS: Any advice to be given to someone using this program.

8. PAGE: Number the pages of a multi-page program as an aid to keeping the pages in order.

9. REINFORCEMENT: Enter the reinforcer (music box, peanuts, hugs and kisses, etc.) or the type of reinforcer (social praise, food, etc.) to be delivered when the student gives a correct response.

10. CORRECTION: Enter what is to be said or done if the student gives an incorrect response.

11. OBJECTIVE: A number which corresponds to the objective or step of the program you are teaching.

12. MATERIALS: Exactly what materials you need to teach this objective. Be specific.

13. WHAT YOU DO AND SAY: Exactly what you do and say to the student to let her/him know what s/he is expected to do.

14. WHAT STUDENT DOES: Exactly what you expect the child to do.

15. TRIALS: The number of times the objective should be included during one session.

16. CRITERIA: The number of correct responses out of the total number of trials for a given number of days that the child must be correct in order to pass the objective and go to the next objective.
Example: Nine out of ten trials correct on two consecutive days.
Example: Eighteen out of twenty trials correct on four days.

17. START DATE: The first day this objective is conducted with the student.

18. COMPLETION DATE: The day the criteria for this objective was met and you moved to the next objective.

Figure 8.3. Curriculum program sheet.

tion. The identification of more than one reinforcer preference will give the trainer some flexibility and latitude in their use and help avoid satiation.

What the Teacher Should Do
If the Student Does Not Respond Correctly

A program should specify the type and frequency of correction or timeout consequences to occur after an incorrect response is made. Possible correction procedures include ignoring the child for a period of 10 seconds immediately after an incorrect response, responding with a verbal ''No!'' immediately after an incorrect response and then showing the student the correct response, or employing the "Model-Lead-Test" technique. The Model-Lead-Test technique is a commonly used correction procedure that provides the student with a "no-fail" instructional situation and maximum opportunity to complete successfully each desired response with a minimum of errors and negative teacher feedback.

To correct a learner's inaccurate performance using the Model-Lead-Test procedure, the trainer demonstrates the correct response for the learner and then the trainer leads the learner by simultaneously doing the task with him or her. While leading the learner, the trainer may use prompts to assist the learner in completing the task. The testing condition requires the learner to exhibit the response independently. The test usually follows the model and lead conditions as described in the examples in Figure 8.4.

Determining Criterion Level

Once the instructional sequence has been written, the programmer, along with the teacher, will need to determine the criterion level for passing one step and proceeding to the next. Criteria can be presented in terms of time (within 1 minute, after 3 seconds), in terms of a degree of quality (90% correct, 19 out of 20 trials) or in terms of both time *and* quality (9 out of 10 trials for 2 successive program sessions).

A decision should also be made on how many times each stimulus will be presented. The more stimuli being worked with, the fewer number of times each will be presented in a session. For example, by computing a total number of trials, a decision can be made on how many trials will be conducted using each stimulus, e.g., four color cards presented 5 times each equals 20 total trials.

Once the procedure is completely detailed, it should be rewritten or typed neatly on a program sheet (Figure 8.3). After the information has been entered on the program format sheet, a final check should be made for inconsistencies, and possible vaguely worded directions.

CONDUCTING A TEACHING SESSION

A teaching session is a prepared and rehearsed presentation conducted by a teacher or tutor whenever he or she attempts to show or tell a student something

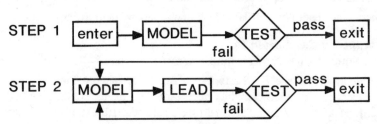

Figure 8.4. Model-Lead-Test sequence.

one or more times. Basically, there are two types of presentations. The first is a show-and-test situation.

1. *Enter* with the materials necessary for the step being worked on.
2. *Place* the materials at or in the appropriate place or manner.
3. *Show* the student how to do what it is he or she is expected to do.
4. *Test* the student on the task or objective.
5. *Reinforce* the student if the student meets criteria on a given trial.
6. *Follow the correction procedure* most appropriate for the student if the student does not meet criteria on a given trial.
7. *Prepare* for the next step.

The second presentation is a test-only situation, where the teacher proceeds immediately with the test and contingent reinforcement, if appropriate.

Both types of presentation need not be conducted on the same day. In some cases, the show-test presentation may not be used, while a test-only presentation paired with a Model-Lead-Test correction procedure may be used. In other cases, the show-test presentation may be conducted until criterion is met one day, then the test-only presentation will be conducted the next program day. In either case, the tutor will have to learn how to translate the written program format into a live and dynamic presentation.

To prepare for a presentation, it is important to be aware of what step the student is presently working on. To determine which specific materials are needed, the trainer would refer to the "Materials" column of the format sheet and would have them available for the presentation.

The physical and/or verbal cues being employed are specified in the "What you do and say" column. Moving one more column to the right, the "What the student does" column states the specific behavior expected of the student. The "Trials" column specifies how many times to run through the presentation routine. The "Criteria" column states how well the child must do before moving on to the next step.

Giving a stimulus cue and obtaining a response from the learner is not enough. The student must be appropriately reinforced or corrected. By looking at the box in the uppermost right-hand corner of the program sheet, information is found regarding these two procedures. Since reinforcement preferences vary to a great degree from child to child, a general term such as "social praise and/or preferred reinforcer" is often used. It is essential that one of the most effective reinforcers known for a given child is used so that the child remains motivated. The correction procedure utilized in these programs should either be specific for a given child, or a variation of the Model-Lead-Test correction procedure.

The Individual Program Book

The Individual Program Book (IPB) is the centralized individual data and working file on each student located in his or her classroom. The best format for the IPB is a looseleaf binder so that pages can be added and changed frequently to provide for flexibility and ease in program revision as needed. Included in the IPB should be items such as IEP instructional sequences written on program format sheets, daily data sheets, and general information sheets. As a communication device, the IPB informs volunteers, clinicians, professional team members, and parents what is being taught, how the student is doing based on the daily data, and general information everyone must be aware of in working with the student such as toileting information, reinforcers, and schedules. It has been found to be efficient to place the program format sheets in the binder in the order that they are taught with the appropriate data sheet directly behind each program sheet. As an administrative device, the IPB centralizes all pertinent information on student progress in one easy-to-use file. The contents of an IPB may include:

1. An *information sheet* that could include:
   a. Name of the child
   b. Placement of the child
   c. Date information was entered
   d. Date of birth
   e. Present chronological age
   f. Toileting procedures, if applicable
   g. Behavioral problems/contingencies, if applicable
   h. Language problems/objectives
   i. Effective rewards and correction procedures
   j. General comments (positioning, medication, seizure activity)
2. A copy of the child's individualized education program is included in the IPB. For many children, especially lower functioning ones, the IEP is comparable with the individual programs for the various tasks that will be taught to the child. The IPB should be treated as confidential information. Only those staff and paraprofessionals who will be working with the staff should have access to the student's IEP.
3. Copies of each instructional program for each task the student will undertake are included. These may either be scheduled in terms of one program per half hour, as a series of programs in an hour block of time (see Chapter 3 for details), or as needed to fit the specific setting's needs and resources. A data sheet for each program is included in the IPB (see Chapter 7 for details.) For a complete list of contents, see Chapter 3.

Assigning Activities Personnel

One of the first activities to be completed during the first week of a new student's attendance is to schedule and assign the appropriate staff and paraprofessionals. Once needs are established, it is the teacher's responsibility to identify the resources to meet the needs. See Chapter 3 for details on organizing activities, personnel, and paraprofessionals.

Determining a Reinforcement Hierarchy

Another first week activity is to identify effective reinforcers for the new child and categorize them according to their strength, i.e., the strongest and most effective reinforcer will be placed at the top of the hierarchy. McCormack (1977) and Striefel (1974) cite certain procedures that teachers can use to identify probable reinforcers (see Chapter 6). Once selection of potential reinforcers has been determined, the information is entered on the information sheet clipped to the inside front cover of the IPB for each student.

GROUP PROGRAMMING

In most classrooms, it will be necessary to place handicapped children into groups for instruction. This will be the case when the number of children in a classroom is large or when the children served are mildly or moderately handicapped. Instruction of individual children becomes more desirable and/or necessary when children are severely or profoundly handicapped. Often, these children will not make progress unless instruction is provided on an individual basis. Group instruction is less intense because children take turns and, thus, individual children are not continually responding. However, the task for the trainer is more complex because he or she must deal with several children and programs simultaneously.

Other reasons why group programming may be desirable include: a) group members may exhibit increased motivation to participate through observation of others, b) members may learn better because of increased cues and reinforcement (in fact, some children may acquire some skills for which they have received no direct training, c) members may experience an increased incentive for improvement through a desire to be accepted and approved by the group, and d) friendly group competition may increase students' desire to improve. There is also a research base that shows that grouping with simultaneous responses provides increased opportunities to respond.

Children can be grouped for instruction in any area of their IEP. Some areas are more difficult for group work than others. One area in which group work is easily accomplished is speech and language therapy. Speech and language therapy can involve from two to five children in a group according to specific disabilities such as articulation therapy, language therapy, voice therapy, fluency therapy, or according to specific objectives, e.g., children who need therapy in articulation may be grouped for instruction. Verbal and less verbal children may also be grouped together in the same group working on totally different objectives. Additionally, children in language therapy may be grouped according to their level of performance (e.g., all working on a specific language contract, or all at the same expressive stage). An example of the specific benefits of group programming is the opportunity afforded to children in fluency therapy to use fluent speech in a group setting to build confidence and improve self-esteem.

Group sessions should probably be 20 to 45 minutes in length on a daily basis if consistent progress is to be achieved. Group language sessions can be conducted in individual speech therapy rooms or in the classroom with each small group sectioned off into a particular part of the room. Screens may be used to eliminate distractions. Data are kept on each child in the group as they would be in individual therapy.

Group programming may also involve an entire class. A functional language stimulation program may be implemented so that all class members are given a general stimulation exercise (e.g., increase single word vocabulary, increase sentence length, use "is verbing," increase vocalizations, and use gestural speech). In addition to grouping students according to type of problem, other factors to be considered include age and ability to learn (level of functioning).

Incidental Teaching

Incidental teaching consists of taking advantage of natural opportunities during the day to teach specific skills that are appropriate for that time and in that situation, e.g., teaching greeting responses and self-help skills (taking off coat and hanging it up) when children first arrive in the morning. By doing an analysis of the regular activities that occur each day, a chart can be made of the skills that are appropriate in each of these activities. These skills can then be taught within the context of the ongoing activities throughout the day. Appropriate use of cues, data sheets (ready and taped to wall where activity occurs), and reinforcement of correct responses are an integral part of incidental teaching procedures. Incidental teaching should take full advantage of functionality and should enhance the probability of generalization across people, situations, and maintenance over time.

SUMMARY

This chapter has provided information on the importance of having a specific philosophy for developing, selecting, or using curricula. Instructional methodology plays an important role in the selection and use of different curriculum materials. Guidelines were provided for selecting and developing materials and for using curriculum procedures and forms in the classroom. Each teacher should be familiar with procedures for developing curriculum materials since commercially available materials are still scarce in some skill areas.

9

Paraprofessionals:
Training
and Use

After reading this chapter, you should have an understanding of:

1. The distinction between and different types of paraprofessionals
2. The importance of paraprofessionals within the special education setting
3. The coordination of a volunteer program
4. The process of recruiting, orienting, training, and evaluating paraprofessionals effectively, including the role of the teacher in the process of implementing a paraprofessional system, the process of matching paraprofessionals and tasks to be accomplished, and the importance of feedback and communication
5. Methods for avoiding potential problems
6. The responsibilities and competencies of paraprofessionals

AS A RESULT OF RISING COSTS and the need for individualized programs, every comprehensive special education program must carefully plan and implement a paraprofessional involvement program. The many contributions that paraprofessionals can make to a program are examined in this chapter.

DEFINITION OF TERMS

The terms "paraprofessional," "volunteer," and "practicum student" have distinct, yet related, meanings. The importance of such distinctions becomes evident in the classroom roles, expectations, and competencies associated with each. These distinctions are examined in the definitions that follow.

Paraprofessional This is a general catch-all term. The term "para" implies a person who is not strictly a professional (that is, one who is not certified or who might or might not have an educational background in a given competency area such as teaching). The term "professional," on the other hand, implies a person who is trained in the use of certain skills and who is capable of effectively using those skills. When combined, the term "paraprofessional" implies a person whose tasks resemble those of the professional, but with elements that differ (Semrau, LeMay, Tucker, Woods, & Hurtado, 1979). In the classroom setting, an uncertified person who is being or has been trained to do many of the things that a teacher must do is considered a "paraprofessional." Practicum students, volunteers, and aides fall into this category.

Practicum Student This person might have some training in relevant areas, but has not yet finished all the degree requirements or has not yet obtained certification. Generally, a student in special education participates in and completes a practicum sequence, student teaches, and then obtains certification. Students from related disciplines such as psychology or speech pathology may sign up for practica to gain required or desired experience in working with persons with developmental disabilities. Some practicum students enter the classroom with a wealth of skills, while others have no teaching skills upon entrance.

Volunteer This person offers to perform services or duties without pay. Generally, the volunteer is not skilled in areas related to teaching children with handicaps and, thus, must be given much guidance. Since it is usually possible to obtain the services of volunteers, and often possible to have practicum students placed in classrooms, both are discussed in this chapter. The term "paraprofessional" is used when referring simultaneously to both groups of individuals.

Classroom Aides Unlike the volunteer and the practicum student, the classroom aide is paid for performing certain duties and responsibilities in the classroom. The person hired as a classroom aide should have a prior work record or references to prove that he or she is able to get along easily with others, has good verbal communication skills, and cares about, enjoys and has a positive attitude about him- or herself and others. Desired traits would include experience with persons with handicaps, previous teaching experience of some sort, and knowledge of or demonstrated application of behavior management techniques.

IMPORTANCE OF PARAPROFESSIONALS

The importance of using paraprofessionals in the classroom was enhanced by PL 94-142's guarantee of a quality educational program for each student

(Semrau et al., 1979). The need for the paraprofessional is largely dictated by the population of children with which the teacher is working. In elementary and secondary education classrooms, it is possible to maintain a very high ratio of students to teachers (e.g., 25 to 30 children to one teacher). Special education classrooms, however, require a much lower student/teacher ratio because of the existing handicapping conditions of the students and the need for individualized programs as mandated in PL 94-142. Characteristically, classes are smaller and more specialized and staff members are hired on a per pupil basis. The severity of a child's handicap also dictates lower staff/pupil ratios. With older and higher functioning handicapped students, it is usually not difficult to provide individualized programs. Commercially marketed programs and materials are usually available and geared for higher level children, allowing the student some autonomy in terms of pacing, self-correction, and self-monitoring (Fredericks et al., 1975). With more severely handicapped children, however, individual programming requires not only structuring materials but also providing one-to-one training. As such, using paraprofessionals is almost mandatory (Fredericks, Grove, Baldwin, & Moore, 1975).

The need for paraprofessionals in the classroom is no small matter. Between 1976 and 1979, the number of paraprofessionals employed by local education agencies increased by 42% (Pickett, 1979). Logic dictates and data confirm (Fredericks et al., 1976) that the more time spent directly instructing a child, the more that child will learn. In fact, the ability to maximize instructional time is considered to be one of the most important management abilities a teacher of handicapped students should have (Fredericks et al., 1977). The realities of a classroom, however, limit instructional time to varying degrees. For example, if a classroom has one teacher and six children with severe handicaps, all of whom need one-to-one instruction and assistance throughout the day, it is extremely difficult for that teacher to effect many changes in these students' behavior. Although group instruction may be utilized for part of the day, the teacher will not be able to devote much time to individual instruction. Thus, paraprofessionals or paid aides are needed to maximize individual instruction time. Paraprofessionals are also often needed when children are "mainstreamed" to assist in the smooth transition from special education to the regular classroom. Frith and Kelly (1981) discuss using paraprofessionals to work with parents.

Paraprofessionals offer a needed service without which many special education classrooms could not and do not meet the mandates of PL 94-142. Paraprofessionals may have unique and necessary skills to offer and/or teach to staff and/or students. Volunteers must feel welcome, needed, and attain personal reinforcement for their efforts (Sciarra & Dorsey, 1979). When teachers are cognizant of all of these possibilities, they are able to shape the paraprofessionals working in their classroom.

COORDINATION OF A VOLUNTEER PROGRAM

The special education teacher has numerous duties. One of the most difficult involves becoming a logistics expert for students, volunteers, classroom aides, and special service personnel. Juggling schedules for service providers and service recipients to ensure the efficient flow of services is one of the teacher's most important responsibilities. To plan for an instructional system in which paraprofessionals might be used efficiently and effectively is also important. Generally, the volunteer program is managed by an administrator such as the director of special education, but if the number of volunteers is small, a teacher may be responsible for his or her own volunteer program. Some large programs have a volunteer coordinator who may well be a member of the staff with other primary duties. The person responsible for coordinating volunteer and/or paraprofessional activities will have several responsibilities: a) recruiting, b) orientation, c) training, and d) evaluation.

RECRUITING PARAPROFESSIONALS

Recruiting is the act of enlisting new members into an already existent social or instructional structure, in this case, the classroom. The first steps in recruiting paraprofessionals are to: a) recognize the importance of paraprofessionals, b) identify sources of paraprofessionals, and c) become aware of specific re-cruiting considerations. The importance of paraprofessionals has already been discussed.

Sources of Paraprofessionals

Paraprofessionals come from many sources. One of the most important "beginning-of-the-year" tasks for any teacher or volunteer coordinator is to identify potential sources of volunteers in the local community. Some potential sources are listed below.

Unpaid positions
1. *Parents* of the children, especially those of children in "special classes," show a willingness to help in the classroom.
2. *High school volunteers,* especially seniors, are often able to obtain release time from their traditional classes if they are able to find structured volunteer or job placement opportunities.
3. *University and college students* are often interested in volunteer work— especially those who are already in or are considering the fields of special education, psychology or other related fields.
4. *Senior citizens,* also known as retirees, often find themselves with a large amount of time on their hands and therefore become interested in activities they have never had time for previously—volunteer work for instance.

5. *Community service organizations and religious groups* often offer a wide age and skill-range of volunteers. Church groups such as women's circles or youth groups, local community service and fraternal organizations such as the Scouts and Elks, Rotary, Kiwanis, and Jaycees often sponsor weekly or monthly meetings, and might be quite interested in listening to a talk concerning a specific classroom or program, thereby encouraging volunteer participation. These same groups often select an annual service project for their membership.

6. *University and college education students in accredited practicum programs* almost always must be placed in a classroom one or more times if they are to obtain the practical experience requisite to graduation and/or certification. The appropriate individuals in college departments can be contacted regarding the availability of a classroom as a placement site and might prove to be a very valuable source of paraprofessionals. Usually, objectives and criteria are established by the individual departments. Checking the criteria to determine if department goals agree with classroom needs is important (examples of objectives and performance criteria for practicum students are discussed later in this chapter).

Paid positions

1. *Job service,* or the local employment security office, can assist in advertising for and prescreening candidates.

2. *Campus personnel offices* also assist in locating prospective candidates with related background experience for paraprofessional positions.

3. *School district personnel offices* often keep a file of prospective candidates for teaching positions or other persons interested in school-related work.

4. *Community action agencies* can often provide referrals of persons who may be interested in working with children, but lack training or advanced education.

5. *Community colleges and technical institutes* often have students who are bright and ambitious and are interested in daytime jobs so they can still pursue their training at night.

6. *Displaced homemaker programs* are interested in finding employment for women who are leaving their homes and entering the job market.

Advertising for either paid or unpaid paraprofessional positions is an effective recruiting method. The key is to widely advertise the position by using public service announcements on radio and television, classified ads in newspapers, and posters in public buildings or facilities that experience heavy traffic, e.g., doctor's office or grocery store. A written advertisement should provide a potential candidate with enough information to make an initial decision as to interest. One that is vaguely worded will result in wasted time for the applicant and the school or agency (Semrau et al., 1979).

Recruiting Considerations

Program needs and priorities must be considered before the actual recruiting of the paraprofessional takes place. Consideration of topics such as the following prior to the recruitment process is essential:

1. How much time will the commitment entail? What is the minimum number of work hours needed to make the paraprofessional's presence effective and to balance the teacher input of time and training? What is the maximum number of hours the paraprofessional can work? Will the schedule vary during the course of the year?
2. Is transportation to and from the school necessary and/or readily available? Is monetary compensation available for the paraprofessional's travel time and/or expenses? If not, is the unpaid paraprofessional still willing to work?
3. Would any type of technical, craft, or vocational skill that the paraprofessional possesses enhance the existing program?
4. Should sex distinctions be made? Is the presence of a male or female important for modeling, program, or pragmatic reasons? Is a father, mother, big brother, or big sister image an important aspect of the program?

Interviewing the Paraprofessional

The interview is the next step in the recruitment process and should be relaxed and long enough for the interviewer to gain a substantial amount of information about the prospective paraprofessional. Observations and information gained during the interview are often the most accurate predictors of later success according to Semrau et al. (1979). The following observations and questions suggested by Semrau et al. (1979, p. 20) should be noted after a prospective candidate is interviewed:

1. Was the applicant punctual for the interview?
2. Was the applicant neatly groomed?
3. Was the applicant enthusiastic about the job?
4. Was the applicant reasonably relaxed and comfortable?
5. Did the applicant answer forthrightly?
6. Did the applicant indicate a desire for self-improvement?
7. Did the applicant appear to be confident in his or her own abilities?
8. Has the applicant engaged in any extracurricular activities (sewing, cooking, volunteering, etc.)?
9. Did the applicant appear to be reflecting before answering questions?
10. Has the applicant been in situations where teamwork was necessary?
11. Did the applicant seem comfortable in discussions about handicapped people?
12. Has the applicant had any contact with people with handicaps?
13. Did the applicant discuss handicaped children with objectivity and without patronizing them?
14. Does the applicant have a history of successful employment?

15. Are there home factors which might require special attention of the school?
16. Did the applicant indicate a general attitude of respect for education?

ORIENTING PARAPROFESSIONALS

Orientation should occur prior to training or any direct interaction between paraprofessionals and children. Orientation information should be presented verbally so that the paraprofessional can interact with the trainer and ask questions (Semrau et al., 1979). However, rules and regulations, staff directory information, overall goals and objectives of the program, administrative record keeping requirements, and miscellaneous information such as whom to contact when one is absent should all be presented in written form. Discussing responsibilities, scheduling observation sessions, determining interaction rules, and scheduling duties and assigning them to the paraprofessional are all useful inclusions of an orientation for new paraprofessionals.

The teacher and paraprofessional have frequently been described as an instructional team (Greer, 1978). In order to be effective as a team, it is necessary to define the different levels of responsibility in the classroom. Semrau et al. (1979) suggest the following outline of responsibilities be used for orienting the paraprofessional to his or her role in the special education classroom.

Classroom Organization The paraprofessional performs housekeeping tasks to keep the room organized, and implements plans as specified by the teacher or specialist.

Assessment A second responsibility of the paraprofessional is assisting with monitoring and scoring.

Setting of Objectives The paraprofessional implements lessons to meet a child's instructional objectives.

Teaching Another duty of the paraprofessional is to teach small groups and individual lessons.

Behavior Management The paraprofessional also implements the behavioral management strategies using the same emphasis and techniques as the teacher or specialist.

Working with Parents The paraprofessional may also meet with parents, but only under the direction of the teacher or specialist.

Individualized Educational Planning A final role of the paraprofessional is to carry out the teacher's plans for the client.

Inter-related responsibilities should be discussed. If the paraprofessional is donating his or her time and skills, it is of utmost importance that use of this donated effort is neither sporadic nor indiscriminate. All paraprofessionals, paid or unpaid, must feel welcome in the classroom and should leave with a feeling of satisfaction that their services are needed and appreciated; otherwise, they may not return. Concurrently, the paraprofessional is responsible for working his or her committed hours and being prompt, consistent, and productive. More specific responsibilities such as toileting, record keeping procedures, and supervision procedures should be communicated verbally, by handouts, and by demonstration as needed. It may also be a wise procedure to have the paraprofessional sign a "contract" stating that he or she has read the regulations and guidelines and agrees to abide by these rules. This ensures that all paraprofessionals have read the information used every day in the classroom.

Observation

During orientation, providing time for the paraprofessional to meet the children and, if possible, to observe the classroom for a few hours will pay off in terms of a clear understanding of services to be provided. This should be carried out before final commitments are made between the paraprofessional and the program. In some cases, a practicum student's or volunteer's initial impressions of wanting to do volunteer work with children with handicaps may change when he or she is exposed to the actual children and handicapping conditions. It is more beneficial to all concerned if such a determination can be made before a potential paraprofessional begins to work with the children.

Determining Interaction Roles

Determining interaction roles essentially means determining who is responsible for what. The program supervisor, usually the principal or special education director, ultimately has the authority over and responsibility for the paraprofessional and what he or she does or does not do. Quite often, though, such contact is minimal. The more immediate supervisor is usually the teacher directly involved with the paraprofessional. Practicum student supervision is usually a responsibility shared by both the teacher (usually termed the cooperating teacher) and the practicum supervisor. Whereas the program supervisor maintains overall leadership and responsibility, the volunteer supervisor, cooperating teacher, and practicum supervisor have the immediate responsibility of orienting, training, and evaluating the paraprofessional. The volunteer or practicum student will usually maintain a set role in the classroom. It is important that lines of communication and patterns of responsibility are established from the onset and maintained consistently throughout the paraprofessional's tour of duty.

Boomer (1980) outlines the role of the paraprofessional in the instructional process in the following specific areas:

1. The paraprofessional helps the teacher develop a more complete and accurate assessment of the child through assessment and observation. The paraprofessional is thus able to help the teacher or therapist clearly identify the skills the child needs.

2. The paraprofessional can assist the teacher or therapist design and implement a consistent educational strategy to help the child function independently across settings.
3. The mere presence of a paraprofessional provides alternate service delivery patterns in a less restrictive environment.
4. The paraprofessional can offer support (with the teacher or therapist) to the total school program.
5. The paraprofessional can help the teacher or therapist involve the parents in the program.

Scheduling and Assigning Duties

Once the decision is made that the paraprofessional will work in a certain classroom, and the roles and responsibilities of both teacher and paraprofessional are clearly defined, duties should be discussed and tasks negotiated. The duties of the paraprofessional working in the classroom in either a paid or unpaid position include:

1. Assisting staff in the preparation and implementation of instructional treatment programs and activities
2. Aiding in the collection, monitoring, graphing, and analyzing of data on student performance
3. Assisting in monitoring and maintaining classroom supplies
4. Assisting in maintenance and enhancement of the classroom's physical environment
5. Attending to the student's physical needs
6. Facilitating communication between the parent and the school
7. Assisting in monitoring student attendance and records
8. Supervising student activities
9. Providing program support to the teacher and other professional staff (e.g., helping on field trips, photocopying, or making classroom materials, or supervising playground activities)

Most paraprofessionals work best if they are responsible for a few activities to be conducted consistently on a daily or weekly basis. Practicum students can be trained in any of the above skills, but due to the nature of practicum requirements, often must be responsible for more instructional-type activities.

TRAINING PARAPROFESSIONALS

A major factor in training a paraprofessional is letting that person know early in his or her tour of duty those skills that he or she is responsible for learning. This process can be facilitated by outlining general guidelines. Usually, a typewritten list of such information can be distributed to the paraprofessional during either the orientation or initial training meetings to help the paraprofessional adapt to the classroom very quickly. This list also contains a statement that the volunteer should sign to indicate he or she has read the guidelines and agrees to abide by them. Since many classroom skills such as observing, data recording, and especially teaching, demand some type of specialized knowledge or skill, the training of the paraprofessional becomes a necessity. General guidelines for training must be established and observed:

1. Adequate time must be taken to train paraprofessionals.
2. Paraprofessionals must be given teaching tasks in the classroom comparable to their level of training.
3. A system of feedback as to the adequacy of the paraprofessional's performance must exist.
4. A simplified system of communication, not necessarily requiring verbal interaction between the teacher and the paraprofessional, must exist.
5. A system of flexible scheduling of paraprofessionals must be maintained (Fredericks, Grove, Baldwin, & Moore, 1975).

General Guidelines

To help ensure the effectiveness of the paraprofessional, as well as the continuing smooth operation of the classroom, identification of various activities that the paraprofessional can adequately carry out should be completed as soon as possible. It is discouraging for a paraprofessional to find out that he or she is just babysitting the students for want of something more constructive to do. Second, the paraprofessional should be given tasks that are not routinely boring, but not beyond his or her capabilities either.

Time must be taken to train paraprofessionals. Fredericks et al. (1977) outline several skills necessary to teach handicapped children. Few paraprofessionals enter a classroom with these skills. Since time is limited, concise training procedures that are simple and quick are a necessity. Although the paraprofessional will continue to learn new information and skills during the course of his or her stay, the first 2 weeks are of utmost importance. Aside from the orientation in which basic information is given to the paraprofessional, this time is considered to be the optimal training period during which the paraprofessional has teaching skills modeled and has an opportunity to try out these skills. The basics of many of these skills can be taught in a seminar-type meeting. This is perhaps the most effective and time-efficient technique for the teacher when dealing with five or more paraprofessionals at a time.

The initial training session should consist of a brief review of instructional theory, a review of some of the types of programs and data forms used in the classroom, and a demonstration of how to teach basic skills to children in the classroom setting using a form similar to the curriculum program format sheet (see Chapter 8). This seminar should be considered just the beginning of the training process, since actual practice, observations by the supervisor of the paraprofessional, and feedback that the teacher gives to the paraprofessional are probably the most important part of the training (Fredericks, Grove, Baldwin, & Moore, 1975).

During the initial training session, the following instructional skills and points should be modeled and/or stressed:

1. The role of the paraprofessional
2. The correct use of terminology
3. The appropriate use of physical and/or verbal cues
4. The correct use of reinforcement procedures
5. An overview of the Individual Program Book or IPB (see Chapter 8 for details on the IPB)
6. An overview of the design of and how to use the curriculum format sheets (see Chapter 8)
7. The design and use of the program's data sheets and data collection system (see Chapter 7)
8. The correct way to deal with problems and inappropriate behaviors (see Chapter 6)

The demonstration part of the presentation should consist of: a) the use of transparencies when discussing the curriculum program and data sheets, and b) the use of either role-playing, videotapes, and/or slides to demonstrate how to conduct a lesson (also referred to as a presentation or tutorial). Of the last three demonstrations (role-playing, videotapes, and slides), the use of videotapes is considered to be the most efficient form of demonstration (Fredericks, Grove, Baldwin, & Moore, 1975). Videotapes, because they are visual, also have the most impact on volunteers and practicum students who have had little or no instructional contact with handicapped students. Specific procedures on how to conduct teaching sessions are presented in Chapter 8; thus, they are only briefly summarized here.

A step-by-step breakdown of a teaching presentation follows: 1) Find needed materials. 2) Prepare cubicle or work area *before* getting child. 3) Give the appropriate cue just *before* showing the student how to carry out the expected behavior. 4) Test the student on the task or objective. 5a) Reinforce the student for giving a correct response, or 5b) correct the child when she or he has given an incorrect response. 6) Record the response on the correct data sheet.

While conducting the presentation, the trainer will be taking individual response data on the appropriate data sheet (show transparencies of the commonly used data sheets, see Chapter 7). These sheets allow the trainer to record and compare daily performance. The trainer then demonstrates on an overhead transparency of a sample data sheet the information that needs to be entered on the sheet, and how data are collected. The frequency and specificity of the data recording procedure are left to the discretion of the teacher. While the paraprofessional is learning how to record data, it is best if the data are collected *every day*.

Also discussed during this initial training session are procedures such as the following:

1. *Modifying a cue so it is appropriate to the sensory deficits that some children with handicaps possess.* For example, one would not use only a verbal cue with a deaf child. A combination of verbal cues (say ''the'') and physical cues (say the command in sign language) are recommended.
2. *Being consistent with cues.* The trainer should use *only* the *exact* wording stated in the ''What you say'' column of the program format sheet. If the nonverbal cue is unclear, the paraprofessional should ask the trainer for clarification. A cue should never be repeated until a correct or incorrect response is made or the repetition procedure is used and the child is helped through the task (otherwise the child may be taught to ignore verbal requests). Also, paraprofessionals must be taught to speak clearly and loudly enough to be heard.
3. *Being consistent in recording data.* Data collection should be conducted exactly as outlined by the specific instructions for the data sheets in Chapter 7.

During the initial training session, it is important to discuss reinforcement in terms of consequences. It is *not* suggested that the leader of the training session delve into topics such as reinforcement schedules, negative reinforcement, or punishment. Instead, the discussion of consequences should be limited to the general case. Feedback immediately following a behavior that increases, decreases, or does not affect a behavior's occurrence is known as a consequence. A consequence that increases the strength of a behavior is a *positive reinforcer* (i.e., praises such as ''Good talking,'' or ''Nice job,'' candy, juice, etc.). These examples might or might not be functional with a particular child. A consequence that decreases the strength of a behavior is known as punishment, i.e., reprimands such as ''No, that is not right,'' or leading the child through the task. A consequence, even one that has increased or decreased a behavior in the past, might (under some circumstances) have no effect on the behavior it follows. It is neutral.

Discussing general rules for delivering consequences such as the following is also helpful.

1. Every time a cue is presented, the child is expected to respond in some prescribed manner, and *immediate* feedback must be given to the child to let him or her know if the response is correct or incorrect.
2. Each *correct response* to the presented cue should result in a consequence such as the following:

    a.   Delivery of a reinforcer of the type chosen from the child's conse-
quence or reinforcer file

    b.   Delivery of verbal praise to fill the time that elapses between when a
correct response is made and when the trainer delivers a tangible
reinforcer, e.g., juice, treats (Before dispensing edible reinforcers,
paraprofessionals should check with the teacher.)

    c.   Delivery of reinforcement *immediately* after a child responds cor-
rectly, within 1 second or less after a behavior occurs

    d.   Delivery of any type of communication necessary to reinforce the
child, e.g., hugging, kissing, tickling, singing

3.   If a child does not respond or responds *incorrectly,* the correction procedure should be used *exactly* as listed on the program format sheet (see
Chapter 8).

It is estimated that the initial training session will last about 1 1/2–2 hours.
Ongoing training should take place through daily trainer-learner contacts in the
classroom. These training sessions are closely allied with the periodic evaluation of the paraprofessional and are discussed later in this chapter.

Sophistication of Teaching Tasks

Many of the paraprofessionals who enter the classroom will have a variety of
skills. Skill level is one of the most important factors to consider when
assigning tasks to a paraprofessional. In many cases, practicum requirements
will dictate what is or should be assigned to a practicum student (e.g.,
mathematics, reading, or language). Volunteers, on the other hand, have no
such requirements. Paraprofessionals must be given teaching tasks in the
classroom that are comparable to their levels of ability and to the teacher's level
of training (Fredericks, Grove, Baldwin, & Moore, 1975). This can be
accomplished by: a) assigning one general curriculum area in which the
objectives are similar to each other—motor skills, homeliving skills, self-help
skills, or pre-academic skills, b) assigning a variety of programs that are similar
to one another because they might all be written on one format, e.g., the
program format (note Figure 8.3), or c) assigning a variety of programs that are
part of a predetermined program sequence and that have the same data-
recording characteristics. In many cases, the new paraprofessional may be
required to move from child to child using one or two programs, e.g., the
paraprofessional may be assigned to teach hand and face washing and toothbrushing individually to three or four children immediately after lunch. In other
cases, the paraprofessional may be required to work with only one child, but
across a variety of programs. Such may be the case in teaching homeliving
skills. Once the child has successfully terminated a program, the paraprofessional is placed on a new program or with a new child. As a general rule,

a paraprofessional should not be kept on one programmed objective with one child for an extended period of time, especially if the child is not making progress. Paraprofessionals are human, too, and they get just as bored with repetition as teachers do—especially when improvement in the student's work is not immediately apparent, which is often the case with severely handicapped students.

Evaluation As a System of Feedback and Communication

The performance of paraprofessionals will not magically improve overnight. They must be observed and helped regularly. The degree of assistance needed will depend on the individual involved. It is very important that the paraprofessional be observed and given specific feedback during his or her first few days in the classroom. During that time, many interaction behaviors are being established, reinforced, and conditioned into the paraprofessional's instructional repertoire. Unfortunately, this might include undesirable behaviors (e.g., reinforcing inappropriate behaviors, delivering erroneous cues, being inadequately prepared, or being inconsistent in data recording). Without regular feedback on what is being done correctly and what is being done incorrectly, the best of paraprofessionals tend to "loosen up" and become imprecise and sloppy (Fredericks, Grove, Baldwin, & Moore, 1975).

Observations should be conducted at least twice weekly, not necessarily on a predetermined schedule. The paraprofessional should receive more help during the initial weeks of training and less help after a period of weeks, assuming, of course, that no major management and/or instructional problems exist. The purpose of observation is: a) to determine at what instructional level the paraprofessional is presently functioning, b) to determine what, if any, problems are arising, and most importantly c) *to provide both corrective and positive feedback.* In this structured situation, the teacher is able to communicate how well the paraprofessional is doing. This point cannot be stressed enough. The teacher must reinforce critical instructional behaviors such as delivering appropriate cues and keeping accurate and consistent data. On the other hand, the teacher must change those paraprofessional behaviors that are inappropriate for the classroom (e.g., delivering inappropriate cues, keeping inaccurate data, and reinforcing undesirable behavior).

In providing feedback, there are two sequential strategies to be employed. The first is to establish a baseline observation. The second is to reinforce or correct desirable/undesirable instructional behaviors on the part of the paraprofessional. The purpose of conducting a baseline observation is to determine the skill level of the paraprofessional to determine weaknesses or strengths in areas such as cue delivery, consistency of presentation, and reinforcement procedures. What strengths can be identified and reinforced? What weaknesses can be identified and corrected? Generally, when conducting a baseline observation, these procedures will be useful:

1. Information is collected for a complete session (a videotape of the session is useful if it can be obtained unobtrusively), and at the end of the session, feedback is given to the paraprofessional. The positive as well as the negative points are stressed.

2. Areas that need work are targeted for the paraprofessional. These are specified in very precise language to be easily understood by the paraprofessional (e.g., "Over the next few days, I would like you to increase the number of times that you reinforce and let Johnny know he is correct").

3. If a variety of problems exist, no attempt is made to correct them all at once. The paraprofessional is informed that they exist and that he or she will have time to get all the "bugs out of the system." One or two of the most serious problems are to be targeted for extra work.

4. The paraprofessional is informed that overnight miracles are not expected, but that a certain problem is to be worked on and corrected within a certain number of days. It is useful to try to get the paraprofessional to relax, even though he or she might not be performing all tasks successfully initially. Setting time lines for behavior change in the paraprofessional is recommended.

After the baseline observation is conducted, the training observations are initiated. Many of the observation and feedback procedures are the same across conditions. The major difference between the two types of observations is that in the training observation, corrective feedback is given immediately during a session. Generally, when conducting a training observation these procedures are followed:

1. Corrective feedback is delivered immediately after an erroneous instructional procedure is exhibited. Feedback can be verbal, though quite often modeling the correct way (teacher working with child) is more efficient. The paraprofessional is first informed about what is incorrect. ("You are not delivering the correct cue." "Don't forget to reinforce the child after every correct response.") If the error is not corrected and is repeated, the correct procedure is modeled again. Next, the paraprofessional tries the procedure slowly, and if correct, the next trial is conducted. Feedback on what the paraprofessional is doing correctly should also be given so that the paraprofessional does not end up feeling that he or she is not doing anything correctly. A goal to strive for is to give four positive comments for each negative comment during instruction.

2. If the correction and modeling procedures do not seem to work for a specific paraprofessional's problem, the environmental conditions can be changed. In such cases, it may be helpful to work with the paraprofessional by role-playing the procedure after the instructional situation has been completed. This is accomplished by setting up an artificial instructional situation in which the teacher plays the part of the child and the para-

professional is the tutor. The instructional procedure is recycled slowly with the paraprofessional receiving verbal feedback as the role-playing proceeds. Modeling is used as needed.

3. If possible, a videotape recorder should be used to provide the paraprofessional with observational feedback (Fredericks, Grove, Baldwin, & Moore, 1975). The paraprofessional will often be able to see his or her mistakes and inconsistencies that occur unnoticed during the instructional situation. Vidcotapcd teacher-conducted sessions also provide good models for the paraprofessional.

4. It is recommended that the teacher be aware of what areas need work, and that he or she follow the procedures outlined in items 2 and 3 as previously mentioned under baseline observation techniques.

5. The teacher should be positive during the observation. Feedback should be provided for both correct and incorrect behavior.

6. As in the baseline condition, it is important to. try to get the paraprofessional to relax even though he or she might not yet be an effective teacher. Goal dates for behavior change in the paraprofessional should be set and discussed with the paraprofessional. A nervous or upset paraprofessional will not do well, but a paraprofessional without feedback and concrete goals might never know when to carry out specific activities or that an activity should have been carried out in the first place.

7. The use of nonthreatening terms such as "weak area" or "something to work on" is recommended. It is helpful to avoid using terms such as "wrong," "bad," "poor procedure," or "terrible" to describe paraprofessional performance. These terms will be nonproductive and may be extremely discouraging for the paraprofessional.

8. It is essential that the paraprofessional be informed of performance areas that have to be worked on and improved, and that praise and positive comments will be forthcoming. The paraprofessional should be aware that the teacher has been monitoring his or her improvements and that the teacher approves.

9. Ultimately, the teacher has the option of terminating a paraprofessional for poor, nonimproving performance. It is suggested that the paraprofessional be given the benefit of the doubt as well as a second chance before such drastic measures are taken. Everyone has "off days."

Communications Program Information

Occasionally, the teacher might want to communicate a procedural modification of a program to the paraprofessional or the paraprofessional might have to communicate a problem to the teacher, but cannot because the teacher might be busy working with other paraprofessionals or teaching children. To avoid such a problem, a message board or other communication procedure should be prearranged. For example, specific comments could be written on the back side of the data sheets for the specific program. Since data sheets are individualized for each program being taught and included in each student's Individual Program Book, a daily check of these areas by the teacher and paraprofessional provides easy communication of a message such as "See me at, , ," or "I need help." (For further details on the classroom communications system, note Chapter 3). For communication to be effective, time must be taken to train the paraprofessionals in the use of the communication system.

Flexible Scheduling

Three approaches for scheduling paraprofessionals follow. In the first, a child is paired with a paraprofessional who conducts all of that child's programs. In the second, a paraprofessional conducts programs in one curriculum area and only teaches children in that curriculum area. In the third approach, scheduling consists of a combination of the first two approaches (Fredericks, Grove, Baldwin, & Moore, 1975). In essence, the paraprofessional works with more than one child in more than one curriculum area. Regardless of what scheduling system is used, the paraprofessional needs to know the following: a) how much time to spend on a program with a child, b) how often to run the program—daily or weekly, c) when to notify the teacher that a program will soon be terminated because of completion, and d) when to terminate an old program and initiate a new teacher-assigned program.

The amount of daily input in minutes per program may vary. For some children it is necessary to conduct a program for several short time periods with breaks in between, e.g., a 10-minute program, followed by a 2- to 3-minute reinforcer break, continuing with or changing to another program, working for 10 minutes, and then taking another 2- to 3-minute reinforcer break. Other children can work for a complete half hour without breaks. The length of the training session needs to be adjusted to individual children and the situation. In all cases, the paraprofessional should be expected to instruct a child or children for 80%–85% of each half hour, i.e., 25 minutes. The teacher should inform the paraprofessional of the schedule that works best with the children with whom he or she will be working. Part of the periodic observations consists of evaluating whether or not the paraprofessional is actually instructing up to the time criteria of 80%–85%. In order for the paraprofessional to achieve this teaching efficiency, the teacher must eliminate all competing assignments for the paraprofessional during time periods designated for teaching.

How often to conduct a program is another item of information that needs to be communicated to the paraprofessional. As a general rule of thumb, each program should be carried out daily with the following exceptions: a) when a certain therapy-based program has been scheduled on a staggered schedule, such as Tuesday-Thursday, or Monday-Wednesday-Friday, b) when a certain curriculum area might have more objectives in it than can be realistically taught in only 1 day (running more homeliving programs 3 days per week instead of fewer homeliving programs 5 days per week), or c) when certain activities such as swimming or field trips are scheduled in place of a regular instructional program. The frequency of conducting a program should be determined by the teacher, and should definitely be communicated to the paraprofessional as soon as he or she starts working on that program. Generally, scheduling is planned prior to the introduction of paraprofessionals to the classroom situation (note Chapter 3 for scheduling procedures).

The paraprofessional must be taught how to determine when a program should be terminated. This entails an understanding of the program. By considering the following questions, the paraprofessional will be able to decide when a program is ready to be terminated.

1. What criteria are established for passing on to the next step?
2. How fast (i.e., how many steps per day or per week) is the student presently passing from step to step?
3. How many steps are left in the program that the child has yet to complete?
4. How many more days should the program be conducted before it will be completed? In other words, if the student is currently completing two steps per week, but has six steps left to complete, we can anticipate that he or she will complete that program in roughly 3 more weeks.

When working on a child's program, it is the paraprofessional's responsibility to notify the teacher of an impending program completion approximately 3 to 5 days before the child actually will finish the program. The teacher should be aware of this if he or she is using precise and accurate data collection techniques. Sometimes, a teacher needs a reminder so planning can occur in terms of a new program being assigned and reviewed and materials bought or made by the paraprofessional. With one week's notice, it should be possible to prepare a new program and materials without unnecessary gaps in the child's completion of the programming schedule.

AVOIDING POTENTIAL PROBLEMS

Following are some procedural suggestions for avoiding potential problems. Avoiding potential problems is always easier than solving existing ones.

1. If a volunteer or paraprofessional program is viewed as being automatically deficient because it is merely a ''para'' professional program, then that program is bound to fail. Efforts must be made to make the program an integral part of the overall educational program, thereby giving it some status.
2. Assigning too little or too much responsibility, or assigning it all at once, will have adverse effects on the paraprofessional, the teacher, the program, and ultimately, the students. It is necessary to assign a practical amount of responsibility that can be carried out in the allotted time. This

may require adjustment by adding or deleting activities from the paraprofessional's work load.

3. It is necessary to avoid monotonous and routinely unvarying assignments. A bored paraprofessional is a nonproductive paraprofessional. Assigning the same children, duties, and/or responsibilities restricts the volunteer and reduces his or her potential effectiveness and motivation, especially if he or she is capable of taking on new tasks.

4. Paraprofessional outcomes often equal program outcomes. Insufficient training procedures or inappropriate placement will have direct results on the program. It is essential to provide needed training and appropriate placement.

5. A lack of communication often results in impaired performance of both paraprofessionals and teachers. For this reason, weekly mandatory meetings are suggested, *whether it is thought they are needed or not.* If problems to discuss cannot be found, then the meeting can be used for planning and/or feedback.

6. Failure to provide sufficient reinforcement for paraprofessionals will result in lowered work performance.

PARAPROFESSIONAL RESPONSIBILITIES AND COMPETENCIES

Much has been said in this chapter about various paraprofessional responsibilities and competencies that usually vary with the sophistication level of the paraprofessional. A list of responsibilities and competencies developed by the staff members of both the Utah State University Department of Special Education[1] and the Exceptional Child Center are included herein. *All* paraprofessionals, regardless of whether they are paid employees, volunteers, or practicum students, and regardless of which level practicum they might be taking, are responsible for the following:

1. *Physical environment*
   a. The physical environment must be appropriate for the child (e.g., seats not too small, desks not too high, lighting sufficient, noise level at a minimum).
   b. The physical environment must be appropriate for the lesson (e.g., homeliving skills are taught in the apartment facilities, academic skills are taught in the classroom).
   c. The physical environment should not be distracting. Appropriate measures should be taken to alleviate the source of distraction, using partitions, moving to another cubicle, asking the people in the adja-

[1]The authors would like to thank the following USU faculty for their input and ideas on these criteria and responsibilities: Dr. Carol Beasley and Joni Forsgren-White. Many of the competencies/responsibilities have been excerpted from their class outlines.

       cent cubicle to quiet down, moving a child away from a distracting window, or seating the child so he or she is facing into the cubicle.

    d.   The physical environment should not be too secluded, nor too far away from needed materials and the supervision of the teacher.

2. *Preparation*

    a.   The paraprofessional should have all necessary materials ready for use.

    b.   The instructional setting should be prepared appropriately *prior* to getting the child from the classroom.

    c.   The paraprofessional should be on time and in the classroom early enough to quietly gather materials, prepare a cubicle, get the child from the classroom, seat the child, and start the program on time.

    d.   The paraprofessional should fill out the data sheets appropriately.

    e.   The paraprofessional should return the materials to the appropriate place and clean up the cubicle for the next person.

3. *Use of instructional materials*

    a.   The materials should be appropriate for the lesson.

    b.   The materials should be appropriate for the child.

    c.   The materials should be utilized correctly (that is, in the fashion for which they have been designed).

4. *Appropriate instructional techniques*

    a.   The paraprofessional should use the exact cue as specified.

    b.   The appropriate trial-by-trial data should be taken.

    c.   The paraprofessional's data should be accurate according to observer reliability.

    d.   The paraprofessional should keep the child on task during the work period.

5. *Use of reinforcement and punishment*

    a.   The paraprofessional should reinforce appropriate behaviors/ responses.

    b.   The paraprofessional should correct inappropriate behaviors/ responses.

    c.   Immediate feedback should be given for correct/incorrect responses.

    d.   The reinforcement/punishment technique(s) should be appropriate for the child and approved by the teacher.

6. *Attitude*

    a.   The paraprofessional should be enthusiastic.

    b.   The paraprofessional should be punctual at all times.

    c.   The paraprofessional should speak clearly when interacting with the children.

    d.   The paraprofessional should be relaxed and comfortable with children.

7. *Miscellaneous* The paraprofessional should pull down the sign-in card and/or sign in.

These competencies can be used to evaluate *all* paraprofessionals.

SUMMARY

This chapter has focused on the role of paraprofessionals in educating children and youth with handicaps in accordance with the individual needs of those children. Paraprofessionals are an essential part of special education; thus, school districts must attend to the need for paid and volunteer paraprofessionals. Part of this attention must be focused on recruiting, orienting, training, supervising, and evaluating paraprofessionals. The more planning and training that goes into a paraprofessional program, the more likely it is that the program will be a success. Procedures for implementing a paraprofessional program were covered in detail in the chapter.

10

Parents' Role in the Education of Their Child

After reading this chapter, you should have an understanding of:

1. The meaning of the parenting component
2. Staff responsibilities to parents and their children with handicaps, the rights and responsibilities of parents in the education of their child, and methods for improving communication with parents
3. Determining eligibility for special services, including the process of selecting and implementing home programs
4. The three service approaches
5. Conducting home programs
6. Various parent support and education systems
7. Center-based programs for infants, preschoolers, and school-age children
8. Outpatient visits

THE PROGRESS OF CHILDREN can often be greatly enhanced when parents and special services staff work as partners in serving children. Parent involvement is seen as a critical component for generalization of acquired skills to the community and for the continuing maintenance of those skills. The importance of the parents as team members in the child's education is recognized and stressed throughout current literature on individuals with developmental disabilities (Gray & Klaus, 1970; Karnes & Teska, 1975; Levenstein, 1970; Shearer & Snider, 1978). The reasons for involving parents in the education process include:

227

1. Parents, especially the mother, are the primary teacher for the child during the early years of life (Stile, Cole, & Garner, 1979).
2. If programs are to be successful, there must be consistency in programming between home and school (Marion, 1981).
3. Provision of the necessary and needed services is ensured when parents have a contributing role (Lillie, 1976; Stile et al., 1979).

Four major dimensions are essential in planning parent programs if staff are to provide parents with the information and skills they need to be effective members of the child's education team. These dimensions include emotional support, exchange of information, direct training of parents and families, and program participation (Lillie, 1976).

DEFINITION OF PARENTING COMPONENT

In this chapter, in reference to the educational process, the parent involvement component refers to:

1. The parents' right to be involved in their child's educational process
2. The parents' responsibilities for involvement in their child's education
3. The responsibility of staff members to provide parents with information, a support network, and training and opportunities to exercise these rights and responsibilities

RIGHTS AND RESPONSIBILITIES

Hofmeister (1977) has stated that education is often thought of as a process that occurs in schools, and that educators forget that parents are also teachers. School personnel may debate whether parents should be involved in their child's education, but the reality is that parents inevitably are (Hofmeister, 1977b). Parents are perhaps the most important members of their child's education team. Most parents are interested in what their children are doing and in what they can do to help their children learn. Parent-child contact time is often significantly greater in terms of hours than is student-teacher contact time, and is many times a one-on-one instructional situation. Whereas a child may spend 4–6 hours interacting with adults in the classroom, the same child may spend more than twice that amount of time with his or her parents in the home environment (Allen, 1980; Stile et al., 1979). Enzer (1976) has pointed out that parents who have a positive attitude about their child's skill acquisition will likely see achievements, whereas parents who distrust or are disinterested in skill acquisition foster lack of achievement.

The Education for All Handicapped Children Act (PL 94-142) has given parents the right to be a part of the team that decides what is to be taught to their children. Thus, parents have been placed in a crucial position of both assisting in the decision-making process of a child's program and in its implementation (Cartwright, Cartwright, & Ward, 1981). Research indicates that if parents of children with handicaps are trained to share in the responsibility of teaching skills to children, learning is significantly accelerated (Bronfenbrenner, 1974; Hofmeister, 1977b).

Concern, then, is not with whether or not parents should be involved; they should and will be to the extent they desire. The focus of concern is on: a) how to encourage parents to accept and act on their responsibility for involvement in their child's program, and b) what resources to provide to parents in terms of training, information, materials, and legal guidance to assist them in being effective members of their child's educational team.

Staff Responsibilities

Unfortunately, many parent involvement efforts have been unsuccessful because of the conflicting attitudes of parents and service providers and because of their lack of skill in working with each other. The service provider often displays an attitude of being an "expert" who must impart knowledge to parents, and this may interfere with listening to the parents; thus, parents are "turned off" (Michaelis, 1980; Schultz, 1978). On the other hand, the service provider is often seen by parents as someone who cannot *really* understand what it is like to be the parent of a child who has a handicap. Parents often consider it one thing to be responsible for teaching the child during the school day or during a short home session when one is being paid to do that with no conflicting activities, but quite another to be responsible for the child day after day, year after year (L'Abate, 1976; Minuchin, 1974). In addition, some parents think of their own education as an aversive experience; thus, they have difficulty in viewing their child's education as a positive experience.

There is a strong need for parents to be involved in the direct instruction of their children. It is the responsibility of all staff members to be responsive to the desires and concerns of parents and to teach parents the skills they want and need to teach their own child. In order to accomplish this, a relationship of mutual respect, honesty, and equality must be established between parent and professional partners in contributing to the educational process (Enzer, 1976; Michaelis, 1980). If teachers want parents to run home programs or supplemental activities, they must recognize the responsibility of providing the parent with the information and skills he or she needs to run such programs or conduct such supplemental activities, while simultaneously realizing that parents have many other necessary activities that compete for the same time. Often, with some creative thinking on the part of the professional, the desired program or activities can be easily integrated into necessary home and family activities (e.g., naming body parts while taking a bath). The following list of suggestions to improve communication and cooperation between parents and service providers was developed over several years of working with parents (Cadez, Morgan, Murray, & Porcella, 1979; Striefel, 1980):

1. Parents should be helped to achieve success in initial teaching efforts by being provided with a task on which they can succeed so that they gain confidence.

2. Parents should be encouraged to be innovative because it increases their involvement and their feeling of confidence when they can contribute to the teaching process. Professionals should avoid claiming parents' ideas as their own, but rather give credit where credit is due.

3. Parents should be encouraged to ask questions because it is only by doing so that they can quickly get the information they need. Professionals should exercise care so that they do not impart the feeling that the parent's question was "dumb" or insignificant.

4. Parents should be praised for their efforts because unmotivated parents will soon lose their enthusiasm for working with their child.

5. Parents should be encouraged to express their discouragement so that they can obtain the emotional support they need to continue their teaching efforts. Professionals should also shift activities and find alternate teaching activities for skills that are developing slowly so the parent or trainer does not become bored, discouraged, or disinterested with the activities.

6. Parents should be encouraged to involve the complete family in the home teaching effort because it increases the rate of child progress, provides cohesiveness for the family, and ensures that no family member feels left out.

7. Professionals should be relaxed and friendly with parents and family members so they feel comfortable in their interactions.

8. Professionals should keep conversations brief so learning time is maximized, time is not wasted, and program costs are contained as much as possible.

9. Professionals should be active listeners so they gain the information they need to continue work with the family effectively and successfully.

10. Professionals should be considerate of parents' time by prescheduling visits and being flexible to change if it helps parents feel important and worthwhile.

11. Professionals must maintain confidentiality for legal, ethical, and practical reasons such as continued trust by parents.

12. Professionals should encourage parents of children with handicaps to get together to share ideas and to provide mutual emotional support to help them realize that others face similar problems.

13. Professionals should make parents aware of the legal rights their child has to a free, appropriate education.

14. Providers should refer parents and family members to appropriate agencies or professionals for problems they themselves are unable or untrained to deal with and should also provide families with information on available services so they can locate these services themselves.

15. Providers should exhibit common social courtesies in all their dealings with the child, parents, and other family members because doing so fosters a good working relationship.

Parent Responsibilities

A great deal of attention has been paid to parents' rights and staff responsibilities. Seldom is much attention paid to the parents' *responsibilities* for involvement in their child's education. Along with the emphasis on parents' rights belongs a corresponding emphasis on parent responsibilities. Table 10.1 is by no means an exhaustive list of parent rights/responsibilities; however, it has been designed to touch upon most of the common areas of concern (Striefel, 1980).

DETERMINING ELIGIBILITY FOR SPECIAL SERVICES

The process of getting the parent involved must start as soon as the child is referred for a special service evaluation. The parent participates by arranging for the intake evaluation, showing up for the evaluation, and providing information for the evaluation. Although the initial referral may be made by someone other than the parent, the parent is ultimately responsible for final arrangement of the evaluation. Referrals may be made by any professional, agency, or individual (e.g., physician, parent, grandparent) regarding a child who seems to the referral source to be in need of special services. An intake process, and the parental and family role in this process, is discussed next.

1. A social worker or intake worker contacts the parent for background and historical information, and sets an appointment time that is convenient for the parent and the evaluation team.
2. The coordinator assigned to the case notifies other appropriate in-house staff regarding the scheduled intake, assigns appropriate personnel to the intake team, and then finalizes the arrangements for the intake with the parents.
3. The intake is conducted, the parents are interviewed, and the child's skills are assessed. It is important for all team members to be present during the interview so that parents are not required to repeat background information and answer the same questions twice. A preliminary meeting is held with family members and the intake team to discuss early findings and the steps to be taken next. It may be helpful to make a home visit as part of the process because it can provide valuable information about the child, the family, the home, and interaction patterns that may be useful for placement and program planning (D. Shearer, personal communication, 1982).
4. The intake report is written and copies are submitted to the child's file, the child's parents, and to any other services directly involved (e.g., the referring school district), if appropriate releases have been signed. The

Table 10.1. Parent rights/responsibilities

Parent right	Parent responsibility
The parents have a right to...	The parents are responsible for...
—an appropriate educational placement for the child	—seeing that the child attends this education program on time, on a regular basis
—have an appropriate IEP developed and be involved in its preparation	—being involved: to attend the staffing, raise questions, provide input
—confidentiality	—seeing that forms for release of information are signed and returned promptly
—access to child's records	—giving 24 hours notice regarding the need to review the child's records and arranging to have a qualified staff member with them when reviewing records
—appropriate educational services for the child's particular handicapping condition	—assisting in getting these services delivered to the child and supporting professionals in securing needed services
—observe the child's program in operation	—making appointments with the teacher, showing up for the appointed observation, communicating any concerns with the staff following the observation
—run any other home programs from agencies of their choice that they feel are needed and of benefit to the child, even if they differ with the philosophy of the center	—providing this information to appropriate staff so that staff members are aware of programs that are going on in the home that may affect the child's center program
—information concerning sources for financial assistance, resources for purchase of special equipment, adaptive clothing, etc.	—following through on using the information to obtain needed services or equipment
—the use of appropriate assessment tools in testing the particular child	—reading all test results sent home. If in disagreement, or if lacking information about the test results, the parents are responsible for arranging to discuss concerns with teacher/examiner.
—be regularly informed of child's progress	—being available for phone calls or home visits from appropriate staff to discuss child's progress, for making arrangements to come to the center to discuss progress, or for reading notes sent home by the teacher and responding to them
—be informed as to possible long term prognosis for the child regarding job skills, living arrangements, ability to care for self, etc	—financial and emotional planning for child's future placement in cooperation with appropriate staff members
—be provided with information and training in skills to deal with child on a daily basis at home	—implementing the programs on a consistent basis, and reporting results back to appropriate staff regarding problems or concerns

primary recipients of the report are the parents, and it is of *vital* importance that the terminology and structure of the report can be clearly understood by the parents, enabling them to become effective and informed advocates for their child.

5. If it is determined that the child is in need of special services, a decision is made with the assessment team and the parents concerning the most appropriate and least restrictive setting for meeting those needs.
6. An IEP staffing meeting is then scheduled so that parents and staff can discuss proposed annual goals and objectives.

THREE SERVICE APPROACHES

There are in use today primarily three types of service delivery or some combination thereof. These types of service include center based (school), home based, or outpatient. The type of service delivery is usually dependent on the age of the client and/or his or her disability, and the types of service available in the geographical area where the client resides.

Objectives Common to All Three Service Delivery Approaches

The parenting goals/objectives for all three approaches include the following:

> To provide parents with information about their child's handicap and the prognosis for the future
>
> To help parents prioritize goals and objectives for themselves and their child
>
> To provide parents with information necessary for them to actively participate in the preparation of their child's program objectives and goals
>
> To provide training to parents and other family members in the skills they need to effectively work with their child on a daily basis via explanations, materials, demonstrations, and role playing
>
> To provide parents with methods for keeping objective data for monitoring progress
>
> To provide information and assistance to siblings and other extended family members to better enable them to adjust to the child with handicaps and assist the parents in dealing with the child
>
> To provide opportunities for parents to actively participate in their child's total program—both at home and at school
>
> To provide parents with opportunities to share experiences and ideas with other parents in both formal and informal settings
>
> To provide parents with information and material resources in all areas of concern regarding handicapped individuals, e.g., legal rights, nutrition, medical problems, and equipment needs

To provide training and information to parents to enable them to be advocates for all individuals with handicaps

To provide parents access to and information regarding other resources available to them (e.g., agencies, equipment, funding) that can be of help in their day-to-day existence with their child

To provide appropriate programming activities geared to the total child, including areas such as gross motor skills, fine motor skills, language skills, self-help skills, sensory, cognitive, and social skills, with emphasis on areas diagnosed as being deficient (the programming should be appropriate for both the child and the family)

CONDUCTING HOME PROGRAMS

It is an established fact that programs conducted in the home setting accelerate the progress of clients and provide an ongoing system that can reinforce the effects of the program while it is operational and sustain them after the program ends (Bronfenbrenner, 1974). Parents want to participate in the teaching of their child; thus, it is in everyone's best interest to teach them how to teach their child (Fredericks, Baldwin, & Grove, 1974). In order to plan for home programs and to ensure their continuation and success, the following suggestions are made.

Introducing the Idea of Home Programs

1. Discuss ideas for possible home programs during the first child staffing. By doing so, home programs will not come as a big surprise. For a child in need of toilet training, talk about a supplemental program to be conducted in the home at the same time.
2. Determine if parents see a particular task or skill as a priority for their child.
3. Collect relevant information on a family to ensure a complete understanding of their situation before suggesting or designing a home program. Some of the relevant information one may need to be aware of can be obtained by asking the following questions:
   a. Do both parents work?
   b. How many siblings are in the family?
   c. What is the siblings' involvement with their brother or sister who has a handicap?
   d. How involved is the family in community or religious activities?
   e. What time constraints are on the family?
   f. Does the family engage in any leisure activities?
   g. Which extended family members and/or friends might help or provide support?

h. Are there presently any external or internal pressures, e.g., illness or recent deaths?

i. Have home programs been tried previously and what was accomplished?

4. The importance of home programs should be stressed to the parents, especially the benefits received by both the child and the family. Being specific and using examples of home programs that have been successful is helpful.

5. Explain and demonstrate to the parent how to adapt each program or activity so that it can be conducted during regular routines of the day or evening. Avoid using programs that cannot be conducted during the regular daily routine whenever possible. Dressing skills, feeding, and other self-help skills should be conducted at those times when they are necessary and natural.

6. Involve all members of the family in home programs so that one family member (usually mother) is not solely responsible. Provide examples of other families (do not use names) who have used home programs successfully (Berger & Fowlkes, 1980). For example:

a. Teenage daughter conducted language program.

b. Family friend did toilet training for mother.

c. Grandmother conducted feeding program until it had become more reinforcing for mother to attempt.

d. Father worked on exercises during playtime with child.

7. Make available progress data to help build the case for total family involvement.

8. Offer to help teach the babysitter or respite care provider the skills necessary to conduct a program or a supplementary activity when the child is with a sitter.

9. Invite family members into the classroom to observe a program being conducted with their child so that the idea of conducting one at home won't seem foreign to them.

10. Do not use language that is geared to a professional audience (especially educational or behavioral jargon). Talking to the parent as a partner (consultant) in the child's education helps establish a good relationship.

11. Let the parents know you are glad to be working with their child and that your aim is to help the child and family as much as possible.

12. Introduce the idea of home programs first through positive examples, and then ask the parents if they would like to try a home program and if they are willing to learn how to conduct one. Be willing to accept ''no'' for an answer without pressuring families to try home programs and attempt to understand their reasons at this time so you can have more success in the future.

13. Never demand that a program be run in the home *"or else"*...*Or else what?*

Selecting the "Right" Home Program and Making It Work

1. Get a strong parental commitment to carry out a specific program before attempting to initiate the program. A strong commitment is indicated if the parent is enthusiastic about carrying out the program, e.g., he or she suggests ways to carry out a program or to involve other family members, or suggests a program to conduct themselves.
2. Involve the parents completely in program identification and adjustment by determining what they want or think they need, by meeting in face-to-face interaction.
3. Identify any activities parents may already be doing with the child that could be refined or adapted to fit a specific home program. This determination can be made by obtaining relevant information during the interview.
4. Choose programs for which all necessary equipment and materials can be provided that the parents do not already have. Inform parents that such equipment and materials will be provided. Otherwise, they may hesitate to accept a given program because they fear they will have to rush out and buy something that may or may not prove to be effective, i.e., special potty chair, walkers, or feeding equipment (Porcella, 1978).
5. Choose an activity that is likely to result in noticeable improvement in a short amount of time so that the parents will be encouraged by the rapid success to conduct other programs. The activity could be a skill that the child has learned in school but has not generalized to the home, or a skill that has almost been mastered by the child at school.
6. Remember that for some parents a program may consist of a review of previously learned skills (skill maintenance program) rather than a new skill. Such a program would be especially useful with parents whose time is limited and who hesitate to take on additional work unless tangible proof of the child's ability to perform the task is evident.
7. Include an element of fun in the programs written.
8. Choose a program that can be conducted in a short period of time (e.g., 10 minutes) so that parents can slowly become familiar with procedures.
9. Choose a flexible home program, one that is adaptable to factors that vary from family to family, e.g., one that allows variation in time, place, and person running the program, *versus* one that can only be run with certain equipment, by a certain person, at a special time. Choosing only those packages and activities that will adapt to the family's schedule and the family's structure and life-style is recommended.
10. Select a program where data are easily collected and are not intimidating, for example a yes/no format, or trial-by-trial data that are collected for

short periods, *versus* charting multiple behaviors over long periods of time.

11. Try to select a home program that is functional and will make life easier for both the child and the parent. Especially useful here are dressing skills, self-care (brush teeth, comb hair, wash face, etc.), toilet training, and feeding skills.

Implementing the Home Program and Maintaining Its Success

1. Parents should be started with a program that can be completed effectively in a short amount of time. After the parent becomes accustomed to the procedures, gradually increase the length of time the program is conducted.

2. The program should be complete, written out, easy to read, and have clear directions and concrete goals. It is essential that the programmer make sure that the program is not confusing or vague in any of its steps by field testing it if she or he has not used it before.

3. The provider should go over program procedures, data collection, goals, and motivational procedures (reinforcement) thoroughly with the parent and other family members to be certain that they understand not only the purpose of the program, but also how to successfully carry it out. This is most easily accomplished by going into the home, demonstrating the program, and having family members demonstrate the program.

4. The program should be explained to *all* family members who may be involved in the program so that it is carried out in a consistent manner. Consistency will encourage more rapid acquisition of the skill.

5. Alternate activities should be provided for use with each program.

6. A specific time should be set for reviewing the program (e.g., "Let's try this program for 3 weeks and see how it goes"). Regular reviews ensure parents that they will have an opportunity to revise or eliminate programs.

7. It is recommended that the parent collect data, especially in areas where progress is slow or hard to measure without data. Parents must be able to see progress on a regular basis if they are to continue to be motivated to conduct the program. Data provide that visual reinforcement. They also provide a method for the teacher or parent trainer to monitor progress and reinforce family members. The data collection system should be simple and data should be collected as often as necessary for measuring child progress. It is necessary to go over the data on a regular basis so that parents can see why the data are necessary and how the data are used. Doing so will avoid resistance to collecting data. Without data it may be impossible to make needed changes in programs, and thus, parental involvement can be lost because parents become discouraged about conducting a program that does not work.

8. Be sure that parents understand the possible increase in undesirable behavior that may follow the initial implementation of extinction or ignoring procedures, for example, crying when put to bed. The first night the procedure is initiated, the child may cry longer than on previous nights because the parents haven't come at the usual time (the child doesn't know how long he or she has to cry).

9. Encourage parents to call you immediately when questions or problems arise. Contact needs to be maintained with the parent regarding problems, progress, etc., as the program is being conducted.

10. Provide parents with feedback on how home programs are helping the child make progress in school activities. Being specific in your communication is helpful.

11. The provider should ask the parent what he or she can do to help in running this home program. Doing this lets parents know you are interested in helping and provides parents with an opportunity to bring up areas in which they need help. Act on the information provided.

12. Expanding home programs as the parent becomes more adept in running them is helpful. One way to do this is to go to more difficult tasks with more complex steps. In this way, both the child and the parent keep learning.

13. Be sure that parents understand the importance of praise and the possible use of tangible resources for the student and also for family members as rewards for *all* efforts. The use of tangible rewards for parents (awards, ribbons, certificates, etc.) should also be considered.

14. Do not overload parents and families with programs. Too many programs can easily result in partial discouragement and interfere with the rest of the family's daily life-style.

15. Formal and informal parent groups need to be available for parents to give them an opportunity to share what they have learned and to learn from other parents. Such interaction can go far in eliminating the feeling of "I'm the only one who has ever experienced this."

PARENTING SERVICES COMMON
TO ALL THREE SERVICE DELIVERY APPROACHES

In an effort to provide parents with information, training, and opportunities to be involved in their child's educational program, the following services are recommended for parents.

Parent Groups

Monthly, weekly, or as needed meetings can be held for all parents. These meetings can be conducted by staff members of the education/service agency, by outside professionals, or by parents themselves. At the beginning of the school year, parents may be asked to complete a questionnaire regarding topics, times, and best days for meetings. The information from this questionnaire can be used in planning parent meetings to best meet the needs of parents and families (Sternberg & Caldwell, 1982) A task force of parents to help staff plan the topics is also helpful, since it gets parents involved right from the start.

After field testing several approaches over the past several years, the following are suggestions for getting the best attendance possible:

1. Preschedule all parent meetings at the beginning of the year and provide each parent with a copy. This plan should include some proposed topics, dates, and times.
2. Give parents written notice of upcoming meetings at least 10 days in advance. Again, include topic, date, and time.
3. Call parents the day before the meeting to remind them and to get an estimate of how many plan to be in attendance.
4. State the topic to be discussed in terms specific enough for parents to determine how beneficial this meeting would be for them.
5. Arrange for babysitting services. Often, organizations such as Girl Scouts and church groups will assist with this.
6. Provide light refreshments. Staff may prepare a snack for the meetings or parents may volunteer to bring snacks. Often, setting up the room for the meeting or fixing the refreshments is an activity that can be completed by a parent who desires only minimal involvement.
7. Schedule meetings in the evenings and on days that provide the least amount of conflict with community activities and arrange car pools whenever possible.
8. Evaluate each session and use the feedback in planning and implementing future sessions.

Higher attendance occurs when parents are divided into groups according to their child's handicapping condition or area of greatest need. Parents are not very interested in group projects, unless they find out specifically about their child and see a direct correlation to his or her need (Michaelis, 1980). The grouping of children by handicapping condition or area of need may vary from year to year according to the population of children being served; however, the following parent groups have worked well:

1. Down's syndrome
2. Motor involved
3. Speech and language problems
4. Nonverbal/nonambulatory
5. Deaf/blind
6. Autistic
7. Behavior problems

Since topics are likely to be more specific to the needs of most parents when children are grouped on the basis of similarities, parents can relate better to the ideas presented and better attendance is the result.

The following are disadvantages to these grouping methods:

1. Grouping requires about four times as much staff time and involvement since several meetings are held either simultaneously or weekly to accommodate all parents in a month's time.
2. Parents are not able to interact with other parents whose children may have different handicaps.

A decrease in attendance tends to occur when parent meetings are held on a regular basis for the large group consisting of all parents. Possible explanations for this include: 1) the topics are too general to be of help, 2) the groups are too large and parents are uncomfortable about asking questions and raising points, 3) large groups tend to be less responsive to the needs of the participants. For example, feeding skills for a child with Down's syndrome may be quite different from those for the child with severe upper extremity motor involvement.

There are times, however, when it is an advantage to have the parents in large groups. Several times during the year, parents may be invited to listen to special speakers (usually from out of town) discuss topics of interest to all parents, e.g., legal rights. In addition to these, there are holiday programs and pot luck dinners where all parents can meet together. These activities give the parents a chance to meet, eat, and share a program of entertainment provided by their children.

In addition to these scheduled meetings, staff should be available for individual or small group seminars. For example, one or two parents may meet on a regular basis to learn how to deal with their child's behavior problems or to learn to sign. It is advantageous to have parents function as trainers because a parent may better understand what another parent is experiencing more readily than a professional will, and a parent may communicate more effectively with other parents.

Sibling Groups

Just as parent groups have been an effective way of helping to meet the parenting goals, sibling groups have also provided assistance to brothers and sisters in understanding, adjusting, and becoming an advocate for the handicapped child in their family. Sibling groups usually involve children age 6 years and older. They are often best conducted in the summertime when siblings are free of other extracurricular activities themselves. Siblings are encouraged to assist in a classroom setting during the summer months when they are out of school but their brother or sister with developmental disabilities is not. An attempt should be made to give the sibling more of a "feel" for what it is like to have a handicap. Several activities can be conducted to provide this experience. Simulation activities of what certain handicaps are like, movies, puppets, books, adult guests who have a handicap, and rap sessions with brothers and sisters of children who have a handicap all help develop an appreciation and understanding of the sibling who has a handicap.

Through experimentation with younger children at Utah State University's Exceptional Child Center, it was determined that children under 6 years of age did not respond well to the aforementioned techniques. Children 6 years and older seem to be better able to understand handicapping conditions and are more able to provide assistance to their parents in dealing with their sibling who has a handicap. However, children of all ages should be encouraged to help with their brother or sister who has a handicap.

During summer programs, siblings may participate in special school, community, or home programs, swimming classes, and field trips in which their brother or sister is involved. If programmed correctly, such activities create a positive attitude toward the child with a handicap, while providing an element of fun along with work and learning. Feedback from parents and children involved in a program like this has been positive. Most have stated that they enjoyed the experience, learned from the experience, and have requested that it be continued. Use of such a program with extended family members such as grandparents and aunts and uncles is also encouraged.

Parent Resource Library

Another service that aids parents of handicapped children is a parent resource library. Such a library contains up-to-date books on a variety of topics of interest to parents with children who have handicaps. All materials, however, are not just for children with handicaps, but also deal with skills and training for other children in the family.

The resource library is a service to parents that is free of charge. Books are mailed and include a pre-addressed, stamped mailer for return. Parents are informed of this service and provided with a library catalogue and registration card upon determination of their child's need for special services. Parents need only fill out a registration card to check out materials. This parent resource library is easily duplicated in other settings and has been adopted by several school districts, public libraries, and service agencies. Information on replicating the library is available from the Outreach and Development Division at the Exceptional Child Center, Utah State University.

Parent Newsletter

Newletters can serve many useful functions. A monthly newsletter that contains dates, times, and locations of local or state meetings and activities that might be of interest to parents of children with developmental disabilities is readily received. Any other items of interest, such as new equipment available, new research findings, or staff changes can also be included. The back sheet of each issue might provide information on a specific area of interest, e.g., safety in the home, poisonous houseplants, dental hygiene, first aid, lifesaving techniques. The sheet can be in the form of an instruction package for dealing with the specific topic (see Figure 10.1). It should be simple, include many pictures and be written for parent use. The newsletter can be sent to all parents whose children participate in center programs. Striefel and Hofmeister (1980) designed and used such a newsletter with great success.

Outreach and Development

Some agencies and school districts have a unit responsible for disseminating instructional packages and technical papers developed in-house. Others use state-operated resource centers. Instructional packages can be developed over time that are primarily aimed at use by the parent in training his or her child at home. For example, Utah State University's Exceptional Child Center has developed a number of kits and products that are shipped to all 50 states and several foreign countries. A product catalog describing the current line of items, their prices, and ordering instructions is available upon request (Hofmeister, 1977a). Parents are welcome to order kits/packages on their own initiative for any child.

Counseling

Parents may be faced with various difficulties in adjusting to their child's handicap, and handling personal problems in the home that interfere with their working with their child. If they feel that they need counseling services to deal with these problems, they should be referred to appropriate counseling staff within the organization, or to other agencies such as community mental health centers and social services.

Resource Directory

Because information is an important need for many parents of children with handicapping conditions, availability of such information is helpful. It is useful to maintain an up-to-date directory of state, national and local advocacy agencies, financial assistance agencies, respite care centers, group homes, sheltered workshops, mental health agencies, and other health-related agencies. Such directories can be obtained by writing to various agencies requesting directories that they have available. The U.S. Government Printing Office in Washington, D.C., is one good source. In addition, an educational community program could develop its own directory for services that includes:

1. A list of local dentists who have indicated a willingness to be of service to individuals with handicaps

FIRST AID:
TREATMENT FOR CHOKING

The incidence of choking is higher in children than in any other age group. Time is of the essence since death can occur within **FOUR** minutes. Recommended treatment is as follows:

first: When a victim is choking, leave him alone in order to prevent further lodging of foreign material (food).

action 1

If the victim is unable to remove the foreign material himself, his lips and skin will turn a bluish color and he will collapse. WHEN THIS OCCURS BEGIN ACTION ONE.

TO CLEAR AIRWAY: **Back Blows** Deliver a series of sharp slaps with a flattened hand over the spine and between the shoulder blades. Apply quickly, forcefully, and in rapid succession. **IF NOT SUCCESSFUL BEGIN ACTION 2**

action 2

Heimlich Maneuver Approach victim from behind, place thumb side of your fist against abdomen, slightly above the navel and below the rib cage. Grasp your fist with your other hand and press it into the victim's abdomen with a **QUICK UPWARD THRUST**. Repeat if necessary. **IN CHILDREN, LESS FORCE IS NEEDED THAN WITH ADULTS.**

action 3

Alternative Method Place victim on his back. Kneel, straddling him at the hips. Place one hand on top of the other. With the heel of the bottom hand on the abdomen slightly above the navel and below the rib cage, press into the abdomen with a **QUICK UPWARD THRUST**. Do not press to either side. Repeat if necessary.

After performing any of the above actions on a choking victim, call a physician IMMEDIATELY.

For further information, see *First Aid for Foreign Body Obstruction of the Airway* which may be obtained from your local Red Cross agency.

Figure 10.1   Newsletter parent training sheet.

2. A list of local music lesson resources who have indicated a willingness to teach music lessons to children with handicaps

3. A list of approved respite care providers willing to take children with handicaps for short term or emergency respite care

To do so, a questionnaire can be sent out to potential information or service groups (Porcella, 1978).

Parent Room

The use of a room set aside specifically as a parent room has been found to be an effective way of getting parents to interact with one another and to disseminate information to them as they wait to pick up children or wait for appointments with staff. Books can be housed in this room for parents to browse through, and posters, slide sound presentations, and short films can also be shown. Parents can be involved in planning activities for the room, too.

CENTER- AND HOME-BASED PROGRAMS

Infant Home-based/Center-based Program

The infant population can be served in two ways.

1. Home-based—The infant technician visits the child and parent in the home and all activities are performed in the home.
2. Center-based—The infant technician works in the center and the child and parent come to the center. All services are delivered to the parent at the center.

The only difference in the two methods is in terms of the location where services are delivered; however, it is less expensive to have parents do the traveling because it allows professionals more time to provide direct service. The children still do not "attend" a center program daily and are in actuality considered home-based, and the parent is still the main interventionist. Based on several years of experience, it is the authors' philosophy that parents of children in the infant program benefit the most by having one main person to work with on a regular basis, as the parent is trained to be the primary interventionist for their child, with other trained staff providing support and specialized services as needed.

Children in this age range (birth to 2 1/2 years) are not usually placed in a center-based program for a set number of hours. The reasoning behind this decision for home-based instruction is as follows:

1. By being trained to be the primary interventionists for their child in the home, parents are given an opportunity to develop skills for working with their child and have the responsibility for the implementation of the child's program.
2. Children in this age range can be effectively taught in the home.
3. Parents can be trained to work on acquisition of skills common to most children in this age range.
4. Most skills in need of intervention for children in this age range are skills that fit appropriately into the course of the child's day; many skills such as feeding behavior are ones that the parent must ultimately deal with on a day-to-day basis.

5. Children in this age group often require a lot of "baby-type" care and their sleep–awake patterns can be erratic; this would only detract from a short, daily, center-based program.
6. It is important to minimize the problems of having an infant deal with strangers on a daily basis.

Children in the infant program can be seen by the infant technician at the center or in the home as needed. On an average, this is twice per month. Each visit ranges from 1 to 2 hours in length depending upon what needs to be accomplished during that visit and how many other staff members may need to see the child during that session. Occasionally, the parent, infant technician, and other appropriate staff members may feel it important to see a child every week for a period of time, or perhaps twice a week. Circumstances that might necessitate this would be: severe feeding problems, the need to chart height/weight on a weekly basis, behavioral problems that require closer monitoring, parent need for extra support from staff, parent need for skill training that requires more than bimonthly sessions, or, staff who may feel it would be beneficial to monitor parent training more closely. This is not an exhaustive list, but should provide some examples of when it might be necessary to see a child more often than twice a month.

Advantages of an Infant Center-based Program During a pilot effort at Utah State University's Exceptional Child Center, 20 parents were given exposure to both center- and home-based methods and asked to comment as to which method they preferred. All but one parent were in favor of center visits.

The following list summarizes advantages of services delivered in a center, as opposed to the home.

1. Other team members are more accessible to seeing the child/family on a regular basis or as needed.
2. Special equipment is more readily available.
3. Travel money can be used on other items, e.g., reduction of parent fees or increasing the amount of equipment to loan out.
4. An infant technician is more accessible to parents and stays in one place all day if parents need to call about problems, progress, or schedule changes.
5. A greater number of children can receive services at a lesser cost, thereby cutting down the number of children on waiting lists.
6. An infant technician can spend more time with each client because he or she does not have to worry about time needed to travel from one home to another.
7. Parents are not isolated from daily activities at the center; rather, they feel more a part of center programs.
8. Parent, child, *and* family get used to center (staff and surroundings) prior to the child attending on a daily basis.

Disadvantages of an Infant Center-based Program In spite of the aforementioned advantages, the one obvious disadvantage of a center-based program is that the infant technician is not able to see how the child functions in the home, nor what the home environment is like. Because of this, it is suggested that the infant technician periodically make home visits to all clients. This still reduces travel time and cost since it is not an everyday occurrence.

All parents and children in an infant program should receive similar services regardless of whether service is provided in the home or the center. The difference is the *degree* to which the parent/child is able to take advantage of the available services. For example, those coming to a center will probably see other professionals like the language therapist on a more regular basis, be more familiar with center activities, and are more apt to be involved in parent workshops. In addition, a center might have a parent room where parents can meet and share ideas, support each other, read material relevant to their child, participate as a volunteer in a classroom program, or just relax.

Preschool Intervention—Center-based Program

Children above the age of 2 1/2 years are usually placed in a center-based program where they attend a center program for a certain number of hours on a daily basis. In such a program, the parents are no longer considered to be the only interventionists, as with the infant program, although they are encouraged to generalize programs to the home situation.

It may be useful if a child and his or her parents are "introduced" to a preschool a few months prior to a child being transferred to a preschool from an infant program. The infant technician may set up an appointment with the preschool teacher at a time when programs are in session, thus enabling the parents to ask the teacher questions about the room and their child and also to observe programs in progress. Approximately 1 month prior to the child's coming to the preschool, a meeting can be held with all incoming parents, the infant technician, and the preschool teacher. Parents can be asked to fill out all appropriate forms for release of information. The teacher may explain in detail how the classroom functions, who works with the children, programming, lunches, diaper fees, extra clothing needed, field trips, administration of medication, and so on. Parents then have an opportunity to ask whatever questions they need to ask the teacher.

Parents are informed of staffings, how they work, and who is expected to attend. They are encouraged to visit the classroom and to continue working with their child in the home. The preschool teacher stresses the importance of conducting home programs when needed. Schedules for attendance hours are worked out and parents are encouraged to car pool where possible. Upon admission to a preschool center-based program, the parents will probably fill out forms such as the following:

1. Application to attend
2. Release for testing and information
3. Release for photographs and videotaping
4. Medical history
5. Nutritional history
6. Release for field trips
7. Swimming release

These forms are contained in an enrollment booklet given to parents to read. This booklet contains information about and policies of the center. Parents are asked to fill out the pages containing the needed information and return them. Parents of preschool children have the right to all parent services offered by the center.

Advantages of a Preschool Center-based Program   Children in an infant program generally start receiving center-based services when they are 2 1/2 years of age. It is at this time that most of the children need a more intensive program with more consistency than may have been occurring in the home. By 2 1/2 years of age, most of the children are beginning to walk, feed themselves, and their daily schedules are beginning to regulate. Attention needed for food allergies and other minor illnesses is also often reduced by this age. Social interaction with peers and other adults at this age is very beneficial to the children.

Disadvantages of a Preschool Center-based Program   For most of the children, the disadvantages are minimal. Some children, however, must travel by bus or car pool to a center program and back home. This may result in a long day for them and can be extremely tiring. The time spent on a bus is usually idle and nonproductive and is often spent sleeping. Cassette tapes with songs or educational material could be played during long bus trips. Efforts should be made to have parents take turns transporting their children in an effort to reduce the length of their school day.

One other disadvantage, initially noted by preschool teachers, is that once the child starts in a center program on a daily basis, the parents often feel they no longer need to work on programs at home. Classroom teachers feel a strong need to stress to parents their responsibility to continue home programming and supplemental activities.

Center-based Instruction for School-age Children

Children between the ages of 5 and 21 years can be placed in any of a variety of instructional settings. Each school-age child must, by law, have a formal staffing upon admission to an educational program, and staffings should be held every 10 to 12 weeks thereafter. A written IEP is required for each child to conform to the guidelines of the Education for All Handicapped Children Act

(PL 94-142). Parents should be informed of their legal rights and encouraged to actively participate in their child's program and in the preparation of the IEP. Parents of school-age center-based children also have the right to make use of all parent services offered by the center.

Classroom teachers should encourage parents to visit the classroom to observe programs being taught. Teachers may request that a parent observe a program for a particular skill area prior to training the parent to conduct the same program at home. Parents are encouraged to telephone or send notes when questions arise. Teachers regularly send home notes on progress or specific program concerns. All parents are encouraged to give time in carrying out home programs when needed.

A center-based program can offer the parents a formal opportunity to request home services. Requests are made by completing a home services request form. Parents are not bound by the initial request for services. They may add, delete, or make a request at any time during the year. Parents who initially request no home services can initiate them at any time during the year. When the classroom teacher or other staff members notice an area that should be supplemented by home activities, they can talk with the parent and suggest activities that would be beneficial.

An ultimate goal is to help parents be advocates for their children. All staff members should encourage parents to be resourceful by making them aware of materials, services, and their own (the parents') skills in working with and for their children.

Several guidelines for parent involvement have been produced that have been beneficial for staff members utilizing all approaches (center-based, home-based, outpatient). These include: "Making a Home Visit is More Than Just Getting Your Foot in the Door" (Cadez et al., 1979) and "So You Want to Have Parents Run Home Programs" (Striefel, Lake, Morgan, & Owens, 1980). These articles offer suggestions for getting parents more involved in home programming and for conducting successful home visits. Other developed products that have been found to be useful for parents include: "What To Know Before You Go" (a guide for IEP staffings) and "You and PL 94-142" (a guide and test for knowledge of legal rights) (Striefel & Hofmeister, 1979).

OUTPATIENT VISITS

Outpatient service is most common for specialized agencies and community mental health centers. Outpatient services staff can provide training in child management techniques by meeting with parents in a series of sessions. Parents can be taught how to use positive ways of interacting with their children to increase appropriate behaviors and decrease inappropriate behaviors by using discipline methods other than physical punishment. Parents then become more effective and this leads to greater family harmony. Most of the sessions are conducted at a center where staff psychologists meet with parents to discuss particular child problems. Parents can also be helped to apply their knowledge of child management to resolve these problems. Staff psychologists may also include home visits in the series of sessions in order to observe parents and children interacting in more natural situations. In these visits, parents are often cued on the application of techniques they have learned.

If parents and children are living in areas where there are no available professionals to provide direct intervention programs for children with developmental disabilities, the clinical services staff can provide written programs for parents to use in their homes to work with their children. For example, the Portage Project (Shearer & Shearer, 1972) and the Multi-Agency Preschool Project (Casto, 1979) each developed extensive materials for parents to use in the home in working with their own child. Following evaluation, and at the request of parents, staff in specialty areas develop programs in areas of the child's developmental delay. For example, a physical therapist may demonstrate a motor intervention program to parents on their initial treatment visit to the center. After the demonstration, parents will go through the activities in the program, supervised by the physical therapist, to ensure that the parents understand what they will be doing between this visit and the next. Parents will then work with their child at home on a daily or regular basis, whichever is designated in the program. The parents and child will make periodic visits to the center where the physical therapist will monitor the progress made by the child and modify the programs, whenever necessary.

The same process could be used by specialists in any other discipline. Frequently, a child will be delayed in more than one area of functioning. For example, while the physical therapist is working on one problem area, the speech pathologist may be providing a program to help the child develop skills in areas of language delay. This program will also be demonstrated, supervised, and monitored by the speech pathologist. The speech pathologist and physical therapist may work together with the parents in the intervention programs. Care must be taken to ensure that a family does not become overloaded with different types of programs.

SUMMARY

Parents are the primary teachers of children with handicaps, especially in the infancy years. Thus, they are a resource that should not be overlooked. Trained parents and other family members can teach a child many skills in the home setting. Doing so will reduce costs for programs serving such children. Parents have rights as well as responsibilities for the education of their child with handicaps. A variety of procedures and suggestions for working with and involving parents in their child's education have been discussed, including a parent training approach that has been proven successful.

References

Adams, G.L. Curriculum development and implementation. In: L. Sternberg & G.L. Adams (eds.), *Educating severely and profoundly handicapped students*. Rockville, MD: Aspen Systems Corporation, 1982.

Allen K.E. *Mainstreaming in early childhood education*. New York: Delmar Publishing, 1980.

American National Standards Institute. *Specifications for making buildings and facilities accessible and usable by the physically handicapped*. New York: American National Standards Institute, 1961.

Anastasiow, N. A philosophical perspective: Why measure child progress? In: T. Black (ed.), *Perspective on measurement*. Chapel Hill: University of North Carolina, 1979.

Anderson, S.R., & Spradlin, J.E. The generalized effects of productive labeling training involving common object classes. *Journal of the Association for the Severely Handicapped*, 1980, *5*, 143–157.

Ascione, F.R. *Methods of direct behavioral observation*. Logan, UT: Exceptional Child Center, Utah State University, 1977

Ashcroft, W. Behavior modification techniques. In: J.G. Greer, R.M. Anderson, & S.J. Odle (eds.), *Strategies for helping severely and multiply handicapped citizens*. Baltimore: University Park Press, 1982.

Azrin, N.A., & Besalel, V.A. *How to use overcorrection*. Lawrence, KS: H & H Enterprises, Inc., 1980.

Baer, D.M. A hung jury and a Scottish verdict: "Not proven." *Analysis and Intervention in Developmental Disabilities*, 1981, *1*, 91–98. (a)

Baer, D.M. *How to plan for generalization*. Lawrence, KS: H & H Enterprises, Inc., 1981. (b)

Baer, D.M., Wolf, M.M., & Risley, T.R. Some current dimensions of applied behavior analysis. *Journal of Applied Behavior Analysis*, 1968, *1*, 91–97.

Bailey, J.A., Wolf, M.M., & Phillips, E.L. Home-based reinforcement and the modification of predelinquent classroom behavior. *Journal of Applied Behavior Analysis*, 1970, *3*, 183–184.

Bandler, R., & Grinder, J. *Frogs into princes*. Bandler, UT: Real People Press, 1979.

Bateman, B. Three approaches to diagnosis and educational planning for children with learning disabilities. *Academic Therapy Quarterly*, 1967, *2*(4), 215–222.

Becker, W.C. *An empirical basis for change in education*. Chicago: Science Research Associates, Inc., 1971.

Bednar, M.J., & Haviland, D.S. *Role of the physical environment in the education of children with learning disabilities.* Troy, NY: Center for Architectural Research, Rensselaer Polytechnic Institute, Educational Facilities Laboratories, 1969.

Bender, M., Valletutti, P.J., & Bender, R. *Teaching the moderately and severely handicapped (3 vols.).* Baltimore: University Press Press, 1976.

Berger, M., & Fowlkes, M.A. Family intervention project: A family network model for serving young handicapped children. *Young Children,* 1980, *35,* 22–32.

Bijou, S.W., Peterson, R.F., & Ault, M.H. A method to integrate descriptive and experimental field studies at the level of data and empirical concepts. *Journal of Applied Behavior Analysis,* 1968, *1,* 175–191.

Blackhurst, A.E., & Berdine, W.H. (eds.). *An introduction to special education.* Boston: Little, Brown & Co., 1981.

Boomer, L.W. Special education paraprofessionals: A guide for teachers. *Teaching Exceptional Children,* Reston, VA: Council for Exceptional Children, 1980, *12,* 146–149.

Borg, W.R. & Gall, M. *Educational research: An introduction.* (2nd ed.). New York: David McKay Publishing Co., 1971.

Bronfenbrenner, W. *A Report on Longitudinal Evaluations of Preschool Programs,* Vol. 2. Is early intervention effective? Washington, D.C.: DHEW, 1974.

Brown, L., Branston, M.B., Hamre-Nietupski, S., Pumpian, I., Certo, N., & Gruenewald, L. A strategy for developing chronological-age-appropriate and functional curricular content for severely handicapped adolescents and young adults. *The Journal of Special Education,* 1979, *13*(1), 81–90.

Brown, L., Nietupski, J., & Hamre-Nietupski, S. Criterion of ultimate functioning. In: M.A. Thomas (ed.), *Hey, don't forget about me: New directions for serving the handicapped,* Reston, VA: Council for Exceptional Children, 1976.

Buros, O.K. (ed.). *Mental measurements yearbook,* 8th ed. (2 vols.). Omaha: University of Nebraska Press, 1978.

Cadez, M., Morgan, C., Murray, K., & Porcella, A. Making a home visit is more than just getting your foot in the door. *Exceptional News,* 1979, *2*(3), 2–4.

Cartwright, G.P., Cartwright, C.A., & Ward, M.E. *Educating special learners.* Belmont, CA: Wadsworth Publishing, 1981.

Casto, G. *CAMS: An early intervention program for the handicapped child. Training manual.* New York: Walker Educational Book Corporation, 1979.

Cautela, J.R. *Behavior analysis forms for clinical intervention,* Vol. 2. Champaign, IL: Research Press, 1981.

Ciminero, A.R., Calhoun, K.S., & Adams, H.E. *Handbook of behavioral assessment.* New York: John Wiley & Sons, 1977.

Cone, J.D., & Hawkins, R.P. *Behavioral assessment.* New York: Brunner/Mazel, 1977.

Coopers, J.D. *Measuring behavior* (2nd ed.). Columbus, OH: Charles E. Merrill Publishing Co., 1981.

Dever, R., & Knapczyk, D. Screening for physical problems in classrooms for severely handicapped students. *The Journal of the Association for the Severely Handicapped,* 1980, *5,* 194–204.

Drabman, R.S. Behavior modification in the classroom. In: W.E. Craighead, A.E. Kazdin, & M.J. Mahoney (eds.), *Behavior modification: Principles, Issues and Applications,* Boston: Houghton Mifflin Co., 1976.

Education for All Handicapped Children Act of 1975. Reston, VA: The Council for Exceptional Children, 1976.

Engelmann, S. *Preventing failure in the primary grades.* Chicago: Science Research Associates,Inc., 1970.

Enzer, M. Parent-child and professional interactions. In: D.L. Lillie & P. L. Trohanis (eds.), *Teaching parents to teach*. Chapel Hill: University of North Carolina, 1976.

Epstein, M.H., Cullinan, D., & Rose, T.L. Applied behavior analysis and behaviorally disordered pupils: Selected issues. In: L. Mann & D.A. Sabatino (eds.), *The fourth review of special education*. New York: Grune & Stratton, 1980.

Fink, W.T., Kuombs, P.G., Sandall, S.R., & Taylor, S.J. *Curriculum development for the severely handicapped: Flexibility within the content of accountability*. Working paper. Eugene, OR: Preschool for Multihandicapped Children, Center on Human Development, 1977.

Frank, D. Are we really meeting their needs? *Academic Therapy*, 1973, *8*(3), 271–274.

Fredericks, H.D., Anderson, R., Baldwin, V. *The identification of competencies of teachers of the severely handicapped*. Washington, DC: Department of Education, 1977.

Fredericks, H.D., Baldwin V., & Grove, D. In: J. Grimm (ed.), *Training parents to teach. Four models*. Chapel Hill: Technical Assistance Development Systems, 1974.

Fredericks, H.D., Baldwin, V., Grove, D., Hanson, W., McDonnell, J., Riggs, C., Furey, V., Jordan, E., Gage, M., Lebac, L., Alrich, G., & Wadlow, M. *A data based classroom for the moderately and severely handicapped*. Monmouth, OR: Instructional Development Corporation, 1975.

Fredericks, H.D., Grove, D., Baldwin, V., & Moore, W. *Volunteers—training and use*. Champaign, IL: Research Press, 1975.

Fredericks, H.D., Riggs, C., Furey, V., Grove, D., Moore, W., McDonnell, J., Jordan, E., Hanson, W., Baldwin, V., & Wadlow, M. *The teaching research curriculum for the moderately and severely handicapped*. Springfield, IL: Charles C Thomas, 1976.

Frith, G.H., & Kelly, P. The parent/paraprofessional relationship in programs for severely and profoundly retarded. *Education and Training of the Mentally Retarded*, 1981, *16*(3), 231–234.

Glaser, K. *Learning difficulties: Causes and psychological implications—A guide for professionals*. Springfield, IL: Charles C Thomas, 1974.

Gold, M.W. Task analyses of a complex assembly task by the retarded blind. *Exceptional Children*, 1976, *43*(2), 78–84.

Gold, M.W. *Try another way*. Paper presented at Marc Gold and Associates conference, San Antonio, January, 1977.

Gray, S., & Klaus, R. The early training program: A seventh year. *Child Development*, 1970, *41*, 909–924.

Greer, J. Utilizing paraprofessionals and volunteers in special education. *Focus on Exceptional Children*, 1978, *10*(6), 1–15.

Guralnik, D.B. (ed.). *Webster's new world dictionary of the American language, 2nd college ed.* New York: William Collins & World Publishing Co., Inc., 1976.

Hackman, J.R., & Oldham, G.R. Development of the job diagnostic survey. *Journal of Applied Psychology*, 1975, *60*, 159–170.

Hall, R.V. *Behavior modification: The measurement of behavior*. Lawrence, KS: H & H Enterprises, 1971a.

Hall, R. V. *Behavior modification: Basic principles*. Lawrence, KS: H & H Enterprises, 1971b.

Hall, R.V. *Behavior modification: Applications in school and home*. Lawrence, KS: H & H Enterprises, 1971c.

Hall, R.V., & Hall, M.C. *How to select reinforcers*. Lawrence, KS: H & H Enterprises, 1980a.

Hall, R.V., & Hall, M.C. *How to use time out*. Lawrence, KS: H & H Enterprises, 1980b.

Haring, N.G., & Bricker, D. Overview of comprehensive services for the severely profoundly handicapped. In: N.G. Haring & L.J. Brown (eds.), *Teaching the severely handicapped*. New York: Grune & Stratton, 1976.

Hawkins, R. P., & Dotson, V. A. Reliability scores that delude: An Alice in Wonderland trip through the misleading characteristics of interobserver agreement scores in interval recording. In: E. Ramp & G. Semb (eds.), *Behavior analysis: Areas of research and application*. Englewood Cliffs, NJ: Prentice-Hall, 1975.

Hersen, M., & Barlow, D. *Single case experimental designs: Strategies for behavior change*. New York: Pergamon Press, 1978.

Hofmeister, A. *Models for educational research and development*. Resource paper. Logan, UT: Utah State University Special Education Instructional Technology Project, 1975.

Hofmeister, A. *Product catalog for the exceptional child*. Logan, UT: Exceptional Child Center, Utah State University, 1977. (a)

Hofmeister, A. *The parent as teacher*. Paper presented at the 56th Faculty Honor Lecture, Utah State University, April, 1977. (b)

Houts, P.S., & Scott, R.A. *Goal planning with deaf developmentally disabled persons*. Hershey, A: Milton S. Hershey Medical Center, 1975.

Howell, K.W., Kaplan, J.S., & O'Connell, C.Y. *Evaluating exceptional children: A task analysis approach*. Columbus, OH: Charles E. Merrill Publishing Co., 1979.

Hupp, S.C., & Mervis, C.B. Development of generalized concepts by severely handicapped students. *The Journal of the Association for the Severely Handicapped*, 1981, *6*, 14–20.

Jones, R.T., & Kazdin, A.E. Childhood behavior problems in the school. In: Turner, S.M., Calhoun, K.S., & Adams, H.E. (eds.), *Handbook of clinical behavior therapy*. New York: John Wiley & Sons, 1981.

Karnes, M.B., & Teska, J.A. Children's response to intervention programs. In: J.J. Gallagher (ed.), *The application of child development research to exceptional children*. Reston, VA: Council for Exceptional Children, 1975.

Kazdin, A.E. *Single-case research designs*. New York: Oxford University Press, 1982.

Kerr, S. *Organizational behavior*. Columbus, OH: Grid Publishing Co., 1979.

Kohfeldt, J. Blueprints for construction: Teacher made or teacher adapted materials. *Focus on Exceptional Children*, 1976, *8*(5), 1–14.

Kolb, D.A., Rubin, I.M., & McIntyre, J.M. *Organizational psychology: A book of readings*. Englewood Cliffs, NJ: Prentice-Hall, 1979.

Kroth, R.L. *Communicating with parents of exceptional children: Improving parent-teacher relationships*. Denver Love Publishing Co., 1975.

L'Abate, L. *Understanding and helping the individual in the family*. New York: Grune & Stratton, 1976.

Lawler, E.E., III. Job design and employee motivation. *Personnel Psychology*, 1969, *22*, 426–435.

Laycock, V.K. Basic educational practices. In: J. Greer, R.M. Anderson, & S.J. Odle (eds.), *Strategies for helping severely and multiply handicapped citizens*, Baltimore: University Park Press, 1982.

Levenstein, P. Cognitive growth in preschoolers through verbal interactions with mothers. *American Journal of Orthopsychiatry*, 1970, *40*, 426–32.

Lillie, D.L. An overview to parent programs. In: D.L. Lillie & P.L. Trohanis (eds.), *Teaching parents to teach*. Chapel Hill: University of North Carolina, 1976, 3–15.

Lilly, M.S. Evaluating individualized education programs. In: T. Torres (ed.), *A primer on individualized education programs for handicapped children*, Reston, VA: The Foundation for Exceptional Children, 1977, 26–30.

McCormack, J.E. *Learning to use an instructional sequence write-up format*. Working paper. Medford: Massachusetts Center for Program Development and Evaluation, 1974.

McCormack, J.E. The assessment tool that meets your needs: The one that you construct. *Teaching Exceptional Children*, 1975, *8*(3), 106–110.

McCormack, J.E. Using a task analysis format to develop instructional sequences. *Education and Training of the Mentally Retarded*, 1976, *11*(4), 318–323.

McCormack, J.E. *Teaching preacademic skills to severely handicapped students.* Manchester, MA: Seaside Educational Associates, 1977.

McKay, M., Davis, M., & Fanning, P. *Thoughts and feelings: The art of cognitive stress intervention.* Richmond, CA: New Harbinger Publications, 1981.

Marion, R.L. *Educators, parents and the exceptional child.* Rockville, MD: Aspen Systems Corp., 1981.

Markel, G.P., & Greenbaum, J., *Parents are to be seen and heard: Assertiveness in educational planning for handicapped children.* San Luis Obispo, CA: Impact Publishers, 1979.

Mash, E.J., & Terdal, L. G. Behavioral assessment of childhood disturbance. In: E.J. Mash and L.G. Terdal (eds.), *Behavioral assessment of childhood disorders,* New York: The Guilford Press, 1981.

Meyen, E.L., Gautt, S., & Howard, C. *Diagnostician's manual instruction-based appraisal system: A basic planning and management tool.* Bellevue, WA: Edmark Associates, 1976.

Michaelis, C.T. *Home and school partnerships in exceptional education.* Rockville, MD: Aspen Systems Corp., 1980.

Minuchin, S. *Families and family therapy.* Cambridge, MA: Harvard University Press, 1974.

Moore, G.T., Cohen, U., Oertel, J., Van Ryzin, L. *Designing play environments for handicapped children.* New York: Educational Facilities Laboratories, 1979.

Morgan, D.P. *A primer on individualized education programs for exceptional children: Preferred strategies and practices.* Reston, VA: Foundation for Exceptional Children, 1981.

Nemeroff, W.F., & Wexley, K.N. *Relationship between performance feedback interview characteristics and interview outcomes as perceived by managers and subordinates.* Proceedings of the 37th annual meeting of the Academy of Management, Orlando, FL, August, 1977, pp. 30–34.

Noonan, M.J., Brown, F., Mulligan, M., & Rettig, M.A. Educability of severely handicapped persons: Both sides of the issue. *The Journal of the Association for the Severely Handicapped*, 1982, *7*, 3–12.

Panyan, M. *How to use shaping.* Lawrence, KS: H & H Enterprises, 1980.

Patterson, G.R. *Families.* Champaign, IL: Research Press, 1971.

Pickett, A.L. *Paraprofessionals in special education: the state of the art—1979,* New York: National Resource Center for Paraprofessionals in Special Education, Center for Advanced Study in Education, City University of New York, 1979.

Porcella, A. Exemplary services project: Increasing parent involvement. *Exceptional News*, 1978, *2*, 3–4.

Sanok, R.L., & Striefel, S. Elective mutism: Generalization of verbal responding across people and settings. *Behavior Therapy*, 1979, *10*, 357–371.

Schulz, J. The parent-professional conflict. In: A.P. Turnbull, & H.R. Turnbull (eds.), *Parents speak out: Views from the other side of the two-way mirror.* Columbus, OH: Charles E. Merrill Publishing Co., 1978.

Sciarra, D.J., & Dorsey, A.G. *Developing and administering a child care center.* Boston: Houghton Mifflin Co. 1979.

Semmel, M., & Thiagarajan, S. Observation systems and the special education teacher. *Focus on Exceptional Children*, 1973, *5*(7), 1–12.

Semrau, B.L., LeMay, D.C., Tucker, B., Woods, J.N., & Hurtado, T.K. *Why not competence?* Jonesboro, AR: Focus on Children, Inc., 1979.

Shaw, S.F., Bensky, J.M., & Dixon, B. *Stress and burnout. A primer for special education and special services personnel.* Reston, VA: Council for Exceptional Children, 1981.

Shearer, D.E., & Snider, R.S. *The portage project: A home approach to the early education of young children.* Paper presented at the International Council for Exceptional Children Conference in Stirling, Scotland, June, 1978.

Shearer, M.S., & Shearer, D.E. The portage project: A model for early childhood education. *Exceptional Children,* 1972, *38,* 210–217.

Shevin, M. The use of food and drink in classroom management programs for severely handicapped children. *The Journal of the Association for the Severely Handicapped,* 1982, *7,* 40–46.

Sontag, E., Burke, P., & York, R. Considerations for serving the severely handicapped in public schools. *Education and Training of the Mentally Retarded,* 1973, *8,* 25–26.

Sontag, E., Certo, N., & Button, J. On a distinction between the education of the severely and profoundly handicapped and a doctrine of limitations. *Exceptional Children,* 1979, *45,* 604–614.

Spradlin, J.E., Karlan, J.R., & Wetherby, B. Behavior analysis, behavior modification and developmental disabilities. In: L.L. Lloyd (ed.), *Communication assessment and intervention strategies.* Baltimore: University Park Press, 1976.

Sprick, R. *The solution book.* Chicago: Science Research Associates, Inc., 1981.

Sternberg, L., & Caldwell, M.L. Parent involvement and training. In: L. Sternberg & G.L. Adams (eds.), *Educating severely and profoundly handicapped students,* Rockville, MD: Aspen Systems Corporation, 1982.

Stevens, J.H., Jr., & King, E.W. *Administering early childhood education programs.* Boston: Little, Brown, & Company, 1976.

Stile, S., Cole, J., & Garner, A., Maximizing parental involvement in programs for exceptional children. *Journal of the Division of Early Childhood,* 1979, *1,* 68–82.

Stokes, T.F., & Baer, D.M. An implicit technology of generalization. *Journal of Applied Behavior Analysis,* 1977, *10,* 349–367.

Striefel, S. Timeout and concurrent fixed-ratio schedules with human subjects. *Journal of the Experimental Analysis of Behavior,* 1972, *17,* 213–219.

Striefel, S. *Managing behavior, part 7: Teaching a child to imitate.* Lawrence, KS: H & H Enterprises, 1974.

Striefel, S. *Best practices manual.* Logan, UT: Exceptional Child Center, Utah State University, 1980.

Striefel, S. *How to teach through modeling and imitation.* Lawrence, KS: H & H Enterprises, 1981.

Striefel, S. *A rural service delivery model.* Paper presented at the 6th International Congress of the International Association for the Scientific Study of Mental Deficiency, Toronto, Canada, August, 1982.

Striefel, S., & Cadez, M.J. *The program assessment and planning guide for developmentally disabled and preschool children.* Springfield, IL: Charles C Thomas, 1982.

Striefel, S., & Hofmeister, A. *The exemplary service project: A program for severely/ profoundly mentally retarded children and youth.* Annual report. Logan, UT: Exceptional Child Center, Utah State University, 1979.

Striefel, S., & Hofmeister, A. *Final report of a program for severely/profoundly mentally retarded children and youth.* Logan, UT: Exceptional Child Center, Utah State University, 1980.

Striefel, S., Lake, D., Morgan, C., & Owens, C. R. So you want to have parents run programs at home. In: S. Striefel (ed.), *Best practices manual,* Logan, UT: Exceptional Child Center, Utah State University, 1980.

Striefel, S., & Owens, C.R. Transfer of stimulus control procedures: Applications to language acquisition training with the developmentally handicapped. *Behavior Research of Severe Developmental Disabilities,* 1980, *1,* 307–331.

Striefel, S., Wetherby, B., & Karlan, G.R. Establishing generalized verb-noun instruction following skills in retarded people. *Journal of Experimental Child Psychology,* 1976, *22,* 247–260.

Striefel, S., Wetherby, B., & Karlan, G.R. Developing generalized instruction-following behavior in severely retarded people. *American Journal of Mental Deficiency Monograph, No. 3,* 1978, 267–325.

Sulzer-Azaroff, B., & Mayer, G.R. *Applying behavior analysis procedures with children and youth.* New York: Holt, Rinehart & Winston, 1977.

Swanson, H.L., & Watson, B.L. *Educational and psychological assessment of exceptional children: Theories, strategies and applications.* St. Louis, Mo: C.V. Mosby Co., 1982.

Thiagarajan, S., Semmel, D., & Semmel, M. *Instructional development for training teachers of exceptional children: A source book.* Reston, VA: Council for Exceptional Children, 1974.

Turnbull, A.P., Strickland, B.B., & Brantley, J.D. *Developing and implementing individualized education programs.* Columbus, OH: Charles E. Merrill Publishing Co., 1978.

Van Beck, D.L. *The company policy manual.* Champaign, IL: Research Press, 1982a.

Van Beck, D.L. *The employee handbook.* Champaign, IL: Research Press, 1982b.

Wehman, P., Bates, P., & Renzaglia, A. Characteristics of an appropriate education for severely handicapped students. In: P. Wehman & J.W. Hill (eds.), *Instructional programming for severely handicapped youth.* Richmond: Virginia Commonwealth University, School of Education, 1980.

Wehman, P., & Hill, J.W. Preparing severely and profoundly handicapped youth to enter less restrictive environments. In: P. Wehman & J.W. Hill (eds.), *Instructional programming for severely handicapped youth.* Richmond: Virginia Commonwealth University. School of Education, 1980.

Wehman, P., & Hill, J.W. Preparing severely handicapped youth for less restrictive environments. *The Journal of the Association for the Severely Handicapped,* 1982, *7,* 33–39.

Whitney, R., & Striefel, S. Functionality and generalization in training the severely and profoundly handicapped. *Journal of Special Education Technology,* Logan, UT: Exceptional Child Center, Utah State University, 1981, *3,* 33–39.

Williams, W., Brown, L., & Certo, N. Basic components of instructional programs for severely handicapped students. *American Association for the Education of the Severely/Profoundly Handicapped Review,* 1975, *1*(1), 1–39.

Wunderlich, R.A. Programmed instruction—teaching coinage to retarded children. *Mental Retardation,* 1972, *10*(5), 21–25.

Index

instructional, 174, 181, 194,
197–198, 202
task, 192–193, 196–197
Shaping of behavior, 116, 119,
132–134
Short term instructional objectives,
100, 106, 109
evaluation determined by, 97, 105,
188
formulating, 80–82, 87, 90, 151,
182–183
writing of, 92, 94–98, 102–104, 163
Short Term Instructional Objectives
Forms, 85, 95
Sibling support groups, 240–241
Skills
academic, 8, 10, 41, 187, 217
age-appropriate, 4, 6, 183
assessment of, 231
basic, 10, 187, 214
communication, 6, 110, 234
functionality of, *see* Functionality of
skills
generality of, 92, 94, 99, 104, 109,
182
generalization of, *see* Generalization
of skills
home-living, 8, 41, 187, 217
motor, 6, 8, 33, 43, 88, 110–111,
217, 234
self-help, *see* Self-help skills
social, 8, 88, 110, 234
technical adequacy of, 99, 102–104,
109
vocational, 88
Social assessment, 60, 67
Social skills, 8, 88, 110, 234
Special education teachers, 19–20
Specialized equipment, 43, 233–234,
236, 245
*Specifications for Making Buildings and
Facilities Accessible to and Usable
by the Physically Handicapped,* 40
Speech therapy, 8, 11, 14–16, 21, 27,
31, 33, 78, 161, 203–204
Staff
evaluation of, 13, 15, 17–18, 24–26,
52, 217–220, 223, 225
motivation of, 2–3, 13, 17, 22–25,
223
organization of, 14–16, 23–26

training, of, 3–4, 7, 19, 32, 197,
213–225
see also Paraprofessionals; Personnel
Staffings, 6–7, 20, 22, 64, 87,
106–109, 246–248
State agencies, 18–19, 58, 151
Stimulus control, 39–40, 45, 48,
135–136, 140, 146
Student-to-teacher ratios, 5, 9, 40,
187–188, 207, 228
Students
feedback to, 135, 159, 193, 200,
216, 224, 238
motivation of, 4, 119
rights of, 75, 96
Summary Information Forms, 82–85,
87–88, 96
Support systems for parents, 227, 234,
238–243

Target behavior, 133–134, 194, 196,
211
Task analysis, 10, 94–95, 173, 181,
183, 190–194, 196–197
Teacher-generated curricula, 181–182,
194
Teacher-made materials, 21, 33, 182,
184, 188–190
Teachers, special education, 19–20
Teaching, responsive, 117–118
Teaching techniques, 201, 224
Terminal behavior, 133–134, 194, 196,
211
Testing
as part of assessment, 58, 60–61,
66–67, 72, 90–91, 187
criterion-referenced, *see* Criterion-
referenced testing (CRT)
norm-referenced, 59–60, 66–67
standardized, 8, 61, 66–67, 77
Therapy
evaluation of, 31–32
language, 8, 14–16, 21, 27, 31, 203,
246
music, 14–16, 21
occupational, *see* Occupational
therapy
physical, *see* Physical therapy
recreational, 15, 27, 31
speech, *see* Speech therapy